Praise for *Friday on My Mind: The Life of George Young*

'A great book for Australian music buffs . . . offering plenty of nostalgia and great stories.'

—*Canberra Weekly*

'Will appeal to anyone who has ever loved any of the bands or songs that George Young was involved in creating.'

—*Canberra Times*

'Jeff Apter shows his usual insightful feel for Aussie rock as he takes us on a fabulous journey.'

—*Daily Telegraph*

'Engaging . . . a portrait of an artist who eschewed the hype and constantly refined his craft.'

—*Sydney Morning Herald/The Age*

'Filled with surprises for both the knowing and uninitiated . . . a moving, heartfelt summary of a life that will live on forever in The Great Australian Songbook.'

—*Glam Adelaide*

'Upbeat . . . an entertaining read for fans of early Aussie rock.'

—*The Herald Sun*

Praise for *Malcolm Young: The Man Who Made AC/DC*

'In Apter's hands it is a story as spellbinding as one of Young's guitar riffs.'

—Helen Pitt, author of *The House*

T0322503

'A ripping yarn about a legendary musician . . . Jeff Apter's book delivers in spades, with plenty of nuggets of gold and interesting new snippets for the AC/DC fan.'

—*The Canberra Times*

'A fascinating ride . . . Apter's book is more than a biography, it's a tribute to a talented and canny man.'

—*100% Rock Magazine*

Praise for *The Book of Daniel: From Silverchair to Dreams*

'To penetrate the mind of an artist renowned for their aversion to the public and press is no simple feat. Apter has done just that to a degree so satisfying, there is little left to be said after the last page is turned . . . Johns' story is in very safe hands.'

—*Beat Magazine*

'Clear-eyed . . . a book for the fans.'

—*Sydney Morning Herald/The Age*

'A fascinating insight into Johns as it diarises the highs and low of his complicated career.'

—*Herald Sun*

'A great story, well told.'

—Rod Quinn, ABC Overnights

Jeff Apter is the author of more than 25 music biographies, many of them bestsellers. His subjects include Daniel Johns, the Bee Gees, the Finn brothers, and Malcolm and Angus Young of AC/DC. As a ghostwriter, he has worked with Kasey Chambers, Mark Evans (of AC/DC) and Richard Clapton. Jeff was on staff at *Rolling Stone* for several years. In 2015, he worked on the Helpmann Award–nominated live show *A State of Grace: The Music of Jeff and Tim Buckley*. Away from music, Jeff has also worked on books with the former captain of the Australian Invictus Games team, Paul Warren, and such sporting greats as Michael Slater and Tim Cahill. Jeff, who is heard regularly on ABC Radio Sydney, lives in Wollongong, New South Wales, with his wife, two children, Poe the budgie and a very blue dog named Neela. RIP Cat and welcome Rani.

www.jeffapter.com.au

Other books by Jeff Apter:
Behind Dark Eyes: The True Story of Jon English
Friday on My Mind: The Life of George Young
Malcolm Young: The Man Who Made AC/DC
High Voltage: The Life of Angus Young
The Book of Daniel: From Silverchair to DREAMS
Tragedy: The Sad Ballad of the Gibb Brothers

BAD BOY BOOGIE
THE TRUE STORY OF AC/DC LEGEND
BON SCOTT

JEFF APTER

ALLEN&UNWIN
SYDNEY · MELBOURNE · AUCKLAND · LONDON

First published in 2021

Copyright © 2021 Jeff Apter

All rights reserved. No part of this book may be reproduced or transmitted in
any form or by any means, electronic or mechanical, including photocopying,
recording or by any information storage and retrieval system, without prior
permission in writing from the publisher. The Australian *Copyright Act 1968*
(the Act) allows a maximum of one chapter or 10 per cent of this book, whichever
is the greater, to be photocopied by any educational institution for its educational
purposes provided that the educational institution (or body that administers it) has
given a remuneration notice to the Copyright Agency (Australia) under the Act.

Allen & Unwin
83 Alexander Street
Crows Nest NSW 2065
Australia
Phone: (61 2) 8425 0100
Email: info@allenandunwin.com
Web: www.allenandunwin.com

 A catalogue record for this
book is available from the
National Library of Australia

ISBN 978 1 76087 791 0

Internal design by Post Pre-press
Set in 13/17 pt Adobe Garamond by Post Pre-press Group, Australia
Printed and bound in Australia by Griffin Press, part of Ovato

10 9 8 7 6 5 4

The paper in this book is FSC® certified.
FSC® promotes environmentally responsible,
socially beneficial and economically viable
management of the world's forests.

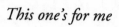

This one's for me

Prologue

'Bon used to swim with sharks, you know.'
—Angus Young

It was 2000, and I was working at Australian *Rolling Stone* magazine, speaking with AC/DC's Angus Young about the band's late, great singer, by then twenty years gone. It was a transitional moment in the long career of AC/DC; after the massive success of their hit 1980 LP *Back in Black*, their record sales had gone into decline but their live shows had become large-scale events, their tours huge money-spinners. And they were now being name-checked by a whole new legion of rockers, everyone from Foo Fighter Dave Grohl to Axl Rose of Guns N' Roses and pretty much any band with loud guitars and a bit of mongrel. They were earning dollars and credibility in equally large proportions, which hadn't always been the case.

Truth be told, Angus wasn't the world's best interview subject—he was the kind of musician who'd rather let his guitar do the talking, which was fair enough. AC/DC's record sales were around 70 million and rising, which put them on the same level as The Beatles and Led Zeppelin. Angus didn't need press coverage to sell tickets (which, in the case of AC/DC, tended to disappear as soon as they went on sale). Still, he gave me his time, and at some point in our chat talk turned to the late Bon Scott, the co-writer of many of their signature songs and an ever-present figure in the band's history. That's when he told me about Bon swimming with sharks.

I didn't think too much of his comment at the time. I figured Angus was speaking metaphorically; after all, Bon's reputation for living large was a huge part of AC/DC folklore. Boozing, womanising, partying hard and long—that was all part of the Bon Scott legend. Swimming with the sharks seemed to be an apt description for the way he lived his life. The guy took very big bites.

But no, I was wrong. While the metaphor definitely fitted the man, I learned that Angus was speaking about Bon's pre-musical life, back in Fremantle. Having discovered at fifteen that he and school weren't a comfortable fit, Bon dropped out and worked as a cray fisherman, which meant he spent a fair bit of time in the drink. Sharks were an occupational hazard—not that it seemed to bother Bon too much. It probably set him up well for a life in rock, especially the Oz rock of the 1970s, when simply taking the stage to play was a risky proposition. Those beer barns could be dangerous.

★

Misconceptions have dogged Bon Scott ever since the fateful day in early 1980 when he died in his sleep on a suburban London backstreet. There are the questions that won't go away. How did he really die? Was there some kind of cover-up? Did he, in some mysterious way, contribute to *Back in Black*, the album that emerged after his death? To me, it's all whispers and innuendo (unless there was a ouija board in the studio, of course). These are the wrong questions to ask about Bon Scott. I'm far more interested in what Bon achieved while he was alive. His premature death was the unfortunate coda to his story—nothing more.

Bon referred to his lyrics as 'toilet poetry', but he was selling himself short. Few if any lyricists have been able to match Bon's ability to both document and chuckle at his own misadventures—try imagining Sherbet's Daryl Braithwaite singing 'Whole Lotta Rosie', Bon's ode to a plus-sized one-night stand. It just wouldn't happen. Bon wrote it like he lived it: raw and real. The man was a larger-than-life character, streetwise and savvy. 'Bon loved a smoke, a drink and a stink,' said his friend Billy Thorpe. 'Wine, women and song,' Angry Anderson said on stage in 2015 during a series of Bon Scott tribute shows called Blood Sweat and Beers. As far as the Rose Tattoo singer was concerned, those were Bon's three key reasons for being.

Then there was Bon Scott the frontman; again, he was just about peerless. Out front of AC/DC, Bon owned the stage—although he was more than willing to share it with his partner in mayhem, Angus Young, who'd often perch himself on Bon's brawny shoulders as they waded into yet another audience. Together, they were the best double act ever produced in Australian rock and roll. Both were fond of a bit of vaudeville; they understood the business of show. They also knew the whereabouts of their funny bones: to them, if you weren't having fun on stage, you clearly weren't doing it right.

Bon Scott was also a raconteur, a man who knew how to generate good copy. When asked if he was AC or DC, he flashed a toothy smile and replied: 'Neither. I'm the lightning flash in the middle.' He'd conduct interviews wearing little more than cut-off denim shorts and a mile-wide grin on his face. Anything to get a reaction, a laugh. And rarely did he let the facts get in the way of a good story—it wasn't until well after his death, for instance, that the real truth about his teenage incarceration came to light. Bon was also an inveterate letter writer—he referred to his letters home as 'despatches from my front'.

With this book, I intend to bring back to life the real Bon Scott: the larrikin with a grin wider than the Luna Park face, a crack lyricist, peerless frontman and true rascal. Poet, provocateur, piss-taker: to me, these are the qualities of the real Bon Scott. Definitely a man who liked to swim with the sharks.

1

'Ron! If you can't sing proper songs, shut up. Don't sing this rock-and-roll garbage.'

—Isa Scott

Bon Scott has gone missing.

It's 23 March 1975, and his AC/DC bandmates—sibling guitarists Malcolm and Angus Young, and new recruits Mark Evans (bass) and Phil Rudd (drums)—are arranged on the soundstage of ABC TV's *Countdown* studio at Ripponlea in Melbourne, ready to roll. They're standing in front of an eager audience of mainly teenage girls, poised to scream their lungs raw, and a production crew about to start shooting. The clock is ticking, but Bon Scott, the band's vocalist, lyricist and master of mayhem, is nowhere to be seen.

Bon's definitely on the premises, because he had been with the others when they arrived a couple of hours prior and rehearsed the song they intend to play, 'Baby Please Don't Go', the cover of an old blues standard that is their latest single. That had gone smoothly; all had seemed well.

But now the band is getting very nervous. While they'd never admit it openly, everyone in the group knows that a pop show like *Countdown*, which only three weeks earlier began broadcasting in vivid colour, has the potential to break an act. The show's reach is enormous, coast to coast, and much bigger than a radio station or music magazine. This could be their moment—and they could definitely use the break.

The show's producer, Kris Noble, glances at his watch. The shooting schedule for the show is tight. If Bon doesn't appear soon, Noble will have to bump them and move on to the other acts on the bill. The now highly anxious members of AC/DC shoot a look in the direction of the stage door, where Bon was last sighted. The audience is growing restless.

What the fuck is going on?

Then, with only seconds left before Noble decides to pull the pin, Bon emerges from the wings, grinning like a madman. But this is not the hairy-chested, swaggering Bon Scott that his bandmates and the audience are expecting. Oh no. This is Bon Scott in drag, after a couple of hours spent running amok in the ABC wardrobe department.

Bon had recently spoken with his friend Mary Renshaw and she joked about the band's name and the obvious sexual innuendo. 'Next thing,' she told him, 'you'll be on the telly dressed as a girl.' Clearly, Bon took her prediction to heart.

The outfit he has chosen is this: a girls' grey school tunic, barely covering his scabby knees, teamed with a blue shirt, cuffed to his elbows. He's wearing a pigtail wig that looks like it's made out of straw, teamed with black hoop earrings, blue eye shadow and falsies. His school tie is askew. He's smeared his lips with a swipe of cherry-red lippy. Bon is possibly the ugliest schoolgirl to ever appear on national TV and certainly the hairiest. And not many high-schoolers have sported the tattoos that mark Bon's brawny arms.

Once the others in the band have taken in the apparition that has just joined them on stage, they tear into the song— but it isn't easy. AC/DC, the Youngs especially, are renowned for taking their rock and roll very seriously, but they're trying not to collapse into fits of laughter. This is beyond ridiculous; it's pure vaudeville. Bon doesn't help matters when, midway through the song, he casually sparks a cigarette while Angus Young launches into one of his trademark solos, then falls to the floor, legs akimbo, his skirt riding up to his thighs. It's a startling sight for the young girls down front. At least he hasn't forgotten his jocks.

As if this isn't crazy enough, Bon, once he's back on his feet, produces a green toy mallet, which he waves menacingly in Angus's direction, staging their own mock Punch and Judy routine as the group powers on. Bon, the cross-dressing lead singer of AC/DC, manages to upstage Angus, the band's manic schoolboy guitarist, which is no small feat. It's all great theatre, totally off the cuff, and it goes over a storm (except in the Sydney suburban home of the Young brothers; their mother is shocked at the sight of Bon in drag).

Audience reaction is all good and well, but the benchmark of any *Countdown* appearance is the reaction of host Ian 'Molly' Meldrum, who can be a fickle character at the best of times. Fortunately, Meldrum loves it, and the band is invited back for repeat performances, even though Bon opts to retire the tunic. One school uniform in the band, he figures, is ample.

Yet if the *Countdown* viewers had known just half of 28-year-old Bon Scott's journey to get to this point, they wouldn't have been smiling so much. They would probably have been shocked out of their skins. It had been one wild ride.

★

Seemingly another world away from suburban Melbourne was Forfar, where Ronald Belford Scott was born at the Fyfe Jamieson Maternity Hospital on 9 July 1946. Edinburgh is some 80 kilometres south of Forfar; Glasgow lies 150 kilometres to the south-east. The town's climate is rated as 'oceanic', which means that it doesn't really have a dry season because it rains a lot of the time. The likely Gaelic meaning of the town's name is 'cold point', which neatly sums up its other characteristic: it is chilly most of the year. Cold, wet or both. Take your pick.

The population was just a few icy locals shy of 10,000 when Bon was born to Charles Belford Scott, better known as Chick, and his wife, Isabella (nee Mitchell), usually referred to as Isa. Bon's parents were both 29 when he was born, having been married since 1941. They had met during the war at a dance in the seaport of Kirkcaldy—Chick served in Ireland, North Africa, France and Italy—and things developed from there. He was a lively type with tattooed arms who liked a good time. Isa didn't drink, but that didn't stop Chick, who liked a tipple or two. When Bon was born, Isa was a housewife, Chick a baker; they were solid, working-class people.

Both their families were musical. Chick's brother George was a pianist in local bands, while Isa's mother played the piano, and her father sang and played the organ.

'We just loved music,' Isa told writer Clinton Walker.

One day Forfar would be known as the birthplace of Bon Scott, rocker, but when he was a child it was probably best known as the home of Forfar bridies—horseshoe-shaped meat pastry snacks that were originally made for wedding feasts but had become everyday fare. The town did boast soccer club Forfar Athletic, but they were struggling in the C division of the Scottish League in this immediate post-war era. If talk did turn to Forfar, the word 'jute' was usually mentioned—some twenty per cent of its townsfolk was employed in its manufacture, at such firms as John Lowson Junior & Co Ltd.

A rare burst of glamour had hit Forfar in March 1941, when King George VI and Queen Elizabeth visited the town, accompanied by a Polish military leader named Władysław Sikorski, whose troops were fighting alongside the British at the time. It was around that time that tragedy struck the Scott family, when their first child, a boy they named Sandy, died at the age of just nine months while Chick was still serving overseas. (General Sikorski met an unfortunate demise, too, when his plane crashed into the sea in July 1943.)

Bon's brother Derek was born in 1949.

Bon and his family spent many of his early years in Kirriemuir, about twenty kilometres north of Dundee, to the north-west of Forfar. It was there that Chick worked in a bakery owned by his father, Alec, kneading dough alongside his brother George.

Today Kirriemuir is the home of Bonfest, a three-day-long communal banging of heads in honour of the man. But when the Scotts lived there, Kirriemuir was a market town, home to just a few thousand locals. Its biggest claim to fame was that it was the birthplace (and final resting place) of author J.M. Barrie, the creator of *Peter Pan*. A statue of Peter Pan still stands in the town square, not too far from a statue of Bon, which was unveiled in 2013. In a curious coincidence, Kirriemuir's sister city, also named Kirriemuir, in the Melbourne suburbs, was barely twenty kilometres from where Bon and AC/DC would one day set up shop.

★

In the early 1950s, Isa's sister moved with her family to Melbourne, and this piqued Isa's interest in emigrating. Chick, after six years in the army, also had itchy feet. Post-war migration to Australia was a lively business, thousands upon thousands taking advantage of the Australian government's Assisted Passage Migration Scheme, moving to a country that, by European standards, was sparsely populated—the Australian population in 1953 was a touch under nine million. Most, of course, were keen to start a new life in a part of the world that hadn't been totally ravaged by war. And Australia had the added advantage of being a lot like home for immigrants like the Scotts: the language was familiar (well, sort of), while what was being seen on the big screen, and heard on the radio, was very familiar. And, in Robert Menzies, Australia had a prime minister who was, by his own admission, 'British to his bootstraps'. Australia was more like Little Britain than some far-flung colonial outpost.

The ads produced by the Australian Migration Office were enticing, promising a new start 'on the sunny side'. They pushed plenty of emotional buttons, too: 'Build your children's future!' read one ad. 'His future is in your hands. Take him to Australia,' claimed another, the type wrapped around the smiling face of an innocent child. Some ads were more succinct, simply reading: 'Bring out a Briton.' As campaigns went, this was a winner—more than one million migrants relocated to Australia between 1945 and 1965.

In return for their fare to Australia, new arrivals were required to stay in the country for at least two years and work in whatever role the government provided. It was a sweet deal, considering the fare was all of £10— hence the renaming of the scheme. They may have come from Kirriemuir, but the Scotts, like so many of their countrymen, were now 'Ten Pound Poms'. Among the many other families who took advantage of the scheme over the next decade were the Gibbs from Manchester, who'd settle in Redcliffe, just outside of Brisbane, and the Swans of Glasgow who, like many of their fellow immigrants, wound up in the South Australian satellite town of Elizabeth. The Farnhams, formerly of Dagenham in Essex, settled in Noble Park, a new suburb in Melbourne, while most crucially for Bon Scott, the Youngs from Glasgow— all ten of them—would eventually put down roots in the sleepy Sydney suburb of Burwood, after a brief stint in the Villawood Migrant Hostel.

The four Scotts—Bon and his younger brother Derek, Isa and Chick—travelled to Australia in 1952 aboard the SS *Asturias*, which had been used as an armed merchant cruiser during the war. After being torpedoed by an Italian submarine in 1943, the ship was repaired and returned to service three years later, when it carried its first load of some 1300 passengers to Australia.

On the ship's passenger manifest, Chick was incorrectly noted as being 21 years older than Isa; they were, in fact, both 35. To pass the time on board, Bon's mother sang to him; he'd quickly learn each song and repeat it back to her. 'He picked them up good,' Isa told Bon's biographer Clinton Walker.

The Scotts' journey from Southampton took 25 days, travelling via Malta, Port Said, the Suez Canal, Aden and Colombo. The *Asturias* eventually docked in the Western Australian city of Fremantle on 30 March 1952. Many families, including the Scotts, continued on to other Australian locales. For a time, the Scotts lived in Sunshine in western Melbourne, a gritty blue-collar suburb that wasn't too far from the home of Isa's sister. Bon's baby brother Graeme was born in 1953 while they were living there. Chick worked as a window-framer; Bon, who'd started to show a flair for the drums and was learning the recorder, went to Sunshine Primary School. On Sundays he enjoyed singing at church, even though formal religion held little interest for him.

Even at a young age, Bon showed signs of a wild streak. Some days he'd drift off to the Footscray baths by himself. A local girl, Mary Renshaw—formerly Swetlana Wasylyk, daughter of Ukrainian immigrants—looked on as the nine-year-old Bon boldly jumped off the high board. Mary wasn't the only person left impressed by his stunt—and she and Bon would connect in the years to come.

But when Bon was diagnosed with asthma in 1956, the family returned to Western Australia, where they had been told the climate would be good for him. Chick managed to swing a transfer and they were on their way west.

★

Fremantle in the mid-1950s was a port city, nestled at the mouth of the Swan River, home to about 20,000. 'Freo', as it was known, was working class through and through, a stronghold of the Labor Party since 1924. Such politicians as

Labor Party stalwart Kim Beazley Sr, and Newton Moore, the eighth premier of Western Australia, were locals. At the same time many of the European families who'd immigrated started to have a strong cultural influence on the city, establishing a 'Cappuccino Strip' at Freo's South Terrace. One day Fremantle would, just like Kirriemuir, boast a statue of Bon in its town square, located at the Fremantle Fishing Boat Harbour. ('The late, great AC/DC frontman Bon Scott is Fremantle's most famous son,' boasts the Visit Fremantle website today.)

During the war Fremantle had come alive as it was the largest base for Allied submarines in the Southern Hemisphere, and the second largest in the Pacific—only Pearl Harbor was bigger. There were up to 125 subs operating out of the harbour. Boozy fights were common—two Maori soldiers had been stabbed and killed during a bar fight with American soldiers at the National Hotel in 1944. But Freo in 1956 was a far sleepier place. The Scotts were relieved to learn that the average winter temperature equalled the best that a Kirriemuir summer had to offer. The mercury frequently leaped over the 100-degree mark (37 degrees Celsius) in the hotter months, although the early afternoon sea breeze, known as the Fremantle Doctor, typically cooled things down.

When the Scotts settled into a small house in Harvest Street, on the north side of Freo, Bon was ten years old and attending North Fremantle Primary School. He was growing especially close to his mother, who was the only person to call him 'Ron'.

Isa was similar in nature to Bon. Mary Renshaw, who would become one of his closest friends, described Isa as 'a friendly, lovely lady who always liked a chat'. Irene Thornton, who'd one day marry Bon, said that Isa was a woman with 'a big voice and [a] lovely, tripping laugh', whereas his father Chick was quieter by nature, 'gentle and very sweet'. 'They were lively people,' added Renshaw. Bon's upbringing didn't fit the rock-and-roll cliché, that of the angry young man with everything to rebel against. The Scotts weren't wealthy, but they were tight-knit. Bon and his brother Graeme were particularly close; Graeme looked up to his big brother.

By the time he started school in Fremantle, 'Ron' was known as 'Bonny Scot', which was shortened to 'Bonny' and, inevitably, just Bon.

While they may have had similar personalities, Bon and Isa didn't agree on rock and roll, which hit young Bon right between the eyes. He'd sing, loudly, as he showered, which didn't please Isa one bit. 'Ron!' she'd call from the kitchen. 'If you can't sing proper songs, shut up. Don't sing this rock-and-roll garbage.'

Show tunes, Scottish ballads—anything, as far as Isa was concerned, would have been better.

Bon's exposure to early rock came more from the big screen than the radio, which rarely strayed beyond middle-of-the-road ballads and country songs. (The top five songs in Australia in 1956 included such chestnuts as 'The Yellow Rose of Texas' and 'Memories Are Made of This'; it was as though rock and roll didn't yet exist.) Bon saw Elvis do his pelvic-thrusting thing in *Jailhouse Rock* and *King Creole*, and watched wide-eyed as the buxom Jayne Mansfield erupted in *The Girl Can't Help It*, and he was hooked. He also loved pompadoured African-American madman Little Richard, who shrieked the film's title song (as well as such nonsensical hell-raisers as 'Ready Teddy'). First-generation rockers Eddie Cochrane and Gene Vincent also cameoed in the movie and made an equally big impression. Rock and roll was new, exciting and a little dangerous, tailor-made for an adventurous kid like Bon Scott.

In 1959, Bon began attending John Curtin High School in Freo. Even though he'd one day make their famous alumni list, alongside model Megan Gale and dancer/actor Paul Mercurio, his stay there wasn't lengthy, nor was he much of a student. Bon left as soon as he legally could, when he turned fifteen in 1961, and found a job driving a tractor at a market garden.

Much of his free time was spent either swimming in the nearby river, hanging out with his mates or playing with the Coastal Scottish Pipe Band. Bon kept time on a snare drum, in a role known as the 'side drummer'. His father, Chick, also played in the band. Known as the 'Coastals', the club had been operating since 1898, when it was formed by a group of expat Scots employed at the Fremantle Railway Workshops. When the Coastals performed in public, it was a big affair for families like the Scotts. Bon and Chick would don their kilts, strap on their drums and play their hearts out, while Isa, Graeme and Derek fell into step behind them. Bon even had the chance to perform on TV, alongside a piper and a highland dancer. In a family portrait from the time, Bon and Chick are decked out in tartan, while Isa, Graeme and Derek beam with pride.

Oddly enough, Bon's time spent with the Coastals—he'd continue drumming with them until he was seventeen, when he traded his kilt for stovepipes—would prove very handy when he started working with AC/DC.

★

In his teenage years, Bon began to develop a reputation as something of a wild child. He and his mates would hang out at the Café de Wheels in Freo, a hotspot for hoons in souped-up cars, as well as girls, 'bodgies' and 'widgies' and 'rockers', and the scene of the occasional punch-up. Bon could hold his own in a skirmish. It was a necessary skill growing up in Freo, a rough-and-tumble working-class suburb well known for the hardness of its locals. Sporting teams were fearful of coming up against Freo; they knew they were in for a tough afternoon on the paddock. A massive fight erupted one Sunday morning in early 1963 at a North Fremantle snack bar; 150, perhaps even 200 people, according to *The West Australian*, were involved in the brawl, which was eventually broken up by police. And this wasn't an isolated incident.

Yet Bon's life took a very serious turn when he was sixteen. Bon would give many versions of the events; as his career progressed, he became a master of tweaking the truth, sometimes a little, occasionally more so. In one variation, he said he'd assaulted a copper; in another he said he had been charged with 'stealing petrol and some other minor offences'. But the truth, which only fully emerged with the publication of Clinton Walker's 1994 book *Highway to Hell*, was more complicated than that.

2

'I was socially maladjusted.'
—Bon Scott

Bon, by this time, had made his first tentative steps into showbiz. Teenager Johnny Young, the Indonesian-born son of a Dutch-Aussie farming family, who'd one day gain national acclaim as the genial host of *Young Talent Time*, ran dances at Port Beach in North Freo. Young would perform with his band, the Nomads, and sometimes Bon would step up on stage and belt out one of his favourite rock songs. Young didn't take too well to the audience's enthusiastic response—Bon had made his first fans.

At one of these dances, Bon took a stroll with an under-age girl; when they returned to the hall, a few other young men expressed interest in her. Bon sprang to her defence and a fight broke out. The police were called and Bon drove off in the car of his mate Terry. When he stopped to get some petrol, Bon was arrested.

Bon was charged with giving false details to the police, escaping legal custody, unlawful carnal knowledge and stealing petrol. His case came to court in early March 1963, when Bon was a few months short of seventeen. He pleaded guilty and was committed to the care of the Child Welfare Department until he was aged eighteen. He was also put on a five-year bond. Bon's case even warranted a few paragraphs in *The West Australian* newspaper.

Bon's incarceration began at Fremantle Prison, which was a fearsome place, a notorious institution built by convicts in the 1850s. It still had its flogging post and gallows left over from its earliest days, a disturbing sight for even the toughest prisoner. Bon spent a short time there before serving out his sentence at the Riverbank Juvenile Detention Centre in Caversham, north-east Perth. Riverbank was an equally tough joint, essentially a prison for boys—the youngest inmates were just fourteen. After scrubbing floors during the day, Bon would gather with the others in a common room, where they'd listen to the radio or play cards. It was there that the idea of playing in a band began to take shape for Bon, even more so when he first heard The Beatles on the radio. On Sundays, after chapel, he'd sometimes drum with a loose-knit band formed among Riverbank residents.

Bon was behind bars for nine months and it turned his world upside down. Running with a wild crowd at Café de Wheels was little more than blowing off steam, but doing hard time was brutal and far too real. When Chick and Isa visited him, Bon initially refused to see them—he felt ashamed, as he'd admit to a future girlfriend, Silver Smith. Unlike most inmates, he'd come from a solid family, and he'd let them down hugely. As Clinton Walker noted, Bon had no intention of becoming a career criminal, which seemed the likely outcome for many of his fellow inmates at Riverbank: 'He was going to keep his head down and his nose clean, just do his time and get out as soon as possible.' If he could, Bon wanted to do something significant with the rest of his life, something that would make up for recent history. He wasn't a religious kid, but the idea of atoning for his sins registered strongly with him.

By Christmas 1963 Bon was released, and he moved back in with Chick and Isa and his brothers. Bon, along with his mate Terry, went to East Perth to get their first tattoos soon after. Bon had some birds inked just above his groin. His eyes teared up as the tattooist got to work. ('Do you want to see the branch they're on?' he'd later ask Irene Thornton, grinning broadly.)

To his eternal relief, when he registered for National Service—Australia had joined the war in Vietnam—he was turned away.

Bon's explanation? 'I was socially maladjusted,' he insisted. It's more likely that his criminal record meant he didn't meet the army's standards; a security assessment was part of the conscription process. Either way, he'd quite literally dodged a bullet.

★

Living in the west may have felt like living on the moon for a kid like Bon—Perth was, in fact, the most far-flung capital city on the planet—but Freo wasn't immune to the impact of The Beatles. Even though the Fab Four's hit-and-run tour of the Antipodes in June 1964 didn't extend to Perth—instead they wreaked havoc in Sydney, Melbourne, Adelaide and Brisbane—the ripples of excitement crossed the Nullarbor during those eighteen amazing days that they were in the country.

Leading Sydney DJ Bob Rogers spent the tour on the road with The Beatles. Documenting the mayhem, as he would admit, was almost impossible: 'At the end I was merely left with a collection of traumas, vivid memories and blurred images.' In Adelaide, almost 300,000 people lined the streets, the line snaking all the way along the stretch of road that separated the airport from the city. There were near riots at every show and a steady body count of female fans who were overcome with excitement. A young girl even scaled the outside of the Sheraton Hotel in Sydney and climbed inside an open window to avoid the heavy security. Australia had never seen anything like it—nor, apparently, had the band. Even John Lennon, a hard man to impress, was heard to mention the 'unprecedented scenes' he witnessed in Australia.

Bon was just one of many budding Oz music legends inspired by The Beatles. Some, including the three Young brothers—Malcolm, Angus and George—and Barry Maurice and Robin Gibb, were fortunate enough to sample the chaos up close when the group packed Sydney Stadium over three nights. That AC/DC, The Easybeats and the Bee Gees, to name just three trailblazing acts, emerged from seeing The Beatles was testament to just how powerful and influential Beatlemania truly was in Australia.

And who wouldn't want to form a band after experiencing Beatlemania?

There was a lot to love: The Beatles looked great, with their shaggy hair and natural onstage exuberance, while off stage they were funny and spontaneous. 'What puts you up above the other groups?' asked an earnest reporter at their Sydney press conference. 'Well,' George Harrison deadpanned, 'having a record contract.' 'Your Dad's a bus driver, isn't he, George?' another journo asked. 'Well, he was,' George replied. John Lennon then chimed in: 'He's got a gold-plated bus.'

Jokes aside, crucially, The Beatles wrote their own songs, unlike Elvis Presley and so many of the first generation of rockers, many of whose careers were now either on the slide or abruptly ended. (Little Richard found God on a train crossing the Hunter River in Newcastle, New South Wales, and swiftly returned to the church; Elvis was on the Hollywood treadmill; Jerry Lee Lewis had been outed for marrying his thirteen-year-old cousin.) Writing and recording original material, as The Beatles did, was new. In the past, acts had depended on songwriters for hire, from such creative production lines as the Brill Building in New York or, in the case of Australian artists, simply re-recording songs by overseas artists, but The Beatles swiftly relegated all that to pop's past.

Years later, while being interviewed in London, Bon dismissed The Rolling Stones and The Beatles, insisting that AC/DC were far more relevant. 'Who needs them?' he chuckled. 'They're last year's model.' But the truth was different: The Beatles were a key motivating force for Bon to pursue a life in music, so much so that he'd cover their songs in his early bands. If four working-class guys from Liverpool could conquer the world, Bon figured, why not a kid from Freo?

There was a lively music scene in the west during the mid-1960s. Dances—stomps, as they were called, unlicensed teenage gigs where booze was consumed outside—were held at the KY Club, Canterbury Court, the Z-Club, the Shakeaway and the Embassy Ballroom, while such bands as Peter Andersen & The Tornadoes, Johnny Young and his new band Kompany, Ray Hoff & The Off Beats, and Russ Kennedy and the Little Wheels packed venues. Radio stations 6KY, 6PM and 6PR played the hits of the day. By early 1965, Johnny Young, who'd signed a record deal with a Perth label called Clarion Records (co-owned by 6PR DJ Keith McGowan), was hosting *Club Seventeen* on Channel 7 Perth, another outlet for the booming live scene.

Meanwhile, on the east coast, The Easybeats, a group formed in the laundry room at the Villawood Migrant Hostel, were poised to become the first homegrown act to raze the charts with their own songs. A phenomenon, soon to be known as 'Easyfever', was just around the corner, and the local music scene would never be quite the same.

★

Every legend has to serve an apprenticeship, and Bon Scott served his with The Spektors. Apart from it being the band where Bon started his career, there was little to differentiate The Spektors from many other acts mixing it up in the Perth scene of the mid-1960s. They were a regulation four-piece dance band: Bon played the drums and sometimes sang; John Collins was the bandleader and key vocalist. Brian Gannon was on the bass, and Wyn Milsom played guitar. They were all mates of Bon's.

The Spektors played a mix of audience-pleasing faves, including Them's 'Gloria', which gave Bon a chance to step out from behind the kit and sing, channelling his inner Van Morrison—though not yet with a great deal of conviction—as well as their solemn cover of a cover, 'It

Ain't Necessarily So', the Gershwin/Gershwin song from the 1935 opera *Porgy and Bess* that Melburnian Normie Rowe had crooned into the Top 10 in June 1965. The Spektors were competent but hardly groundbreaking. The Easybeats, meanwhile, had broken through with their first local number 1 hit, 'She's So Fine', co-written by George Young and singer Stevie Wright.

Bon's signature denim-and-big-balls look was a long way off, too. With The Spektors, he had his hair cut short and wore the standard collared shirt and tie that The Beatles somehow managed to make look cool, although it didn't quite work the same magic for The Spektors. Looking at shots of Bon from the time, the word 'sensible' fits the bill, unlikely as that seems. The Spektors rehearsed in the Scott lounge room; Isa, whose anti-rock-and-roll stance had softened, would serve them tea and cake.

So, The Spektors were not going to reshape the world of popular music, but Bon did, however, make a couple of key connections during his two years with the band.

Vince Lovegrove was a Western Australia native, born in Claremont, barely ten kilometres from Fremantle. Like Bon, he was one of three children; he had two sisters, Christine and Sue. While still a student at Applecross High, Lovegrove began singing for his first band, The Dynells. Lovegrove had moved on to a band called The Dimensions when he first encountered Bon and straightaway he sensed a kindred spirit, a guy with a bit of ambition and some ability.

'I first met Bon in 1964, 1965,' Lovegrove said in a 2012 documentary. 'We were in opposition bands in a very small club scene. He was actually playing drums . . . Bon used to get up and sing maybe three songs a night. He and I often would end up playing the same venues and we struck up a friendship.'

Lovegrove pulled Bon aside one night after a gig.

'Mate, you've got a great voice,' he said. 'You should sing more.'

Interestingly, Ted Holloway, who'd joined The Spektors on guitar, felt that Bon was a better vocalist than John Collins. 'Bon was a great little drummer, but he added more to the band when he was out front.'

But that wasn't easily achieved because The Spektors were led by Collins; Bon was the junior member of the outfit. It wasn't the only time in his career he'd find himself stymied by seniority.

While Bon was still doing time in a covers band, The Easybeats continued to pump out great, original hits—'Wedding Ring' in winter 1965, followed by 'Women (Make You Feel Alright)' in early 1966, with more to come.

When Vince Lovegrove was asked to nominate his key influences, The Easybeats was one of the groups he namechecked. They were the local band to emulate. Bon, in particular, was knocked out by their singer Stevie Wright, an onstage whirlwind of flying hair, gymnast-worthy moves and, when required, dewy-eyed sincerity (sometimes helped by rubbing onion skin in his eyes). And the group's female fans were drawn to Wright like bees to honey, something Bon couldn't help but notice.

Lovegrove, meanwhile, was working on a plan.

'What if we form our own band?' he asked Bon.

Both were big fans of British soul singer Stevie Winwood, from the Spencer Davis Group, and, crucially, US soul duo Sam & Dave, who provided them with a rough outline for what would become The Valentines: a group with two lead singers and a lively, high-energy stage act.

It was also while with The Spektors that Bon started dating his first 'serious' girlfriend, Maria Van Vlijmen; she was seventeen when she met Bon at the very first Spektors gig, at the Medina Youth Club, where they played to a handful of people. Bon loaded his drums into the back of the family's Falcon station wagon and was driven to the gig by Isa.

Looking at a photo taken soon after Bon and Maria met, they could easily be mistaken for a couple at a high school formal: Bon in a suit and tie, a slightly awkward smile on his face, Maria in a sleeveless dress, her fair hair piled high. It was hard to imagine that barely a year earlier, Bon had been doing hard time at Riverbank.

Speaking with writer Clinton Walker, Maria agreed that Bon had a softer side. 'Bon was very experienced, but to me he was this nice boy. You couldn't swear around me. And there was no drinking.'

In a documentary made soon after Bon's death, Maria remembered the first gift that Bon bought for her, at a time, she recalled, when 'he had no money'. Little did she know, but for twelve months he'd been paying off a yellow teddy bear that he knew she fancied, paying a couple of shillings a week. 'When I got up on Christmas morning,' she said, 'there was this giant teddy bear . . . it was just gorgeous.'

Bon and Maria weren't destined to stay together, but they would keep in touch for the rest of Bon's life, as would Lovegrove. ('Can't wait for the photo of you in your bikini,' Bon wrote to her from the Thomson River Motor Inn at Sale in Victoria many years later. 'Probably less if you can manage it . . . Hope to see you soon. Maybe I can take your photo.')

If The Spektors weren't working, Bon would swing by a club called Broadway, where Johnny Young and his latest band, The Strangers, held down a Saturday-night residency. Young was the biggest drawcard on the Perth scene, but Bon was also learning how to make an impression. 'He'd hop on stage and sing a couple of songs and he'd get a terrific reception,' said Young. 'That's how I got to know Bon—by him jumping up on stage and singing some songs with my band.'

Young had hosted The Spektors on his TV show, *Club Seventeen*, leading to a clunky exchange about Bon's roots. Young mistakenly interpreted Bon's accent as Liverpudlian.

'Kirriemuir,' Bon corrected him.

'Where's that?' Young asked.

When Bon told him it was in Scotland, Young seemed genuinely surprised.

'Ah, he's a Scotsman!' he said, feigning possibly the worst Scottish accent ever heard.

The Spektors never made it into a recording studio, but while appearing on Young's TV show in October 1965 they played three songs, including their takes on 'Gloria' and a song originally recorded a year earlier by British band Mike Berry and The Innocents called 'On My Mind'. (These two songs surfaced on a 2003 compilation called *The Clarion Call*.)

After his crayfishing job operating out of Freo harbour, Bon held down a day job as a postie while living with his parents. Maria lived nearby, sharing a place with her brother Joe.

On his postie rounds, Bon would drop into the menswear store where Vince Lovegrove worked, and they'd slip away for a drink, or a line of speed, and plot their next move.

And within months, Bon was moving on from The Spektors.

3

'Bon wanted to make it. He wanted to be a rock-and-roll
star and he wanted to be in the biggest band in the world.'
—Vince Lovegrove

Vince Lovegrove's suggestion that they join forces proved
too strong for Bon to resist, so he gave The Spektors his
notice and Lovegrove did likewise with his latest band, The
Winztons. They brought others with them—guitarist Wyn
Milsom from The Spektors and members of Lovegrove's
band—and by mid-1966, they all came together as The
Valentines. Behind the scenes, 6KY DJ Alan Robertson gave
the band their name and soon enough he'd be giving them
prized airtime and access to the studio, where they'd sniff
out new and interesting music in the station's record library.

The Valentines cited Traffic, The Rolling Stones, Sam &
Dave and Small Faces as inspirations—and, of course, The
Easybeats, who'd just achieved the seemingly impossible:
success overseas in 1966 with the massive hit 'Friday on My
Mind'. These were all the right acts to name-check, but The
Valentines' name was a giveaway—they played crowd-pleasing
pop for a female-heavy fanbase, singing the songs of the day
with a liberal serving of cheese. (In a later interview, Vince

Lovegrove said they were part of a scene dominated by 'Top 40 cabaret bands . . . People didn't write their own songs.') They dressed in garish matching outfits: blue sharkskin suits at first, then satin pants and puffy pirate shirts, which worked well in concealing Bon's tattoos from teenage fans who might be scared off. (Tatts, of course, were the domain of ex-cons, bikers and sailors, not wannabe pop stars.)

To keep his unruly fringe in place, Bon would wash his hair and, while still wet, secure it with sticky tape—sometimes it looked as though he'd ironed his mane into place. Before taking the stage, he'd gargle a rough blend of whisky and honey, which worked a treat both for his throat and his nerves. Within weeks of their first show they were drawing big crowds to such rooms as the Canterbury Court and the Swanbourne Surf Lifesaving Club, which was known to locals as the Swanbourne Stomp. Over time, the band would host its own dances, too, usually booze-free events for kids under legal drinking age. (This didn't stop their fans getting seriously pissed before the gigs, of course.)

The Valentines wasn't a massive step up the creative ladder for Bon, who still shared vocal duties just as he'd done in The Spektors. It was a pretty commonplace arrangement; Adelaide's The Twilights were also fronted by two singers, Glenn Shorrock and Clem 'Paddy' McCartney.

When The Valentines performed it was clear that Lovegrove was the more traditionally handsome of the two, even though he'd later accept that 'Bon was, no question, the better singer'. They'd swap lead vocals depending on the range of the songs they covered. Bon took the lead vocal on such covers as 'To Know You Is to Love You' and 'Everyday I Have to Cry'.

'Our two voices, while worlds apart, worked well together,' said Lovegrove. He also admitted that they were both works in progress; neither were yet 'confident enough to lead a band on our own'. And while Lovegrove didn't quite have Bon's vocal chops, he was a good hustler and handled much of the band's PR. (The funny, frank and highly quotable Bon Scott hadn't yet emerged.) But with two young singers out front their audience appeal was undeniable and, given the solid amount of live work up for grabs, it gave Bon the chance, soon enough, to turn 'pro' and hang up his postie sack. Bon wouldn't hold down another 'regular' job for several years.

It was while Bon was playing with The Valentines that his future wife, Irene Thornton, first got to see him in action. Thornton, an Adelaide native, knew good music, but it wasn't on display here. 'I thought Bon was really cute,' Thornton wrote in her memoir, *My Bon Scott*, 'but the band was really awful.'

A perceived lack of musical acumen didn't hamper The Valentines' progress, especially when their main rival, Johnny Young, upped and left town. Young had hounded The Easybeats while they were in Perth in 1966, pleading that they write him a hit—quid pro quo for a feature spot on Young's TV show. When he turned up at their hotel room, enquiring about the progress of the song, Young was shocked by what he saw when he poked his head inside. Stevie Wright was in his underwear, scratching his head and barely awake, while 'about a dozen girls sprawled out around the place', Young would tell a reporter. 'It was very rock and roll.'

The song that Wright and George Young provided Johnny Young was called 'Step Back', which became a huge national hit in September 1966. Most Australian bands, either in the wake of some success or in the hunt for it, gravitated to Melbourne, where a vibrant music scene had developed. With a hit single in the charts, Young and his band Kompany also decided to head east.

As for The Valentines, with Johnny Young now out of the picture, they were suddenly top of the pile in Perth. But they, too, had their eyes on the southern capital.

★

The Valentines' debut single was a ten-tissue weepie called 'Everyday I Have to Cry'. It was released in May 1967 by Clarion Records, which had a distribution deal with Sydney powerhouse Festival Records. But it was hardly a trailblazing piece of work. In the wake of The Easybeats' success, local bands, duly inspired, began taking a crack at writing their own material: former Ten Pound Poms the Bee Gees had had their first big chart hit with 'Spicks and Specks', a Barry Gibb original, in September 1966. But 'Everyday', which Bon and the band cut late one night in a tiny Perth studio, was a cover.

The song was written by African-American country-soul great Arthur Alexander and had first been recorded in 1962 by US teen idol Steve Alaimo. The Valentines did give the song a bit of a makeover, stripping away the brass and backing vocals of the Alaimo's original and milking the song for every drop of pathos they could muster. It duly hit the Top 5 in Perth, and 'The Vallies', as they were known to their fans, were on their way, at least in their own backyard (the song didn't make an impact outside of Western Australia). Bon's vocal was earnest, hand on heart.

Homecoming heroes The Easybeats returned to Australia in the winter of 1967, and The Valentines scored the prized support slot when the 'Easys' toured in June, playing two shows to feverish full houses at Perth's His Majesty's Theatre.

The Easybeats shows were the first time that Bon Scott rubbed shoulders with George Young, who was riding high on the global success of 'Friday on My Mind', an inspired three minutes of working-class rock and roll that had breached the UK Top 10 in late 1966 and, just a month before their Perth dates, raced into the US Top 20. Recording a follow-up had proved to be a massive challenge for George and the band, but with 'Friday' they'd accomplished something beyond the grasp of any other Aussie rock band: international success with their own material. The Easybeats made it clear to Bon that there was a bigger musical world beyond Perth, even if he wasn't quite ready yet to take it on.

A bond formed between the two bands beyond the shows, as writer Clinton Walker noted. 'The Valentines partied with The Easybeats back at their hotel, as hordes of screaming teenage girls littered the footpath below,' he wrote. 'The two bands swapped shirts like opposing Grand Final football teams.'

Despite the increased female attention, Bon continued seeing Maria, who was planning a move to Melbourne. Bon invited Valentines guitarist Wyn Milsom to move into the Scotts' North Fremantle home, where The Valentines now rehearsed, although it was never made clear if Bon had first checked with his parents about their new boarder.

In addition to their bonding sessions, The Easybeats also left Bon and his bandmates with an original song, a George Young/Stevie Wright co-write called 'She Said', which The

Valentines released as their second single in August. It failed to chart, but that didn't prevent Bon and the group from dipping into the George Young catalogue again in the future.

★

Everybody's was a popular tabloid magazine, published by Australian Consolidated Press, which sourced a lot of its content from the burgeoning pop/rock scene—when it wasn't covering such big stories as 'Trade Secrets of a Female Impersonator' or 'The World's Most Famous Nudes'. The magazine had once let slip the home address of Easybeat George Young, and his family's sleepy suburban home was invaded by souvenir-seeking female fans, many of whom were chased away by George's mother, who wielded a mean broom when necessary. (This flashpoint became known as the Burleigh Street Riot.)

In 1965, the mag established an event for unsigned local bands in Brisbane, Melbourne and Sydney, known as the Battle of the Sounds. The judges were drawn from radio and TV, while screaming fans brought a lot of Saturday afternoon footy fever to the various heats, which were held in both metropolitan and regional hotspots. The company behind tooth-rotting treat the Violet Crumble bar took over as sponsor in 1966, and Hoadley's Battle of the Sounds was born. There was no entry fee; all that was required to compete was to fill in a form, practise hard and try, and persuade every person you knew to come to your heat and scream loudly.

Mainstream media tried to make sense of the Battle of the Sounds. When *The Canberra Times* covered the 1966 'country final', its journalist was overwhelmed by the sheer noise of the crowd—the event could get very territorial. 'The music was mere background noise [as] six hundred "switched on" fans cheered,' the paper reported. 'As if the audience noise was not enough, the musicians [from Canberra band The Roadrunners] used four large amplifiers—with the volume turned right up.'

As rites of passage went, the Battle of the Sounds was a necessary step for bands on the rise. 'Over its seven-year lifespan,' noted music website MILESAGO, 'almost every major Australian group had a shot at the competition, either at state or national level.' At its peak, in 1969, the competition was so fierce that more than 1000 acts slugged it out.

The event provided a sizeable nudge to the careers of such notable locals as Sherbet, The Flying Circus, Doug Parkinson In Focus and The Twilights, all winners of the event. Highly regarded placegetters included The Masters Apprentices, Zoot, and Jeff St John's Copperwine. Jeff St John was a powerhouse vocalist and performer, despite being confined to a wheelchair due to spina bifida. He owned the stage, something Bon had yet to accomplish with The Valentines. As for Zoot, they were a good-looking bunch with a flair for self-promotion, who'd soon become The Valentines' rivals in the keenly contested pop market.

Not only did the Battle of the Sounds offer broad exposure, but the winner also scored a return trip to the UK on the Sitmar cruise line, $1000 prize money (later upped to $2000) and the promise of live dates in London. But as winners learned, you had to sing for your supper on the Sitmar; this was no pleasure cruise.

The Valentines signed on for the 1967 Battle of the Sounds, which proved to be a big turning point in Bon's life, and the journey of the band. They won the WA heat and flew to Melbourne where local band The Groop—whose numbers included crack songwriter-in-the-making Brian Cadd—took out first place at Festival Hall, before a crowd of 6000 fans.

Bon and the band weren't overly disappointed. They had looked upon the Melbourne trip as a reconnaissance mission: if they liked what they saw, they'd move heaven and earth to shift base. They stayed for a few nights after the Battle of the Sounds and checked out as many clubs as they could—and that was all the proof they needed to agree that Melbourne was the place they needed to be. The city was bursting with music, and with opportunities.

The group returned home with the plan to sell everything they owned and get back to Melbourne as soon as humanly possible. Only bassist Bruce Abbott opted to stay behind, and was replaced by John Cooksey.

'Our frustration with Perth was that we could see we weren't going anywhere,' said Vince Lovegrove in 2012. 'You could only play so many venues so many times a year. Bon wanted to make it. He wanted to be a rock-and-roll star and he wanted to be in the biggest band in the world. We both did.' And that simply couldn't happen in Perth.

They duly boarded the train for the four-day trip to Melbourne, destined to reach their new base on 13 October 1967.

★

For anyone with even the vaguest interest in the music biz, Melbourne clearly was the place to be. *Go-Set* magazine operated out of three rooms in St Kilda and fast became a must-read for music fans; its writers included future *Countdown* host Ian (soon to be Molly) Meldrum and future novelist Lily Brett (who only half-jokingly insisted she was hired at *Go-Set* because she owned a car). Photographer Colin Beard shot a weekly centre-page spread for *Go-Set* known as 'The Scene— The Seen', in which he captured what was hot in the city after dark.

Melbourne was also the base of the new TV show *Uptight*, hosted by the amiable Ross D. Wyllie, the Brisbane-born son of an army sergeant, whose persistent limp was the result of childhood polio. Wyllie was also a singer, signed to independent label Sunshine Records. Such bands as The Loved Ones, The Masters Apprentices and Somebody's Image, whose singer was a fair-haired teenager named Russell Morris, were also based in Melbourne. It was a happening place.

Music biz whiz-kid Michael Browning, every inch a Collingwood native—'Our veins flowed black and white,' he admitted, citing the suburb's AFL team colours—booked bands for many of the city's key venues, including the Thumpin' Tum and Sebastian's. At the latter, a 'No Bozos' policy ensured they catered to a hip city crowd, and pop stars would rub shoulders with tastemakers from the fashion, art and music scenes. Browning, who was still in his early twenties, also booked bands into the recently opened Bertie's, a club decorated in Edwardian Revival style, which reflected his interest in antiques and the upscale tastes of brothers Tony and Phillip Knight, who owned the venue. Billy Thorpe loved Bertie's; to him, it was 'the best live music club

Australia has ever had'. He too would soon shift base from Sydney to Melbourne.

The scene was also bursting with life and larger-than-life figures such as Jim Keays, the charismatic lead singer of The Masters Apprentices, and Gerry Humphrys, the equally charismatic frontman of the soon-to-split Loved Ones, responsible for stone-cold Aussie classics 'The Loved One' and 'Everlovin' Man' (Humphrys would become The Valentines' first 'proper' manager). Manager Wayne de Gruchy, a Ballarat Grammar dropout, was another big character who, in the words of future client John Paul Young, 'didn't so much walk into a room but make an entrance'. Lily Brett held court in her East Melbourne café, a music biz hangout. The eager Ian Meldrum seemed to be everywhere, notepad at the ready. Pot and speed were the intoxicants of choice, booze not so much. Some of the venues were actually unlicensed and if there was any drinking, it happened elsewhere, or on the sly.

'There was a great feeling of community among the bands, their girlfriends, agents, managers, roadies, bouncers, club operators and friends,' Browning reflected in his memoir, *Dog Eat Dog*. 'Melbourne was becoming Australia's music Mecca.' Rents were affordable, which made the city even more desirable.

It was a lot for 21-year-old Bon Scott to take in. He'd adapt, though, and pretty quickly. And soon enough, Bon Scott's path would intersect with Browning's, to their mutual benefit.

Apart from his stretch inside Riverbank, Bon hadn't spent much time away from his people in Freo, but from then on he would spend the rest of his life in motion. He'd write a lot of letters from the road; over time, as they grew bawdier, he'd refer to them as 'despatches from my front'. But Bon's letters home could also reveal a more sensitive side of his nature. When he wrote to Maria just before setting out on their cross-country rail odyssey, his tone was a little desperate. 'I hope that it works out this time,' he admitted.

Otherwise, he feared, it'd be back to his postie beat and a humdrum life in suburbia.

★

It's fair to say that planning wasn't Bon's, or The Valentines', strong point. They arrived in Melbourne with some instruments, very little money and one piece of intel: the phone number of Ronnie Burns, pop singer and well-connected Melburnian. (He and his buddy Ian Meldrum had been ejected from The Beatles' 1964 Melbourne show because Meldrum screamed too loudly.) The Valentines duly called Burns as soon as they reached Flinders Street station, and he shouted them a meal and steered them in the direction of a fleapit hotel. It wasn't glamorous but it was Melbourne, the centre of the music world, and Bon, Lovegrove and the others—Wyn Milsom, Ted Ward, Warwick Findlay and John Cooksey—couldn't have been more excited.

In a few days, they set themselves up with marginally better accommodation in a small apartment in St Kilda. Room sharing was the norm; as Lovegrove delicately put it, 'We lived in each other's pocket: we knew every bedroom secret of each other.'

The Valentines needed to take care of business, so they signed with AMBO, the Australian Management Booking

Agency, which sourced a lot of local work. But they were flat broke. In some ways, their early stint in Melbourne was similar to the story told by legendary group The Band in the film *The Last Waltz*, where they admitted that during their hardscrabble days they'd carouse the aisles of supermarkets, stuffing bread and deli meats into the pockets of their overcoats while avoiding the glares of the checkout operators. Bon and The Valentines, too, were living hand to mouth, sometimes resorting to petty larceny to survive.

It was a relief, in a way, that The Valentines snagged a tour of rural Victoria not long after arriving; they needed the work, and the money. They left the city in a Kombi, which they'd given a psychedelic paint job. It was quite the sight for the locals.

When they returned to the city, Michael Browning made a point to check them out, as he did the many new bands on the scene. Although he was taken aback by the satin pants and puffy shirts—'just like that famous Seinfeld episode', Browning later wrote—he liked their set, 'especially when they got into the soul stuff'.

He was also taken by the ability of Bon and Lovegrove to 'schmooze' when they met: 'I was a sucker for [their] fatal charm.' What Browning noted, however, would be an ongoing problem for The Valentines: there was a vast difference between the band live and on record. Playing live proved they had chops; on record they were just another crowd-pleasing pop act.

Bon's girlfriend Maria had also moved to Melbourne; she lived in South Yarra, which proved a handy escape for Bon from the micro-sized Valentines HQ. Bon was the only Valentine with a steady girlfriend, which caused some moments of conflict and resentment in what was an intensely blokey world. (Interestingly, years later, when Bon and AC/DC shifted to London, he lived out a similar situation with then-girlfriend Silver Smith, which would also lead to rumblings of discontent among his bandmates, who snippily dubbed them 'Rod and Britt'—a nod to that supercouple of the mid-'70s, Rod Stewart and Britt Ekland.) Bon had a knack for both finding a partner and putting a little space between himself and the groups in which he worked.

Yet Maria didn't quite share Bon's rock-and-roll dream. 'We'll be touring the world, living on a luxurious tour bus,' he told her. But to Maria it all seemed a pipedream, another world altogether to their current situation.

★

Ivan Dayman was another larger-than-life figure on the Australian music scene of the 1960s. Ex-RAAF—he'd served in World War II—Dayman had shifted from his native Adelaide to Melbourne in 1964, where he took out a lease on Festival Hall for Saturday shows and renamed the venue Mersey City. By the time his path intersected with Bon and The Valentines, the 40-something Dayman was a well-established and sometimes feared industry player.

On one road trip with his star client, Normie Rowe, just outside Mackay in Queensland, two carloads of hoons surrounded their speeding bus, yelling threats. Rather than panic, Dayman pulled over to the side of the road and said, 'Hang on, boys,' as he stepped outside. He walked calmly to the first car and slammed the door on the leg of a passenger, leaving him screaming in pain. Then he reached inside the car and punched the driver in the face.

'I suggest you fuck off now,' Dayman advised, and the locals did just as instructed.

When Dayman returned to Rowe and the band, no one said a word. Everyone was in complete shock—and awe.

Dayman provided a lifeline for The Valentines after some skilful schmoozing from Lovegrove. He booked them a week of shows in Adelaide in early 1968, followed by dates in Brisbane and Sydney. Dayman then secured them a return engagement in Sydney, an eight-week run of dates, which would be Bon's first lengthy visit to the harbour city. There was even a whisper in the press that Dayman might sign The Valentines to his Sunshine record label, though nothing came of it.

In Sydney the group, who were splitting about $300 a week, stayed in the Americana Hotel in Kings Cross, a hotspot for the many American soldiers visiting Sydney on R&R from Vietnam. Nearby was the Bourbon & Beefsteak, a 24-hour joint that was also regularly packed with rowdy, randy American servicemen (its owner once ran covert ops for the CIA), and the Pink Pussycat, one of many venues owned by Abe Saffron, allegedly a key underworld figure in the city. The legendary Whisky a Go Go was a short stumble away, as were numerous strip clubs and brothels—the band was deep in the heart of red-light Sydney. And the Sydney scene was vastly different to Melbourne; it was sleazier, more titillating. Harder drugs, especially heroin, were readily available and just as readily consumed. In the words of Michael Browning, who'd spent his fair share of time there checking out new bands, 'To me, everyone in this city seemed to be stoned.'

Curiously, Bon and The Valentines had made a pact: unlike just about every other group at the time, they'd steer clear of pot. In fact, Bon and Lovegrove didn't smoke pot until the trip to Sydney, where a fellow muso invited them back to his place 'for a puff'. After one joint, according to Lovegrove, 'We were shit scared, paranoid and wondering whether we should be there.' They slunk back to the hotel, where they were sharing a room. When the rest of the band found out, they were shocked and threatened the two singers with the sack, although they eventually backed down. Speed and booze were perfectly fine—the former helped them get through the long, demanding nights of live work—but pot, weirdly, was taboo.

Maria travelled north to spend a weekend with Bon in late April, but it was apparent that he'd become a sucker to the temptations of the road, even though, in his letters to her, he'd promised his fidelity. Their relationship, Bon's first major love affair, ended soon after, although they stayed in touch. It wouldn't be the last time that Bon's taste for the rock-and-roll life wrecked any hope of domestic bliss.

4

'It was a wild time. Sex and drugs and rock and roll.'
—Vince Lovegrove

Bon and the band may have been building a steady live following up and down the east coast, but they still lacked a hit record. They'd looked on in the early months of 1968 as local acts Somebody's Image and The Groove hit the Top 20 with 'Hush' and 'Soothe Me', respectively, while The Masters Apprentices reached the Top 30 in April with 'Elevator Driver'. Topping all this was cherubic expat Pom Johnny Farnham, barely eighteen years old and fresh off a Melbourne building site, who created chart history with 'Sadie (The Cleaning Lady)', his debut single, a novelty record that was on its way to becoming the highest-selling single by any Australian artist in the decade with almost 200,000 copies sold. It was the dawn of a boom time for homegrown music, but as for The Valentines and the charts . . . well, nada.

Desperate for some chart action, they chose to record The Easybeats' 'Peculiar Hole in the Sky', written by George Young and Harry Vanda. It was an unusual song with a twisted history—The Easybeats had recorded it while in

London's Pye Studios in late 1967, but it had not, as yet, appeared on an Easybeats record, much to the band's frustration. The Easys felt this could have been the hit they needed to seize on the momentum of 'Friday on My Mind'.

The Valentines dropped into a Sydney studio in late May to record their own version, roping in a session drummer when their own time-keeper Warwick Findlay opted out of the group. The record was produced by Pat Aulton, who'd hit paydirt with pop star Normie Rowe and later on would scale even loftier heights with his jingles. ('Oh, what a feeling, Toyota!' was one of his, as was 'Aussie kids are Weetbix kids'. Aulton also came up with 'It's Time', the centrepiece of Gough Whitlam's successful 1972 prime ministerial tilt.) The B-side was also a savvy choice; it was their cover of 'Love Makes Sweet Music', a song originally recorded by avant-garde Brits The Soft Machine, recommended to The Valentines by influential Melbourne DJ Stan 'the Man' Rofe, who also wrote for *Go-Set* and had just been anointed 1968's King of Moomba.

The result was a great leap forward for The Valentines, a terrific take on 'Peculiar Hole in the Sky', with a hefty serving of brass and a strong whiff of psychedelia. Bon sang the lyric with all the pathos he could muster. When it was released, again on Clarion Records, in August 1968, it came with a strikingly original promo campaign. 'Please buy a copy,' read the ads in the music press, 'we're starving.' It wasn't far from the truth, a problem made even more manifest when 'Peculiar Hole in the Sky' failed to set the charts alight, barely scraping the Top 40 in Sydney and Brisbane and failing to chart elsewhere.

The Valentines now resided in Dalgety Street, St Kilda, cheap digs in the midst of the red-light district that housed not only the band but also Bon's pet carpet snake, the new love of his life, which turned up unexpectedly in various corners of the house. A disagreement over the snake resulted in a fight with one of Bon's bandmates, leaving the singer with a chipped tooth. Bon's teenage brother Graeme, soon to begin a new life as a merchant seaman, was a regular visitor during his school breaks.

Again, foreshadowing his future life with AC/DC, The Valentines HQ quickly became party central, the scene of some hardcore debauchery. Roadie John D'Arcy, a street-wise kind of guy, came by to sniff out some work and, after talking business, Bon invited him into a bedroom where they initiated a threesome with a willing fan. 'The chick was going down on me,' D'Arcy wrote in his co-authored book *Live Wire*, 'and Bon was doing her from behind.'

This was not an unusual occurrence; the band had started to draw some very enthusiastic groupies. Stage invasions became standard practice at Valentines shows, while most gigs would end with an everyone-welcome all-nighter back at their share house. Bon didn't have any money, but he was living the high life. 'It was a wild time,' said Vince Lovegrove. 'Sex and drugs and rock and roll.'

Even in the midst of all this decadence, Bon was astute enough to not impose himself on under-age girls, especially after his experience back in Freo that had led to his stint in juvenile detention. So he kept a polite distance when two fourteen-year-old fans, Gabby and Betty, began visiting the band's digs. Gabby's mother tracked them down, walked into the house and advised the band members to keep their hands to themselves. 'I know where you live,' she warned them. She meant business; these girls weren't to be touched.

She wasn't the last angry parent to pay an unscheduled visit to Bon at Casa de Valentines.

It was during this lively period in his life that Bon met eighteen-year-old Mary Renshaw, a Melbourne designer, the daughter of Ukrainian immigrants who'd met at a German work camp during the war. This was the same woman who, years before as a young girl, had watched as Bon boldly jumped from the high board at Footscray baths.

After seeing Bon perform with the group at a venue called 10th Avenue, a Bourke Street spot that hosted lunchtime shows, Mary was approached by Bon. He liked the beads she was wearing.

'Could you make me a set?' he asked.

She agreed on the spot, coming up with an ensemble that was, in her words, 'very Jimi Hendrix'. Renshaw would become one of Bon's lifelong friends and confidantes, and, briefly, his lover.

Michael Browning finally decided to book the band into Sebastian's, although, upon their arrival, he was a bit concerned about exactly what he had bought into. Sebastian's was the venue for the hip and the edgy, perhaps the number one gig in town, and in waltzed Bon and the others, pirate shirts and the rest of it, 'looking like a teenage cabaret band', Browning would recall. He feared the band might suffer the same conundrum as The Masters Apprentices. As good as the Masters were musically, their following of mainly teenage girls was not the type to stick around. That audience could be incredibly fickle.

Still, The Valentines could pull a crowd, and they were starting to incorporate a little showbiz into their act. Come showtime, the house lights would go down and smoke bombs would explode on stage. When the smoke cleared, Bon and Lovegrove would be seated on the amps, waving sparklers. It was cheesy, but the young girls lapped it up.

'It was like a feeding frenzy,' reported Ian Meldrum in *Go-Set*, when he covered a Valentines gig and witnessed the now obligatory stage invasion.

★

Michael Gudinski was a sensible, sixteen-year-old Jewish kid from the Melbourne suburb of Caulfield, who was working with promoter Bill Joseph, the latest manager of The Valentines. Joseph figured that the eager Gudinski could use a little on-the-road experience and despatched him off to Adelaide with Bon and the band when they had a run of dates. Gudinski had no idea what he was getting into. He later described it, very euphemistically, as 'a colourful and testing time'.

The Valentines stayed at Powell's Court Motel in Adelaide, which was the type of lodging whose management looked the other way when rock bands were in the house and on the loose. One morning, Bon shocked Gudinski by proudly showing him his soiled bedsheets from the night before, which he'd shared with an eager female fan. The jokes that Bon cracked, as Gudinski noted in his foreword to the 2015 book *Live Wire*, were 'so impressively off colour that I [still] can't bring myself to repeat them now'. While on the bus, Bon tried—and failed—to entice the very straight, middle-class Gudinski to smoke hash.

Over time, Gudinski had the same sense as Michael Browning about Bon and The Valentines. 'They were good,' he wrote, 'but a product of their time.' They were a bubblegum act with an audience to match; their key rivals were Zoot, who, thanks to their manager Wayne de Gruchy, were making waves with their 'Think Pink' campaign, dressing from head to toe in pink. Singer Darryl Cotton painted his car to match; even Zoot's fans wore pink. (Later on, de Gruchy would put John Paul Young into a blue-and-white sailor's outfit, which for a time was his go-to look.)

As for The Valentines, this wasn't the world-conquering rock-and-roll band that Bon dreamed of fronting. He knew that. Gudinski thought Bon had the potential to become 'Australia's Jim Morrison', but that couldn't happen in The Valentines. (Their rivals had a similar experience; Zoot's key members Rick Springfield, Beeb Birtles and Darryl Cotton found fame beyond the restraints of Think Pink.)

But The Valentines were getting noticed. In August 1968, *Go-Set* profiled the band and asked Bon to complete a Q&A. Under his current 'Likes' he listed: 'My room (painted red), long blonde hair, sex, showers, swimming.' Among his dislikes were 'being disturbed while thinking, washing and ironing'. His current tipple of choice was a concoction known as a Sand Zombie, while his favourite male vocalists of the moment were bluesman John Lee Hooker and soul great Otis Redding. He also admitted to having a thing for Motown supergroup The Supremes. He also shaved three years off his age; as far as the Australian public was concerned, Bon Scott was nineteen years old. Twenty-two would have sounded positively ancient to Valentines fans.

There was no mention of bubblegum pop or, wisely, groupies; in fact Bon had fallen heavily for an expat American, a woman named Michelle Dali, though that wasn't destined to last. (Years later, while on the road with AC/DC, he'd track her down in Houston, Texas; she was married with a child.)

Soon after, *Go-Set* tipped The Valentines as one of the 'Groups Most Likely to Succeed in '69'. It would prove to be as much a curse as a blessing.

★

Mark Evans was a working-class teenager, a budding musician, living in a tough Melbourne suburban housing estate known facetiously as the 'Prahran Hilton'. His father and brother were boxers; Evans, too, could handle himself in a scrap. On New Year's Day 1969, Evans, along with some buddies, rolled up to an afternoon concert at a venue named That's Life; the gig was sponsored by Top 40 station 3XY. On the bill were Compulsion, a band managed by Michael Browning, which featured a hotshot guitarist known simply as Reno (who was soon pinched for trying to rob the same bank where he had an account). The Valentines were also playing. You couldn't miss their fans, who were gathered near the stage, waving banners that screamed, 'BE MY VALENTINE IN '69'.

Writing in his memoir *Dirty Deeds*, Evans readily admitted that the heavy rock of Compulsion was more his taste; to him, 'the Valentines were a teenybopper band, a prototype for later groups like the Bay City Rollers'. Seated in front of the PA, Evans and his mates looked on, waiting to be impressed, as Bon, Lovegrove and the rest of the band played. Between songs, Evans noticed Bon sneaking off into the wings to slug from a bottle of Johnnie Walker. 'Then he'd walk back on stage and roar into the microphone.'

As the set progressed, and the temperature in the room rose quite literally, Evans was amazed by what he saw happening to the drunken singer. A strange metamorphosis was occurring. '[His] tattoos were starting to appear—he had tried to hide them with make-up, but the sweat was making it run. This guy was turning into Bon Scott before my eyes.'

The Valentines may not have rocked his world, but Evans was won over by Bon Scott; clearly, this guy was a rock and roller trapped in a pop band. 'I thought he was dead cool,' Evans wrote. 'The tattoos and the rapidly emptying bottle of Scotch were very impressive to this schoolkid.'

Remarkably, in only a few years Evans would be sharing a stage with this wolf in pirate's clothing.

A few weeks later, a Vietnam-bound Normie Rowe appeared on the cover of *Go-Set*, his long hair shaved back almost to the skull. When the mag hit the stands, Bon and The Valentines returned to That's Life, to play a Valentine's Day show with Johnny Farnham, Max Merritt and The Masters Apprentices. In keeping with the spirit of the occasion, Bon and Vince walked on stage clutching paper Cupids, which they distributed among their very vocal fans down the front. As was typical, the gig didn't last long—it came crashing to a halt when Bon was dragged into the crowd and deprived of his pants and jacket.

A few hours later they played an in-store at Allans Music on Collins Street. Again, they were mobbed, but this time not by lusty fans—instead, they were cornered afterwards by Melbourne band Cam-Pact, who 'massacred' Bon and the others with paint-filled water pistols, right there on the mean streets of the Melbourne CBD.

Back at Valentines HQ, the non-stop partying continued. It was as though Bon led two lives—on stage, he and The Valentines were the cuddly boys who dressed in matching outfits and won over their teen fans with Cupids, while back at St Kilda it was a different, far more debauched scene. It got to a point where their fans visited the house in shifts—in the morning it'd be the youngest girls, skipping school, who were happy to clean up the band's mess and hang out. They knew what happened in the front room of the house and steered clear; that was where the R-rated action took place. They referred to it as the 'Bad Room'.

Later in the day, as Valentines roadie John D'Arcy recalled, 'the sixteen-year-olds would start turning up, all made up, in their mini-skirts . . . They'd tidy up, do our dishes and service anyone in any way they required.' But, as he made very clear, 'It was all consensual and good fun.'

It was just as rowdy when they hit the road. Once, after a gig in rural Shepparton, the local copper, who'd observed what seemed like the town's entire female contingent swooning over the group, gave them some advice: 'Leave. Now.' Much of the male population of Shepparton had The Valentines in their sights. The band jumped into their van, an ageing Ford Thames rattletrap, and duly hit the road. Bon smoothed out their escape with a serving of his hash cookies. On longer road trips they'd drop acid, sit back and stare into the night sky, dreaming of real success.

On another road trip, Bon consulted a fortune teller, whose reading was a mixture of the mysterious—he would marry a blonde and a redhead; he'd one day join a band playing a 'weird' instrument—and the disturbing. She told him he was likely to die young. That definitely wasn't what he expected to hear. When he told Mary Renshaw about the findings, she noticed that it 'freaked him out'.

Back in Melbourne, Bon sat down with *Go-Set*'s ubiquitous Ian Meldrum, who'd described The Valentines as 'the cupids of the Australian pop business'. The talk turned to the band's young female fans.

'Do you take advantage of them?' asked Meldrum, in a rare concise moment.

'No, I don't,' Bon shot back, 'but if I feel like it and there's something available, then why not?'

It wasn't the only occasion that Bon assumed a macho stance when speaking with the press. Even at this early stage, he understood the impact of a good sound bite. But sometimes he didn't consider the potential fallout from his remarks.

★

Live work was in ample supply for Bon and the band; they'd play upwards of ten shows a week, sometimes as many as four on Saturdays alone. Pubs, clubs, high schools, dances—they played the lot, more often than not to a familiar crowd of screaming teens. In March 1969, they were part of a pop show at the Moomba Festival, staged at the Alexandra Gardens in central Melbourne, before a crowd of several thousand. They shared the bill with Zoot, Johnny Farnham, The Masters Apprentices and Russell Morris—it was a very big day out, a sea of faces. (After the show, Lovegrove was arrested for assaulting police after an incident in which a female fan had been turfed off the stage. He was fined $50 and slapped with a twelve-month good behaviour bond.)

But a genuine hit was still eluding The Valentines. Like flies to sherbet, they were drawn back to the Vanda/Young songbook, but rather than seek out something as interesting as 'Peculiar Hole in the Sky', they cut a novelty track, 'My Old Man's a Groovy Old Man', which was released in February 1969—Valentine's Day, no less, the day of their show at That's Life. It was another Vanda/Young song that The Easybeats had recorded but not yet released, although it had already been covered by UK bands Dr Marigold's Prescription and The Rag Dolls, without any chart success.

Initially, against The Valentines' wishes, the song was relegated to the B-side of their single 'Ebeneezer', but when that failed to connect, DJs flipped it over and began playing 'My Old Man', which hit the national Top 40 in July, eventually peaking at number 12. It would be the biggest hit of their career, and joined a group of local releases that were making an impression on the charts: Russell Morris had a huge hit with the avant-garde 'The Real Thing', produced with a Phil Spector-ish flourish by Ian Meldrum, who gave it the works, Hitler Youth choir and all. (It was written by Johnny Young, Bon's old rival back in Perth.) Doug Parkinson In Focus had given The Beatles' 'Dear Prudence' a stunning makeover, while The Flying Circus, a quality country-rock act at the time posing as a pop band, had spent more than three months in the Top 40 with 'Hayride' and had their next single, 'La La', ready to roll. The Valentines were keeping good company.

The band put in an awkward cameo on the ABC TV show *Hit Scene* to plug 'My Old Man', which proved beyond doubt how bad Bon and the others were at miming. The tight-trousered combo was squeezed onto a set at the

Melbourne Exhibition Centre, which they shared with an assortment of hot rod cars, the kind of flash motors that the band could only dream of being able to own. An even more awkward on-set interview followed with host Dick Williams, Lovegrove taking on the role as band spokesman. Bon—resembling, as one YouTube wag would note, a '60s housewife (his hair looked as though it had been styled with a knife)—didn't utter a word; he just smiled uncomfortably and most likely wished it would all be over soon.

Winning Hoadley's Battle of the Sounds was still very much on The Valentines' radar. Given their momentum, especially their recent chart success, they fancied their chances in 1969. But still they intended to cover every possible base, to the extent where, during the final at Melbourne's Festival Hall, Lovegrove sidled up next to Michael Browning at the backstage urinal.

'What's Doug Parkinson going to be wearing?' he asked Browning, who managed In Focus. Browning had no idea, but, as he made very clear in his memoir *Dog Eat Dog*, this wasn't some random enquiry. 'Vince looked at me with the kind of smile that said, *I know we look stupid, but we'll do anything to win this competition—and get the fuck out of this country.*'

It didn't help—Doug Parkinson In Focus won the night, and the booty; The Valentines were runners-up. This left Bon and Vince fuming, so much so, according to Browning, that Bon turned up a few nights later at an In Focus gig at Bertie's looking to throttle Parkinson. This was way out of character—Bon was a lover, not a fighter. He felt the loss deeply.

In an ironic footnote, when Browning and his band learned they had to play their way to the UK on board the Sitmar, they 'agreed to tell Hoadley's where they could stick their so-called prize'. As for Bon and The Valentines, they were still stuck on the treadmill, struggling to be seen as anything more than a cheesy pop group with a curious dress sense.

5

'Police raided the practice hide-away of . . . The Valentines, and found them in possession of the drug, marijuana.'

—*Go-Set*

In winter 1969, The Valentines were invited to take part in the Operation Starlift tour. It was a bold undertaking, the biggest tour of its type yet seen in Oz, featuring an all-Australian line-up performing in most capital cities. Fifty people gathered at Melbourne Airport on August 1969 to board a Fokker Friendship flight to Hobart; among them were Russell Morris and reigning King of Pop Johnny Farnham, plus members of Zoot, The Masters Apprentices and The Valentines. Starlift was a well-oiled machine, uncharacteristic for the time; the artists would stay in first-class accommodation rather than fleapits and travel by air, not bus. The headliner for each night would be determined by who was the biggest pulling act in that particular city.

On the first night at Hobart's City Hall, the usual chaos ensued—70 fans collapsed and an army medical team was called in to deal with the madness. As Masters' bassist Glenn Wheatley later wrote, 'Backstage was like a battlefield.'

That night, the tour manager announced that a competition was to be staged among the acts—or at least those willing to participate—in an attempt to learn who could perform, as Wheatley recalled, the most 'despicable and dirty deeds' with obliging female fans. A point-scoring system was devised, the least admirable deed scoring the most points. After just one night Bon was way out in front, with a score of 32.

The tour rolled on, through Melbourne and then Brisbane, where a crowd of 6000 packed Festival Hall; this was an even bigger gathering than The Beatles had drawn to the venue two years earlier. Once again, madness reigned—Wheatley ended the Masters' set with a concussion, no shoes, no socks and not much left of his trousers. Meanwhile, back at Lennon's Hotel, where the troupe was staying, Bon worked on accumulating more 'dirty deeds' points, as he and The Valentines hosted the after-party in Room 509.

By the time Starlift reached Sydney for the final show of the tour, in early September, Bon had virtually lapped the field, scoring heavily when he bedded the daughter of the mayor of a country town. On closing night Bon stepped up to receive his award, wielding a vibrator like a sword. 'I'd like to thank everyone involved,' he said, feigning humility. Then he addressed the sex toy in his hand: 'And thanks to you, without which I wouldn't be here receiving this award tonight.'

Bon may have won the gong for dirty deeds, but The Masters Apprentices were Starlift's big winners: their latest single, '5.10 Man', became a national hit and by May 1970 they were on their way to London. Bon and The Valentines, meanwhile, continued the struggle to be seen as more than a disposable bubblegum pop outfit, the Antipodean answer to such blink-and-you'd-miss-them acts as the 1910 Fruitgum

Company and the Ohio Express. And their next single did little to dispel the image.

★

As low points in The Valentines' career went, it was hard to go past 'Nick Nack Paddy Wack', which emerged during the spring of 1969. A pop reworking of the 'This Old Man' nursery rhyme, it put a whole new spin on the term 'cringeworthy'. The intention had been to capitalise on the success of 'My Old Man's a Groovy Old Man', which was still charting, but it failed dismally. (Interestingly, if this had been the era of made-for-kids acts like The Wiggles and Hi-5, it might have been a huge success, as the song was originally intended for a children's show and not for commercial release.) When they returned to ABC's *Hit Scene* to play the song, Bon gave the distinct impression he was relieved he wasn't singing lead on this particular turkey. Soon after, The Valentines appeared on TV performing 'Build Me Up Buttercup', an eminently disposable hit for British band The Foundations; it seemed as though they'd given up trying to be anything but a lightweight pop act.

A change of scenery, perhaps even a change of sound, was on the cards, and Bon and the band shifted temporarily to Torquay, about 100 kilometres to the south-west of the city, for an extended period of rehearsals at the Jan Juc Surf Lifesaving Club. It was the end of winter, a quiet time at the surfside locale, perfect for Bon and the group to do some woodshedding. Or so it seemed.

Two weeks into their retreat, on 20 September, at about 10 p.m., the band had just finished rehearsals. Someone lit up, and they were settling in for a mellow evening, when there was a rap at the front door. It was the cops, wielding a search warrant. They found a pipe and a small amount of pot. The Valentines were busted.

'The pop world rocked last week when the police raided the practice hide-away of top pop group, The Valentines, and found them in possession of the drug, marijuana,' reported *Go-Set*, as seriously as if it were breaking news of a political assassination.

The Valentines had become the first Australian band to undergo what was almost a rite of passage for the world's biggest outfits. Two members of The Rolling Stones had been busted, notoriously, in February 1967, while John Lennon and Yoko Ono had also been busted—by the very same copper, Detective Sergeant Norman 'Nobby' Pilcher—in October 1968. George Harrison was next on Pilcher's list. (The way-too-zealous Pilcher was later sentenced to four years in prison, convicted of conspiracy to pervert the court of justice.)

The circumstances leading to The Valentines' arrest were unusual. A few weeks before they decamped for Torquay, a young woman had appeared at the front door of their city apartment. She was an art student, hoping to flog her paintings. Mine host Bon, dressed in nothing but his jocks, emerged from the kitchen, where he'd just baked a tray of hash goodies.

'Care for a cookie?' he asked.

She imbibed, washing it down with a cup of tea, without being fully aware of what she'd just eaten. She did, however, share a joint with the band before leaving. She wrote to her sister in Adelaide with the big news.

'You wouldn't believe it,' she bragged. 'I smoked a joint with The Valentines!'

Unfortunately, her sister's place was raided, and the letter was discovered, which led the cops to The Valentines and the raid of 20 September. The possession charge was of genuine concern for the band, especially Lovegrove, who was sitting out a good behaviour bond after his arrest at the Moomba show.

Bon took the charges so seriously he stopped smoking pot altogether—for all of one day. He also took the time to discuss his situation with a reporter from *Go-Set*.

'Cops should realise what we do is right for us,' Bon stated, showing considerable insight and a healthy dose of optimism. 'They shouldn't persecute whole groups of people for being different.' In another interview, he also bemoaned the likelihood that the Oz government will be 'the last to legalise homosexuality—and pot will be the same'. Bon couldn't have imagined how prescient this comment would prove to be.

The case was due to be heard in Geelong Court in October but was then rescheduled to February 1970, while the band, in a curious coincidence, engaged a lawyer named Lennon. It was a Beatle surname, after all; maybe he'd bring them some good fortune.

While awaiting their day in court, Bon and the band continued to struggle for credibility, looking on, once again, as their fellow Aussies rode high in the charts. In the week they were busted, Russell Morris, Johnny Farnham, solo Bee Gee Robin Gibb and The Masters Apprentices were all in the *Go-Set* Top 20, while in recent months everyone from Ronnie Burns and Doug Parkinson (whose huge voice was equalled only by his afro) to Axiom and 'the new Zoot' (they'd ditched the Think Pink angle) had graced the cover of the influential mag. This had only happened once to The Valentines, back in late January 1969, and even then they had shared it with The Twilights, whose photo took up most of the cover.

A brief return trip to Perth provided some respite for The Valentines, especially for Bon, who had sex with a woman during a radio interview—off-mic, thankfully.

A week before Christmas, Bon spoke again with *Go-Set*, and this time he sounded more than a little desperate. 'The hardest thing for us,' he said, overlooking their pending court case for the moment, 'is to live bubblegum down.'

The band ran ninth in *Go-Set*'s annual poll—Zoot, who were on the verge of transforming The Beatles' 'Eleanor Rigby' into an Oz rock classic, ranked number 1. Barely making the Top 10 summed up The Valentines' situation: they were popular enough, but never likely to be top of the pile.

Stan 'The Man' Rofe, musing in *Go-Set*, had an idea. He suggested The Valentines try to redefine themselves by writing their own material; he felt they had the potential to be the next Easybeats. And there was a vacancy at the top, because those local trailblazers had just broken up, deep in debt, after a dispiriting final Australian tour in late 1969. Bon, too, nurtured a dream of writing songs, but opportunities were few in the band, which was slowly running out of steam. A full-length album might have given Bon the chance to flex his songwriting muscles, but that never eventuated. The Valentines would be a singles band for their entire career.

★

Finally, The Valentines' court date came around. Any possibility of dressing down for the occasion was dispelled when they entered the courtroom decked out in bell-bottoms, broad-collared shirts and loud ties. No one had thought it necessary to have their long hair trimmed for the day; Bon's mop was as unruly as ever.

Their attorney, William Lennon, did his best to explain to the court how this unfortunate situation at Torquay had come about. He suspected that it was a conspiracy that led to the tip-off and their arrest. 'Somebody in the entertainment world,' he declared, 'is ill-disposed to them.'

He went on to explain that smoking dope made them 'more receptive to musical sounds', adding that the band was inspired by the very public drug adventures of such superstars as The Rolling Stones and The Beatles. (Back in June 1967, Paul McCartney had admitted to taking LSD.) And as to their outrageous dress sense, it was all show, Mr Lennon told the court—just another part of the music biz. 'Underneath it, they are decent and respectable young people.'

The magistrate was duly swayed and let The Valentines off easy; each was fined $150 and put on a good behaviour bond. (Lovegrove's existing bond was extended for another year.) Bon and the others celebrated in the appropriate manner—they went home and got high.

But their celebration was brief. Whispers of their demise began to circulate in March 1970 when an ad ran in the music press, listing their equipment for sale. Bon had stated that with 'a good record in our pack and plenty of good luck' they might even crack the US market, but that was nothing more than wishful thinking. Even the mighty Easybeats, with the exception of their hit single 'Friday on My Mind', had failed to make a genuine impact in the States. They toured there once, in 1967, on a heavily stacked bill with crooner Gene Pitney—who hustled them during endless games of cards—and never returned to the USA.

The Valentines did have one final shot left, a single named 'Juliette', which surfaced in March 1970. Finally, it was an original, Bon sharing songwriting credits with guitarist Wyn Milsom and bassist Ted Ward. It was a heartfelt (if soppy) love ballad, dripping with strings and sorrow, Bon singing his heart out in honour of an elusive love who left him 'alone and sad'. It was hard to imagine this was the man who'd go on to write the lyrics for 'Whole Lotta Rosie' and 'Crabsody in Blue', but at least it was a starting point.

'Juliette' reached the Top 30 in Melbourne, despite an ongoing radio ban on locally produced music. This ban emerged from a lengthy 'pay for play' dispute between commercial radio stations and the six largest record companies, which had an impact on many local releases. But that was pretty much the end of the road for The Valentines. In a letter to Maria, Bon let her know that it was all over for the band. He hinted at a new project with Milsom and Ward, a 'shit-hot group' by his modest estimation.

Somehow The Valentines managed to limp along to August 1970, when they played a final show at the Melbourne suburb of Werribee. There was no big public announcement about their decision to quit; they were, simply, done. After the gig they headed back to the city, to the office of their manager Bill Joseph, who duly informed each member of the band how much they owed him. It echoed the last hurrah of The Easybeats, who after their last show in 1969 discovered that they, too, were deep in debt. (Bon, to his credit, managed to repay his debt to Joseph.) While the others started scoping out new careers—Lovegrove began writing for *Go-Set* and made moves to get into broadcasting, Wyn Milsom would become a pioneer of PA systems—Bon was about to become a mountain man.

6

'[Bon] was a little Pan-like in those days, often sitting in his
room playing his recorder.'
—John Bisset

As role models went in 1970, a fledgling group could do
far worse than follow the lead of The Band, an ensemble of
four road-hardened Canadians and a feisty drummer from
America's Deep South. They'd backed two stars—rockabilly
rebel Ronnie Hawkins and rock poet Bob Dylan—before
finding their own voice in such era-defining albums as
1969's *The Band*, and *Music from Big Pink* released the year
before. After years of hard living on the road, the quintet
had hunkered down in rural Woodstock, only 170 kilometres from New York yet seemingly a million bucolic miles
away, renting a house on 100 acres with its own pond—for
all of $US125 a month. It is there they'd conjured up the
songs that made these two albums so essential: classics 'The
Weight', 'The Night They Drove Old Dixie Down' and 'Rag
Mama Rag', among them.

After so many years in which New York and Los Angeles
were the creative (and business) hubs of American music,
suddenly everyone was getting back to the country—Dylan
lived in Woodstock, a short motorbike ride away from the

guys in The Band; Jimi Hendrix was also a near neighbour. Van Morrison, Janis Joplin and Todd Rundgren also sought respite in Woodstock, while Neil Young bought a ranch on the other side of the country in California. In 1969, Albert Grossman, who managed The Band, Dylan, Joplin and Rundgren, established the sprawling Bearsville Studio just to the west of Woodstock, which become an in-demand site for city-weary musos.

In an Australian context, at least geographically speaking, Adelaide was probably the city that could best simulate what Dylan and the others had found at Woodstock. Within an hour of leaving the CBD you could disappear into the Adelaide Hills, a hidden oasis of wildlife and horse trails— and cheap rent. And soon enough the Hills would be Bon's next base; it was there that a like-minded collective was intent on replicating what The Band had created in Woodstock, as far-fetched as that seemed. (Adelaide, for all its attributes, was no New York.)

The outfit was called Fraternity and they'd strongly modelled themselves on Woodstock's famous residents. 'Fraternity were just a copy of the real Band,' Bon admitted in 1975. 'They breathed and lived like The Band.' Over time, they'd cover 'The Shape I'm In', 'Chest Fever' and 'Just Another Whistle Stop', all staples of The Band.

Fraternity had undergone their share of evolutions. Most recently, Adelaide native Bruce Howe, who was the group's bedrock and bassist, had been part of Levi Smith's Clefs, a highly rated outfit that included guitarist Mick Jurd, expat Kiwi John Bisset on keyboards and Tony Buettel on drums. Jimmy Barnes, who worked with Howe after Bon's time with Fraternity, felt Howe was a tough boss; he would knock

Barnes in the back of the head with his bass if Barnes missed a note. But Barnes also cited Howe as a big influence on his career. He'd leave his mark on Bon, too.

The Clefs were signed to Sweet Peach, an independent label based in Adelaide—their debut LP, 1970's *Empty Monkey*, was called 'the best rock album ever produced in Australia' by *Go-Set*, although it didn't sell. After another shuffle, they renamed themselves Fraternity. When Howe reached out to Bon, having heard about the end of The Valentines, Fraternity were holding down a residency at a disco in Sydney called Jonathan's (later known as the Phoenician Club), playing long sets six nights a week.

Speaking at the State Library of South Australia in 2015, Howe recalled how he came to invite Bon into the fold. 'Bon and I were mates . . . If we were in Melbourne or Sydney together, we'd hang out. When The Valentines called it a day, we didn't have a singer . . . I asked Bon to come along and join the band and he did.' Not only would Bon sing, but he'd also play recorder, the instrument taught to many Australian schoolchildren (and dreaded by just as many parents).

Bon, who of late had been bingeing on the heavier sounds of such breakout acts as Led Zeppelin and Santana, jumped at the chance to join a 'real' band, an outfit that played 'serious' music—and, in strictly practical terms, he had no other plans. He was still living the gypsy life. There was no such thing as a Plan B in the world of Bon Scott.

When Bon reached Sydney, settling in at the band's digs on Jersey Road in Woollahra, he'd undergone a physical meta-morphosis: his hair was now shoulder length, he was sporting some facial fuzz and he carried a long, fringed shoulder bag. The pirate shirts, matching outfits and ironed-down hair were relics of the past. Bon had morphed into a hippie. A tattooed hippie, of course, but his new look definitely tagged him as a card-carrying member of the Age of Aquarius.

The Jonathan's gigs were long, late nights, admittedly longer gigs than Bon was used to with The Valentines, whose shows tended to crash and burn when the stage invasions began. New bandmate John 'JB' Bisset was a bit sceptical about Bon's recruitment, as he'd reveal in an interview for the AC/DC Collector website—he knew him strictly as the co-singer with The Valentines, and Bisset felt that Fraternity were 'comfortably superior to them'. But once Bisset heard Bon belt out a version of Vanilla Fudge's 'Take Me for a Little While', he was won over.

'He did it great,' Bisset remembered. 'We went on to become good friends and drinking buddies.' In another interview, Bisset described Bon as 'a little Pan-like in those days, often sitting in his room playing his recorder'.

A fledgling Sydney band named Sherbet, whose members weren't too long out of high school, would take the 9 p.m. to midnight shift at Jonathan's, then Bon and Fraternity would play until the wee small hours. David Lillicot, a friend of the guys in Sherbet who'd also befriend Bon, would film the band rehearsing using Fraternity's gear. Bon occasionally slipped in and out of the picture, puffing on a cigarette, watching the group play. If only he and Sherbet's Daryl Braithwaite, a former classmate of Olivia Newton-John's and a fitter and turner by day, had any idea of the kind of musical journeys that awaited them.

Sometimes after gigs, members of both bands, plus their crews and partners, would gather in Centennial Park and boot around a footy, unwinding from their lengthy sets.

Go-Set's Philip Morris took photos of Bon and the band during one of these sessions. With his shirt off, a leather band around his head and his tatts finally on full and proud display, Bon looked very much like a man on a mission, even if he was only kicking a footy.

Morris, who'd go on to shoot Bon frequently when he joined AC/DC, felt he was more 'subdued' while in Fraternity. 'They were a serious muso's band,' said Morris. 'It was very different to AC/DC.'

Bon, who'd bought a motorbike, would ride around Sydney, familiarising himself with the layout of the city. Sometimes he'd collect John Bisset's son and take him for rides, aware that there was some disquiet at the Bisset house. 'He was one of the few people who brought cheer into our lives,' said Bisset, whose marriage wasn't the rosiest.

But Bon's relationship with this bike, and the others that he'd subsequently own, could be complicated. He had a tendency to park his bike in what he figured was a safe spot, go off on a tear and then forget where he'd left it. Sometimes it'd be days before he tracked it down again.

Back at Fraternity HQ, a large piece of modern art hung on the wall; it resembled an alien landscape. It intrigued the band and became the inspiration for their future songs 'Getting Off' and 'Jupiter's Landscape'. A frequent visitor at the house in Woollahra was John 'Robbo' Robinson, the lead guitarist from local band Blackfeather, who'd just signed to Infinity Records, a forward-thinking subsidiary of the Festival label. He'd take over the couch, drifting off to sleep with English prog rockers King Crimson on the stereo. It wasn't the last time Robinson would drift in and out of the world of Fraternity.

Not long after Bon joined the band, Fraternity scored the support slot on the Oz tour of Jerry Lee Lewis, aka The Killer, the piano-pounding wild man from the first generation of rock and roll, whose career had nosedived since the late 1950s when it was revealed that he'd married his under-aged cousin. While in Adelaide, Fraternity played some shows at a club named Headquarters. Vince Lovegrove, in his new role as journo/Bon Scott spruiker, gave them the works in print: 'They came—they played—they conquered,' he declared in *Go-Set*.

Perhaps even more crucially, while the band was in Adelaide, they came to the attention of Hamish Henry. In the words of exhaustive Oz music website MILESAGO, Henry was 'a young millionaire, entrepreneur and automobile dealer', though probably not in that order. He ran a booking agency called the Grape Organisation while holding down a day job at his family's car dealership. Henry was well-heeled and ambitious and when he saw Fraternity play, he made them an offer they could scarcely refuse.

'Base yourselves in Adelaide,' he said. 'I'll set you up.'

He'd pay them each a weekly wage of $30, look after their rent and manage their career.

No Australian musician in 1970 would ever have dreamed of such a proposal; musos were very low on the feeding chain when it came to the economics of rock and roll. Towards the end of the Operation Starlift tour, Glenn Wheatley had had a rude awakening—when he did the calculations for just one sold-out show, he estimated the promoter had grossed $30,000, yet The Masters Apprentices shared $200, as did Bon and The Valentines. 'Shouldn't our share be greater than the promoter's?' Wheatley wondered, and not unreasonably.

(Wheatley got involved in the day-to-day running of the Masters, to their benefit; he'd later capably manage huge sellers Little River Band and 'You're the Voice'–era John Farnham.)

Henry may not have been offering Bon and Fraternity a million dollars, and he wasn't hugely experienced in the music biz, but he was cashed up and believed in the band. He promised that he'd back them for three years. And on 19 December, it was announced in *Go-Set* that Fraternity were on the verge of doing what no other band of the time had ever considered—and would have been thought utter madness if it were proposed. They were leaving Sydney to set themselves up in Adelaide.

*

Hamish Henry owned an Adelaide Hills property named Hemming's Farm, a three-and-a-half-acre spread in Aldgate, and it quickly became Fraternity HQ. Bon, while he enjoyed swimming on the farm with Henry, wasn't long for the country life. He and Bruce Howe, as well as keyboardist Bisset, his wife Cheryl and their four-year-old child—plus a dog—shifted to a place a little closer to the city, while the rest of the guys stayed on the farm. Henry covered Bon's rent. (Bon also kept a room at Vince Lovegrove's place, just in case.)

Though he lived in the city, Bon spent a lot of time on the farm; it was where the band rehearsed, partied and dreamed out loud. He quickly developed a reputation among his bandmates, as Fraternity drummer John Freeman (who replaced Tony Buettel) recalled in 2015. Bon was known as 'Road Test Ronny'. He was like a human petri dish, a living, breathing science lab: 'If anyone came around with substances that were a bit dubious, we'd give it to Bon. If he survived a couple of hours, we'd get into it, too.'

One day, Bon found some mushrooms growing under the farmhouse and offered them to the band, but despite their fondness for trippy fungi, this was one time they passed. 'He would take *anything*,' insisted Freeman. Well, not quite everything. Bon would sometimes go mushroom picking in Kuitpo Forest, south of Adelaide, with a muso mate named Niel Edgley. 'He was a tripper,' Edgley said, 'but had a sheer dislike of heroin and often told users they were oxygen wasters.' Bon made it clear to many of those close to him that heroin was definitely not his drug of choice.

The remoteness of Hemming's Farm made it the perfect place for all-nighters, and it was during yet another marathon party that Bon first crossed paths with Adelaide native Irene Thornton, who was just back from an extended stay in London. Adelaide in the early 1970s was hardly the centre of the universe—Irene found it even more lifeless than when she'd left five years earlier—so a 'happening' joint like Hemming's Farm became a magnet for anyone in search of the high life.

Irene's friend Andrea, who knew Vince Lovegrove, suggested they take a trip to the farm to meet the band.

'I think you'd really like the lead singer,' Thornton was told.

Hemming's Farm was packed that night; it seemed as though everyone in the city had been invited. Bon was in the thick of it, wearing a pair of shorts so snug he might as well have been nude, stumbling through the crowd with a girl on his arm and a drink in his hand, smiling at everything and everyone. Later that night, Bon was in one of the farm's many bedrooms when Irene, in search of a toilet, happened upon him. He was naked, on his knees, with a girl's toe in his mouth. Irene stammered an apology and backed out of the room.

'I hadn't heard of toe-sucking before,' she later noted.

'The farm became the centre of a cool little scene,' Irene wrote in her book *My Bon Scott*. 'They had three-day benders out there, fuelled by mushroom and dope and speed and booze.' And toe-sucking, in Bon's case.

*

Hamish Henry's plans for Fraternity were bold, almost outrageously so. He intended to have the band tour the US by March 1971, on the strength of some interest expressed by American record executive Dick Broderick. He was the VP of MCA Records, whose roster would soon feature Elton John, Neil Diamond and expat Aussie Olivia Newton-John. It was an interesting twist: most Oz bands who decided to set off overseas typically went to the UK, where obtaining a work visa was easier and the surrounds more familiar. But not so Fraternity; as far as Henry was concerned, the United States was the pot of gold, and Fraternity, with their obvious devotion to The Band, seemed a perfect fit.

Henry's confidence was infectious. 'There's no way in the world it can't work,' Bon told a journo from *Go-Set*. He'd repeat that in letters to his family and friends.

Before Bon and the band took on the rest of the world, however, there was business to attend to closer to home.

Henry was one of the organisers of the Myponga Festival, three days of what the promoters hoped would be nothing but peace and love and music, to be held from 30 January to 1 February. Myponga, which was about 60 kilometres south of Adelaide, was the site of an old uranium ore deposit (it's now dairy-farming country).

It was only eighteen months since the Woodstock festival had been staged in New York State, and Henry's event was billed as the 'First Australian Festival of Progressive Music'— like Woodstock coming to Oz. Internationals Black Sabbath and Cat Stevens were booked to perform, along with some premium local talent, including Daddy Cool, Billy Thorpe, Jeff St John, Spectrum, Wendy Saddington and Chain. Fraternity would, of course, appear.

Vince Lovegrove was handling publicity, and the press release for Myponga defined its MO: 'Myponga '71 is more than a three-day pop festival . . . it's a revolution of peace, love and freedom . . . Let's get together at Myponga for a truly beautiful experience.' The festival offered everything: music, food, camping facilities, proper security—also a bit of retail. 'Various creative shops will be erected on the site to sell in-gear fashions and handcraft items,' read one ad. There'd even be a swami on site, a spiritual necessity in 1971.

What self-respecting, bead-wearing, Vietnam-protesting music lover could resist?

Henry, ignoring the obvious conflict of interest, gave Fraternity a prime spot and they took the stage just before headliners Black Sabbath. Bon rode his motorbike to the gig, parking it at the rear of the stage, revelling in the 'vibe'. But Fraternity were not the breakout act of the festival, which drew about 10,000 punters—perhaps twice as many if you included the freeloaders who jumped the fence, just as they'd done at Woodstock. Daddy Cool were the stars, alongside Spectrum; within months both bands would have huge hits ('Eagle Rock' and 'I'll Be Gone', respectively).

Still, the event was considered a success.

'Myponga the grand-daddy of 'em all,' stated one newspaper headline, alongside a shot of Ross Wilson in action, a fox tail attached to the arse of his pants. 'Grog galore,' screamed another, next to a photo of boozy revellers stomping in the mud while Wilson and the band did their retro-rock thing.

A report in the *Sunday Mail* showed how puzzling this gathering of the tribes was to mainstream media: 'Ten thousand heavy rock fans at the Myponga pop festival tonight settled themselves firmly in their garbage-strewn pop paddock for a night of love, peace, rock music and booze, booze and more booze.' Oddly, there was no mention of the pot smoke that hung like smog in the air. Another journo was obsessed with the noticeable absence of underwear: 'There are about 5000 girls at the festival and there does not seem to be a bra among them.'

As for co-headliner Cat Stevens, he either missed his plane or cancelled—depending on which report you believed. Whatever really went down, the Greek-English singer/ strummer failed to appear.

Historically speaking, though, Myponga was significant. It was the first but not the final time that Bon and Sabbath's Ozzy Osbourne would share a stage—although next time around Bon and the man who liked to call himself 'the plumber of darkness' were on much more equal footing.

★

With their eyes still very much on the larger prize of the US, Bon and the band shared some unlikely bills during the early months of 1971. In March, they played at the Adelaide Festival of the Arts—where the controversial rock opera *Jesus Christ Superstar* would make its Oz debut the following year—playing alongside Sydney singer Jeannie Lewis. But Lewis was no rock and roller; her roots were in folk and jazz. They performed a piece titled 'Love 200', written by the Tasmanian-born composer Peter Sculthorpe, which followed Captain James Cook's journey to plot the transit of Venus, leading the explorer to Australia. Lewis had recently performed the piece in Sydney with prog rockers Tully.

Bon couldn't help but laugh at the punters in their penguin suits and finery, or the way the members of the orchestra treated him with such formality. That didn't happen in the venues he was used to playing.

A few weeks later Bon and Fraternity were letting the whole of Australia know of their devotion to The Band, when they performed a note-perfect take of 'The Shape I'm In' on ABC TV show *GTK*. Bassist Bruce Howe, with his high hairline and blissful gaze, could have even passed for The Band's resident eccentric and musical genius Garth Hudson. Bon was in his usual streetwear—jeans and singlet—and kept the straightest of faces, which was in keeping with the deadly earnest demeanour of the rest of the band. But the ballsy voice that would soon be familiar to every Australian music fan was starting to take shape, because every now and again Bon would cut loose.

Despite Fraternity being a humour-free zone, one aspect of Bon's personality was starting to emerge, as the band's

John Freeman admitted: 'He was never afraid to take his shirt off.' But the smirk and the leer—two of Bon's trademarks—were yet to come into play.

Fraternity were the logical choice to support Brits Deep Purple, Free and Manfred Mann when their tour reached Adelaide's Apollo Stadium in mid-May. The roadshow was backed by Sammy Lee, a colourful Sydney identity with a pencil-thin moustache and a North American twang, who ran drag club Les Girls. Lee was known as 'the King of the Cross', and his involvement meant there were some heavy figures backstage at the Adelaide gig, as John Freeman recalled. 'There were blokes running around with guns. It was terrifying.'

When Fraternity were told to go on stage and play their set, they complained that the house lights were still up. 'Do what you're told,' they were instructed. 'Go and play.' Clearly there was no room for negotiation.

Bon would reconnect with Deep Purple again, in much improved circumstances. But not so Paul Kossoff, Free's wild-haired, seriously stoned guitarist. The next time Bon spoke about Kossoff, he'd deliver a punchline worthy of a stand-up comic. Tragically, Kossoff wouldn't be around to get the joke.

★

Fraternity recorded an album called *Livestock*, released in early 1971 on Sweet Peach, the record label side of Hamish Henry's all-encompassing Fraternity empire. The Band influences were most obvious in such cuts as 'Summerville', while the overall feel was of a band stuck between prog, psychedelia and country-rock but with no clear sound to call its own. Reviewing a 1998 reissue of the record, AllMusic's Victor W. Valdivia summed up *Livestock* well. 'None of it is really that groundbreaking or unusual,' he wrote, 'and would probably have faded into obscurity without [Bon] Scott's later notoriety. *Livestock* serves a good historical purpose but is of limited interest to anyone but hardcore Bon Scott fanatics.'

The album featured just one of Bon's songs, a co-write with bandmate Mick Jurd called 'Raglan's Folly'. This limited creative involvement summed up Bon's position in the Fraternity hierarchy: he was a songwriting novice, a newbie. Bruce Howe, Jurd and John Bisset wrote the bulk of the material, although you would never call them prolific. 'We were an amazingly self-indulgent and lazy lot,' Bisset said in an interview with AC/DC Collector. 'Priority number one was always "getting out of it" on whatever was available.'

'Upstairs' was band slang for being high; when drunk they were 'downstairs'. Fraternity didn't have a pet term for songwriting.

The group performed 'Raglan's Folly' on *GTK* during April. It was a ponderous six minutes of Oz prog, striving for the epic feel of Brits Yes and Genesis, but with none of their melodic smarts or poetry. Bon, decked out in a singlet and jeans, his beard in full and scraggly flourish, sang the lyric (which he'd written) with plenty of gusto, but the track dragged on and on, each player seemingly lost in his own musical world. As for Bon's recorder solo at the close, it could have passed as a dead ringer for passages heard on King Crimson's *In the Court of the Crimson King*. Perhaps

Bon had been tuning in when Blackfeather's John Robinson was napping on the band's couch back in Sydney.

Speaking of Robinson, he'd written a mood piece named 'Seasons of Change', which Fraternity were keen to record. To date, they hadn't troubled the business end of the charts—*Livestock* had kicked around the lowly end of the national Top 50—and they felt that this might just be the song to help them break through. They'd been assured by Blackfeather's label that they were free to release it as a single. The only trouble was that Robinson and Blackfeather were in the process of cutting their own version, without Fraternity knowing. This was the pre-*Countdown* era, when a band could be a big fish in a small pond (as Fraternity were in Adelaide) but little heard of elsewhere, so Blackfeather had the clear advantage of coming from Sydney. If anyone was likely to score with 'Seasons of Change', it was them.

Fraternity's cover was solid, this time actually helped by Bon's recorder, added on his suggestion in place of the piano solo on Robinson's original. And Bon sang it like he meant it; he could do earnest sincerity as well as anyone else in the band. And again, they were given solid exposure on *GTK*, where they played the song with their usual stony-faced determination (apart from bassist Howe, who beamed beatifically).

But when Blackfeather's take was released in May, the Fraternity version was as good as dead. Blackfeather's reached a national peak of number nine, charting for fourteen weeks, while Fraternity's charted strongly in Adelaide and then disappeared into the ether.

★

Bon had recently reconnected with Irene Thornton, although this time around he didn't have anyone's toe stuck between his lips. She chatted with him after a Fraternity gig at the rowdy Largs Pier Hotel, one of the key venues in Adelaide (and the site of Australia's first drive-through bottle shop). Fraternity would play there just about every week. Later, the pub would go down in AC/DC history as the site where Bon's mate, wild man Pat Pickett, joined the band's entourage as 'lighting director'. 'We didn't have any fucking lights,' Mark Evans noted in *Dirty Deeds*. It didn't matter. Pickett stayed.

On the night he caught up with Irene at the Largs Pier, Bon was, as usual, wearing his sprayed-on shorts. Irene couldn't resist making a comment.

'What a well-packed lunch,' she cheekily noted, her eyes glancing southwards.

'Yeah,' Bon replied, not missing a beat. 'Two boiled eggs and a sausage.'

It was a pretty fair comeback, and it made an impression on Irene, as she wrote in *My Bon Scott*.

'*Hello*, I thought. I was suddenly *very* impressed.'

Both Bon and Irene began talking about each other with their friends—Bon called her a 'real spunk', a big rap in 1971—and soon after, at the house Bon shared in Adelaide, they became a couple. They bonded over the copy of *Bazza Pulls It Off!*, the Barry 'Bazza' McKenzie comic that Irene had with her. (Bon was also a big fan of Johnny Hart's *B.C.* comic strip.) The Bazza McKenzie series, written by Barry Humphries, depicted the life and times of a 'randy, boozy Australian rampaging through Swinging London'; they now fetch a handsome price online. Some of the Aussie vernacular that dotted the pages—'technicolour yawn', 'up the freckle', 'point Percy at the porcelain'—wouldn't be too far removed from Bon's raunchier lyrics with AC/DC.

Bon would collect Irene from her office job every afternoon; together they'd roar off on his beloved trail bike. When Bon visited her at home, he had a quirky habit of tapping on Irene's bedroom window, rather than using the front door, even though her mother was very fond of him. Bon even sent Irene flowers, a first. Clearly, this was a love match—and when Bon fell in love, he fell hard.

They consummated their relationship one night at a house in Norwood, Bon impressing Irene with his moves. When Irene, who'd just turned 21, first told Bon that she loved him, he replied, with a wink: 'That's just as well.'

★

Pubs such as the Pooraka Hotel and the Largs Pier became the centre of the couple's world, along with the farm. Bon would sometimes proudly hold up the bar, basking in the attention he received as 'that guy in Fraternity'—and happily knocking back the free drinks, too. Yet despite Hamish Henry's support, he was as broke as ever. ('The dollar sign is not the ultimate,' Bon told a writer from *Go-Set*, clinging to the band's 'it's all about the music' shtick—which was just as well.) Sometimes when he over-imbibed Bon might get into a punch-up, but he was more interested in hedonism than head bashing. Lots of women gravitated to him; among them was Margaret Smith, a flame from his past. Margaret had been married when she and Bon were an item; she'd first met him when she worked as a secretary in the philosophy department at the University of Adelaide. Clearly she wasn't the typical 'rock chick'.

But Bon didn't flirt with her or any of the others, certainly not in front of Irene, at least.

History has concluded that Bon felt creatively repressed in Fraternity and was denied any serious input, but as far as Irene could see, he was happy there, at least for a while. Admittedly, the others in the band were well read—big thinkers—which made Bon feel insecure about his lack of a traditional education, but this was still a step up from the bubblegum image of The Valentines. And Fraternity were big news in Adelaide; their weekly gigs were always packed.

Bon's taste in music was starting to develop—he learned about Dylan and The Band via the guys in Fraternity, while Irene turned him on to trailblazing singer/songwriters Carole King and Joni Mitchell. In early 1971, King was exploding across the planet with her classic LP *Tapestry*—it stayed in the Oz charts for almost a year—while Mitchell was pushing singer/strummer boundaries with her landmark albums *Ladies of the Canyon* and *Blue*. They were era-defining artistes, favouring intimate tones and deeply felt lyrics. And both certainly got their hooks into Bon Scott, who had a sensitive streak that few were exposed to. As for his fashion sense, that wasn't evolving at the same pace. Irene admitted his image needed some work; to her, Bon was 'all over the place'. He wouldn't be surrendering his ball-hugging shorts any time soon.

★

Fraternity's grand plans for breaking into the US had faded. Instead, they now set their sights on 1971's Hoadley's Battle of the Sounds—the final staging of the event, as it turned out. The competition, as always, was strong; apart from Fraternity, the key contenders were Sherbet, Fraternity's opening act back in Sydney, and Jeff St John's Copperwine; 'Uncle' John Ayers had recently jumped ship from Copperwine to Fraternity, which only upped the rivalry.

On stage at Melbourne's Festival Hall, Bon sang 'Seasons of Change' as if his life, not just his career, hung in the balance. He'd shaved off his scraggly beard, and there was more than a little swagger in his onstage moves; his hips seemed to have a life of their own. He looked sharp, too, in denim.

After the performances, the bow-tied MC stepped forward to announce the winner, having just rattled off what was up for grabs: $2000 in cash, overseas tickets, a $300 recording session with Bill Armstrong Studios in Melbourne and a $300 recording fee. It was a generous bounty.

When Fraternity were declared the winner, the band's rent-a-crowd, who'd travelled with them from Adelaide, screamed in unison—the reaction was more in keeping with what Bon used to experience with The Valentines. Upon hearing the news, Bon couldn't stand still; he bounced around, almost bursting out of his skin with excitement. The rest of the band flashed rare public smiles. This truly meant something. An event like Battle of the Sounds might have smacked of the mainstream for idealists like Fraternity, who considered themselves part of the counterculture, but this was big, all the same.

'We did it for Adelaide,' Bon said, genuinely thrilled, as he stepped up to the mic. 'Thank you.'

Then he and the band ripped into 'Hemming's Farm', a tribute to the communal life back at their rural HQ, with raw energy—those weekly gigs playing to the boozy punters at the Largs Pier had toughened up their sound.

The win was also a welcome relief for Bon. The band weren't long back from the Gold Coast, where they'd had a run-in with the local coppers, who'd said they were playing too loudly. When Bon challenged them from the stage, the men in blue intervened and shut down the show. Bruce Howe pulled Bon aside afterwards and called him a 'dickhead'. Bon didn't have a clear understanding of the power of the law, especially in a volatile place like Queensland, which was ruled with an iron fist by the state premier Joh Bjelke-Petersen. He needed to tread a bit more warily.

But now, finally, they had a ticket out of the country. Once back in the City of Churches, a crew from the local Channel 9 was despatched to shoot a special on the band at Hemming's Farm. Bon, while showing off some moves on his trail bike, flew over the handlebars, landing in a patch of thorns. His injuries were only superficial, but it was a worrying omen for his future.

Bon and recklessness were kindred spirits. On another occasion, while on the road, his bandmates looked on as Bon jumped from a pier into water swarming with jellyfish, purely to get a laugh from the local kids. At Hemming's Farm Bon liked to ride a trolley down an embankment in the direction of the lake. When the trolley hit the dirt at the bottom of the embankment, he'd be catapulted into the water like a human cannonball.

One day, Bon and John Bisset dropped acid, loaded Bon's bike onto the back of Bisset's ute and drove down to the beach. Bon was not the type to sit and ponder the universe when high; instead he insisted that Bisset climb on the back of his bike, which he duly rode through a tidal stream that crossed the beach, drenching them both. Then Bon smashed straight into a huge pile of sand. The bike was wedged and Bon and Bisset were thrown high into the air. Bon landed on the sand, unhurt, tripping madly, dripping water and spitting sand, a huge grin on his face. Fortunately for him, Bisset saw the funny side, too.

'I knew you'd either hit me or laugh,' Bon told him, smiling broadly.

7

'They're dancing on the plate.'
—Bon, on acid, confronted with a plate of scones

There was plenty of business to attend to before Bon and the band could head offshore. Most importantly for Bon, he and Irene were getting hitched. Hamish Henry had made it clear that their UK entourage—the band's departure was planned for May 1972—would include wives but not girlfriends. His munificence only extended so far. This hastened Bon's proposal to Irene, although it wasn't a marriage of convenience. They were in love.

When Bon broke the news to his mother, Isa, back in the west, she had one key question: 'Is the girl pregnant, Ronnie?' (She wasn't.)

The wedding took place on 24 January, during a typically sun-blasted Adelaide summer. They said their 'I dos' at the registry office at the Adelaide Town Hall. Bon wore flares and wide lapels; Irene was stunning in a full-length crepe skirt, her fair hair cascading down her shoulders. They were flanked by Bruce Howe and John Bisset during the ceremony (Irene opted against bridesmaids). Then the newlyweds, various friends, family and the guys from Fraternity piled into the band's ride—an ageing Greyhound bus—for the trip to Hemming's Farm for the reception. First stop, though, was Bon's share house in Norwood, where the newlyweds posed for photos with their mothers, smiling happily. It was the first time that Irene had met Isa, and they connected strongly. 'She was full of life,' wrote Irene, 'just like Bon.'

Not surprisingly, the reception was an all-nighter; at one stage during the long night, the keg was somehow knocked into the dam. It was a problem easy fixed—the guests simply jumped in and retrieved it. Pot, booze and good times were in ample supply, and the party spilled over to the next day. Bride and groom awoke the next day with supersized hangovers.

Upon reflection, Irene figured that Bon 'just liked being married'; he seemed more excited by the concept than the reality, and fidelity would prove a very tricky thing for him to manage. But he was more domesticated than Irene, having been pretty much independent since his days in The Spektors. Bon was a dab hand at the ironing board and could also rustle up a basic though edible spread—he even taught Irene how to make coleslaw. Irene, by her own admission, had none of these skills; the notion of a domestic life in suburbia had little appeal for her. But it was a love match, at least at the time. Bon was 25, Irene 21, and their shared future seemed bright.

'I thought it would last forever,' she wrote, 'and things would never change.'

Oddly, not long after they were married, Bon drove Irene to the house of Margaret Smith, one of his former partners, and introduced the two women. It was a peculiar gesture; perhaps it was Bon's way of proving to Smith that he'd moved on. But Smith, after a change of Christian name, would eventually resurface in Bon's life.

★

In the weeks leading up to their departure, the band secured some funding from the Arts Council of South Australia and headed out on a quick regional tour. Bon had scored some super-strength blotting-paper acid and, in typical Road Test Ronny style, he took to it with abandon, even though the others were a little more wary.

As John Bisset recalled in an interview at AC/DC Collector, 'Most of us sussed out to take just enough to get upstairs but not really peaking.' Not so Bon.

To his credit, Bon was generous with his drugs: he once plied John Bisset with Mandrax—'mandies'—during a show, and Bisset dropped headfirst onto his keyboard, as though he'd been shot, his right foot stuck on the volume pedal.

Part of the deal with the Arts Council required the band to be on call for civic receptions. During one such soiree, after a show at Waikerie, on the banks of the Murray River, the hostess offered everyone scones. Bon stared at them, fear in his eyes. He was freaking out.

'What's wrong, Bon?' Bisset asked.

'They're dancing on the plate,' Bon whispered.

★

While Bon was dealing with the dancing scones, in Sydney, two brothers who would change the course of his life were serving their musical apprenticeship. Malcolm and Angus

Young were connected to Bon by more than a shared love of rock and roll. The Young family had also come to Australia via the Assisted Migration Scheme, just like the Scotts. They arrived in June 1963. Only two Youngs stayed behind in the UK—older brothers Alex, who was serving time in a band called Grapefruit, and John, who was detained at Her Majesty's pleasure.

The Youngs came straight off the council estate at Cranhill in Glasgow, about 130 kilometres from where Bon was raised in Kirriemuir, and wound up in the Villawood Migrant Hostel in Sydney.

Again, just like Bon, neither Malcolm nor Angus had completely shed their Scottish brogue. When pop singer Ted Mulry once visited the Youngs, he asked Malcolm: 'What's that language you all talk in?'

In 1971, the most famous Young of all was George, the third youngest of the eight siblings. He'd been the mainstay of The Easybeats, whose path had crossed intermittently with that of Bon Scott while he was with The Valentines. But in 1972 Malcolm and Angus started their musical journey. Sixteen-year-old Angus played manic lead guitar in an outfit named Kantuckee, while Malcolm, three years his senior, was the steady-handed rhythm guitarist in Velvet Underground, a favourite act of the suburban dance circuit. Neither downplayed their musical bloodline; Angus and Malcolm would proudly introduce themselves as 'the brother of George Young—from The Easybeats!' And they were eager to pursue their own rock-and-roll dream, inspired equally by Chuck Berry, Buddy Holly, Little Richard, big brother George and their shared distaste for the nine to five.

While Kantuckee was little more than a garage band, Velvet Underground was a working group, gigging regularly, building a following—mainly female, mainly young—and trying their hand at writing originals. Malcolm had joined them in April 1971 and had recently acquired an impressive rig: a Marshall amp and a Gibson guitar, towering over his five-foot-two frame. As for Angus, two simple words were printed on the top of his amplifier: 'HIGH VOLTAGE'.

It was around this time that Ted Albert, the well-heeled, well-spoken scion of the successful Sydney music empire Alberts, producer and staunch supporter of George Young and The Easybeats, visited the Young family home in suburban Burwood. When he heard Malcolm and Angus banging away on guitars in a nearby room, he turned to their father, William, and said: 'If they ever want to do anything, send them to me.' Albert sensed that George might not be the only Young with some talent.

Step by gradual step, the pieces of AC/DC were falling into place.

★

The last hurrah of Fraternity before their departure for the UK was the release of an album, their second, titled *Flaming Galah*, which appeared in April. Yet again, Bon had just the one co-write on the album, a country-rocker called 'Welfare Boogie', which was credited to the entire band. It was a classic case of singing about what you know; in some ways, Hamish Henry's weekly cheques weren't vastly different to surviving on the dole. The lyric even flashed back to the day when The Valentines were busted, because, as Bon sang, 'the wrong guy I trusted'. The funny, clever wordplay for which he'd become renowned was slowly taking shape, as was Bon's habit of drawing on his own experiences for source material. There was more personality in that single song than there was on the rest of the LP, although one track, 'If You Got It', was noteworthy, simply for the fact that it was recorded while the band was on 'shrooms. ("'Twas the season for gathering mushrooms,' admitted John Bisset.)

'Welfare Boogie' was considered strong enough to release as a single, but it didn't bother the charts, which currently featured such locals as Colleen Hewitt, Johnny Chester, and The Aztecs' terrific 'Most People I Know Think that I'm Crazy'. *Flaming Galah* hit a national peak of number 28 and then quickly faded away. The time couldn't have been better for an overseas odyssey.

In the weeks leading up to their flight out, Bon and Irene briefly moved in with her mother. First, they flew to Perth, to check in with Bon's people and his many drinking buddies. Bon was primed for the UK, hugely excited. As Irene noted, Bon firmly believed that Fraternity were world-beaters: 'He was convinced that Fraternity was going to knock them dead in England.'

They did find time, however, for a week-long stopover in Singapore en route, which was a brave new world for Bon. A shortage of cash meant they had to stick to their hotel and the nearby streets, yet the experience 'just blew his mind', wrote Irene. Chinese restaurants were hard enough to find in Adelaide, let alone chopsticks, which were beyond Bon's reach. He got more food on himself than in his mouth.

★

Bon and Irene joined the rest of the entourage on 21 June 1972. It was a time when the UK charts were a strange brew of glam rock (T. Rex, Slade, Gary Glitter), mainstream singer-songwriters like Don McLean ('Vincent') and Gilbert O'Sullivan ('Ooh-Wakka-Doo-Wakka-Day'), soul/R&B acts including Roberta Flack and The Drifters, and such Brit perennials as Wings, The Moody Blues, The Who and The Kinks. Teen pop was also big, in the shape of David Cassidy, Donnie Osmond (currently experiencing 'Puppy Love') and Michael 'Rockin' Robin' Jackson. There was nothing even remotely like 'Welfare Boogie' in the Top 40. Not a good omen.

Located at Mountfield Road in suburban Finchley, the 'Frat' house was a relatively short ride away from London's CBD on the Tube's Northern line. Depending on whose memory you trust, there were either seventeen or nineteen people (the band, partners, crew, tour manager Bruce King and a dog named Clutch) living in a house designed, at most, for six people. There were so many people living there that meals had to be prepared and eaten in shifts; it was more like a boarding house than a communal HQ. The local pub and high street were within stumbling distance, which was handy.

Not too keen to play homemaker, and in need of some ready cash, Irene quickly landed a job as a typist. The money, in her words, may have been 'terrible', but Bon would come to rely on her meagre wage to get by—and not for the last time.

In a textbook case of poor planning, Hamish Henry arranged for the band's Greyhound bus to be shipped over from Australia. What seemed like solid management turned out to be the exact opposite, because he hadn't factored in London's narrow streets—some were simply too small for their ride to manoeuvre. The Finchley locals had a field day; it was a hilarious sight, parked in the street like a beached whale. In the words of Fraternity's Sam See, 'It was a tactical blunder not equalled since Gallipoli.' Another bad omen.

Bon was a master of creature comforts and soon found the local TV to his taste. He fell for such shows as *Monty Python's Flying Circus* and *The Benny Hill Show*, even if they were poles apart in style and substance. Music shows like *Top of the Pops* and *The Old Grey Whistle Test* were compulsory viewing in the house. But Bon and the others didn't know what to make of the 'opposition'. When Bryan Ferry and Roxy Music vamped their way through 'Virginia Plain' on *Top of the Pops*, they were aghast. They hadn't seen so much glitter, sequins and all-round glamminess in their lives; it certainly wouldn't have passed the pub test at the Largs Pier.

Who is this poof? Bon wondered.

But in his quieter moments, Bon understood that if a band was to succeed, it needed a bit of the ol' razzle-dazzle. Wiggling his hips while tooting on a recorder wasn't going to cut it; he knew that. He'd often sit with Bruce Howe and discuss stagecraft, as Howe revealed in 2015. '[At the time] he was quite a shy performer. We realised that to make it to a huge audience you had to take over the whole stage. And when he came back to Australia, he knew that's what he had to do, next chance he got. And he did it.'

★

In typical Fraternity style, the band sat back and waited for something to happen. Bon, meanwhile, turned 26 on 9 July 1972. Lack of funds meant that celebrations were subdued; Irene had just enough cash to buy him a shaver and a bottle of brandy. They were so broke that when winter started to creep in, Irene was forced to buy a heater and blanket on hire purchase. Hamish Henry kept talking a big game—there were plans to either rework their last album or record another, but nothing came of them. Bon kept busy by scribbling away in his notebook, jotting down possible lyrics and song ideas.

Finally, with the help of a local agency, MAM (co-founded by singer Tom Jones), Fraternity scored some gigs, but all they did was prove what currently remained unsaid: the band was out of its depth. Their first major show, on 17 August, was a total disaster.

London-spawned Status Quo had had a huge hit during the psychedelic '60s with 'Pictures of Matchstick Men' but were now in the process of reinventing themselves as an eight-legged, denim-clad boogie monster (and not too far away from the sound of early AC/DC). When Fraternity were booked to open for them at a show in coastal resort town Bournemouth—the hometown of several members of prog rockers King Crimson—the 'Quo' was in the process of pulling together the songs for their breakout fifth album *Piledriver*.

Bon and the others were in their Greyhound bus, parked outside the venue—the oddly named Starkers Royal Ballroom, which would have tickled Bon, that fan of Benny Hill—when the headliners arrived in two Bentleys. The four members of Status Quo stepped from their fancy motors, decked out in Afghan coats and bell-bottoms, their long hair flowing, looking very much like rock-and-roll peacocks. This, inevitably, prompted much snickering inside the Fraternity bus.

It was a very different Status Quo that took the stage after Fraternity's set—and not just because they'd changed backstage into their faded denims and T-shirts. They were 100-plus shows deep into their Dog of Two Heads tour and, having been on the road since late 1971, were by then a very well-oiled machine. They plugged in, set their amps to 'boogie' and absolutely tore the place up. 'They rocked us off the stage, totally destroyed us,' recalled John Freeman.

During the drive back to London, the temperature inside the Greyhound grew particularly chilly, and harsh words were spoken. As guitarist Sam See commented in an online interview, 'In retrospect, it was probably the defining moment of the end for a few of us.'

Further support slots with such bands as Atomic Rooster, Fairport Convention and the Pink Fairies only confirmed what they suspected: they were no match for the headliners. One of their major problems was their equipment—many of these bands came equipped with their own supercharged PAs, which Fraternity simply didn't own. Nor did they have enough strong original material; they still fleshed out their sets with covers.

The mood at the house in Finchley turned very bleak. Bon and Irene spent as much time away from the place as they could, Bon being the kind of guy who'd cross the street to avoid confrontation. ('Everyone loves a smile,' he'd tell the others, flashing one of his own, but it didn't seem to help.)

Hamish Henry's advocacy started to fade, too. As John Freeman later noted, 'He had the money but didn't have the expertise.' You needed to be well connected in such a competitive music market as the UK—and Henry simply wasn't. Adelaide native Robert Stigwood had recently helped guide the Bee Gees to huge success in the UK and the US due to his innate understanding of hype and his heavyweight contacts in what was known quietly as 'the Pink Mafia', a group of like-minded impresarios that dominated English showbiz. Hamish Henry was no Robert Stigwood.

It didn't help Bon's state of mind when he heard from the head of the band's Australian fan club; apparently Fraternity were already a forgotten band back in Oz. Now it was all about Billy Thorpe and The Aztecs, G. Wayne Thomas, and New Zealand's The La De Da's. Sherbet, the kids who'd opened for Fraternity back during Bon's first shows at Jonathan's, were also making waves on the charts and would record numerous hit singles over the next decade. Fraternity had achieved a dubious double—they were now nobodies in two countries.

8

'They were on the same level and it was way
above my head.'
—Bon's opinion of his Fraternity bandmates

In October 1972, Fraternity crossed the Channel for shows
in Germany, supporting Sweet, another London-based glam
band who were making big chart inroads. Their frothy 1972
single 'Wig-Wam Bam' was a huge hit at the time, peaking
at number 4 in the UK (and eventually reaching number
15 in Australia); such frenetic Sweet staples as 'Blockbuster',
'Ballroom Blitz' and 'Fox on the Run', most of which were
co-written or co-produced by expat Queenslander Mike
Chapman, were just around the corner.

German audiences turned out to be more responsive
to Fraternity's take on rootsy rock and roll, helped along
by Bon, who introduced a few songs using his very basic
Deutsch. 'We focused more on rock for the German audience and went over quite well,' said John Bisset.

The group limped back to Finchley and tried to come up
with a new plan. In a rare concession to the charts, they opted
for a glam-rock reboot and gave themselves a new name:
Fang. (They didn't change their sound, just their name.) Bon
commandeered some silver bracelets from Irene and wore

them as earrings, but his new look was more rock-and-roll pirate than Marc Bolan. (Funnily enough, years later, Lemmy from Motörhead was asked if he thought of Bon as a pirate. 'Well, I never saw him dressed as a pirate. I never saw him dressed actually; he was usually just wearing a pair of jeans.')

It didn't help Bon's situation that despite the ever-increasing number of lyrics he was recording in his notebook, none were deemed worthy of being teamed with music. He remained low in the Fraternity hierarchy.

Bon had developed an uncanny habit of crossing paths with people who'd play a far more crucial role in events further down the line—he'd already intersected with Ozzy Osbourne, Deep Purple and Free's Paul Kossoff. This happened again during the band's brief reign as Fang (which lasted just a few dates), when they opened for a Newcastle-upon-Tyne band named Geordie in March 1973.

Though they'd only formed in early 1972, Geordie had already tasted chart success, breaching the UK Top 40 with a song called 'Don't Do That', which earned them a comparison to glam rockers Slade, the band *du jour* for pissed-up skinheads and yobs. Out front of Geordie was a stocky 25-year-old singer with a voice that was equal parts gravel and sand and an explosion of hair that made Bon's mane look tidy by comparison. His name was Brian Johnson. Like Bon, Johnson was working class all the way; his father Alan had been a coalminer (and a sergeant major in the British Army's Durham Light Infantry).

During that show with Geordie, Bon watched from the wings as Johnson hoisted guitarist Vic Malcolm onto his shoulders and waded into the crowd, who lapped it up. It was great theatre.

That's a good trick, Bon thought, and stored it away for future reference.

★

As the winter of 1973 set in, Fraternity's situation grew increasingly worse when their landlord threatened them with eviction. Bon was relieved when his brother Graeme visited; he desperately needed a break, some kind of outlet. (He'd tried the hallucinogenic plant datura, but it left him a babbling wreck, prostrate on the floor.) Graeme, now working as a merchant seaman, had grown very tight with Bon over the years. Bon referred to him as 'my favourite earthling'.

Together they took in a number of London concerts, including shows from Deep Purple and The Sensational Alex Harvey Band. Bon was gaga for frontman Alex Harvey, a fellow Scot. In a situation that would echo Bon's future role in AC/DC, Harvey was considerably older than his bandmates, but that didn't matter—he had great presence, which impressed Bon enormously. He owned the stage. Bon and Graeme also saw The Rolling Stones, not too long back from a tour of Australia (where a group named Headband, featuring an Adelaide mate of Bon's named Peter Beagley, had opened the shows). Bon was so impressed by the shark's tooth dangling from Keith Richards' ear that he swung by Portobello Markets and bought one for himself.

The Scott brothers even got the chance to see Little Richard in action. This was a first for Bon, who used to belt out 'Tutti Frutti' in the shower, much to the dismay of Isa. It was late April 1973, and Richard had sold out London's Hammersmith Odeon (a venue that Bon and AC/DC would one day fill), his career on the rise again. The 40-year-old Richard had taken to introducing himself as 'the king of rock and roll', which wasn't an unreasonable claim—after all, he'd been on the scene since the glory days of Elvis, Chuck Berry and Buddy Holly. Bon was a little surprised by Little Richard in the flesh; he was even more flamboyant than he'd anticipated.

Back at the Frat House, the mood darkened further when the guys in the band put the kibosh on a proposed 'women only' holiday arranged by their partners. Instead, they used their partners' money for new gear. It was a relief for all concerned when they were asked to return to Germany, this time to tour with a band named Amon Düül.

This oddly named collective had a similar mindset to Fraternity's; it had emerged from a Munich-based political art commune named Amon Düül, linked to the powerful German student movement of the 1960s. It was a far heavier scene than Hemming's Farm, but the notion of community was similar. Yet Bon and the band were probably more aligned with British band the Pink Fairies, who they soon toured with for the second time. The Fairies, as they'd readily tell the press, believed in three key ideals: free music, drug use and anarchy.

None of this improved Fraternity's fortunes. Bon, much to his dismay, was forced to take on work as a cleaner, his first day job since his stint as a postie back in Freo. If that wasn't bad enough, a doctor told him that his hearing was in bad shape.

'You could be deaf in a few years if you keep playing rock and roll,' he was told.

Could anything else go wrong?

It could, apparently. Fang was booked to appear at the Holsworthy Festival in Devon on 11 July, opening for British band Mungo Jerry, who were fresh from an appearance on *Top of the Pops*. Again, like so many of the acts for whom they opened in the UK, Mungo Jerry not only had hits—1970's bubbly 'In the Summertime' was one of the bestselling singles of all time—but were also well oiled, having been on the road since the start of the year. Fraternity, once again, were blown off the stage and, as Irene noted in a letter home, it didn't go unnoticed. 'The guys got a bad write-up in . . . *Melody Maker*,' she wrote.

With gigs drying up, Bon found various jobs, driving a forklift, working in a wig-making factory and then, far more suitably, pulling beers at the Manor Cottage pub, but the situation between him and Irene was becoming as fragile as that within the band. The notion of 'sharing and caring' didn't register strongly with Bon, because whatever money he did make, he didn't share with his wife. But what was Irene's was definitely Bon's.

Hamish Henry, meanwhile, was making new plans—Canada was now floated as a possible base for the band, because clearly it wasn't working out in the UK. Bon went as far as undertaking an interview at the Canadian embassy, but Irene wasn't interested. She made it clear to Bon that if he went to Canada, he'd be travelling by himself. When Bon's brother Graeme offered to spring for tickets back to Oz, Bon reluctantly accepted.

Fraternity's odyssey was over, although they were hardly the first (or last) Aussie band to get put through the wringer in the UK. Peers such as The Masters Apprentices and The Twilights had also tried, and failed, to crack the lucrative market, while even the almighty Easybeats struggled to repeat the huge success of their 1966 global smash 'Friday on My Mind'. Others, such as Zoot's Rick Springfield, chose to try their luck in the US instead. (Springfield had a Top 20 hit there with his first solo single, 1972's wistful 'Speak to the Sky', and remains an established star in America almost 50 years later.)

Bon cut through the crap when a reporter asked him to explain exactly what went wrong. 'We all got stoned and disappeared up our own arseholes,' he replied. In a more considered response, during an interview with *Juke* magazine, Bon outlined what he saw as the key problems. Simply put, Fraternity 'didn't have a chance in England', he accepted. But there were also internal issues; he wasn't on equal footing with the rest of the band. 'They,' he said, referring to the others, 'were on the same level and it was way above my head.'

They were hardly a band of brothers. And Bon, despite his best efforts to adapt, was never a fully fledged hippie.

'The whole mood of the band went downhill in London,' John Bisset stated in an online interview. 'Harsh reality began to set in. The party was over. We were not up with the play as far as sound production went. Our PA was inadequate and we lacked the know-how and experience of the UK bands.'

Bisset stayed in the UK, joining Mungo Jerry, the very same band that had blown Fraternity away in Devon, while Sam See also jumped ship, rejoining The Flying Circus. The others in Fraternity decided to return to Adelaide and regroup, but not with Bon. He was replaced as vocalist by John Swan, and a few years later by Swan's nineteen-year-old brother Jimmy (aka Jimmy Barnes).

Bon and Irene had other plans. They reached Perth on 31 December 1973, checked in with his family, then took the slow train to Adelaide where they lobbed up on Irene's mother's doorstep, stone-cold broke. They were forced to sleep in Irene's childhood bedroom.

A lot had changed musically since Fraternity had left Australia eighteen months before. Singer/songwriters such as Kevin Johnson, the hirsute piano man Brian Cadd and Ross 'I Am Pegasus' Ryan were now in vogue—outside of Sherbet, there wasn't a single Oz band in the charts. The only reminder was David Bowie's take on The Easybeats' 'Friday on My Mind', a standout from *Pinups*, his covers album that was currently riding high in the charts.

Bon was 27 years old, down on his luck, a singer without a group. It was time to seek out a new sensation.

★

Bon's return to Adelaide in early 1974 was hardly a period in which he was covered in glory. In fact, he spent a good deal of those early months covered in something else altogether when he took a job working at the Wallaroo fertiliser plant. He'd tell Michael Browning, soon to manage AC/DC, that he was a 'shit shoveller'. (He actually worked on the weighbridge, but that just didn't have quite the same effect on people.)

Sometimes Bon would catch up with his old friend Peter Beagley (soon to change his name to Peter Head), who'd just moved back to Adelaide when his group, Headband, split up. Headband, like Fraternity, had made some inroads—they toured Australia with the Stones, released a few singles and

finished third in the 1972 Hoadley's Battle of the Sounds—
but never quite made the A-list.

Peter Head was a tall, good-looking guy with a shock of
dark hair. As a boy of thirteen he'd fallen hard for Little
Richard, just as Bon had, and he learned his chops playing
with Johnny Mac and The Macmen, Adelaide's first rock-and-
roll band. While still a kid, he also played piano, backing the
showgirls at La Belle, a notorious Adelaide den of iniquity.
He'd also done time in London in the mid-1960s, working
with Boz Burrell, who would hit the jackpot a decade later
with platinum-plus rockers Bad Company. During the days
of Fraternity, Head managed Hamish Henry's art gallery/
booking office in a converted stable at Henry's home in
North Adelaide.

It was there that Henry had given Bon odd jobs, such as
mowing the lawn and cleaning up the yard, which is how
Bon and Head grew close. 'Bon would come into the gallery
after he'd finished work,' said Head, 'and we'd sit and I'd
teach him a few chords on guitar.' Sometimes they'd jam
their favourite songs.

Not only were they friends, both aged 27, but they had
a new shared bond: their latest groups had fallen apart. As
Head stated in an online interview, 'Both bands had been
to the metaphorical top of the mountain, looked over to
see the Promised Land, and then come tumbling down in
a resounding crash. Close, but no cigar!' He described this
time with Bon as 'a re-union of old rock'n'roll warriors'. They
smoked, drank and sometimes jammed, trying to figure out
their next move.

Bon's marriage, meanwhile, had been pushed to the limits
during their eighteen months in the UK. It had become

increasingly clear to Irene that Bon, for all his good qualities, wasn't cut out for marriage. The simple things, like helping out with finances, appeared to be beyond his reach. Irene was more grounded; Bon not so much. And not only did Bon have a roving eye, but women also continued to gravitate to him. Add the heavy disappointment he felt from Fraternity's failure in the UK and it was no great surprise that they separated soon after their return to Adelaide. Bon moved in with Fraternity's Bruce Howe and dropped off Irene's radar for some time.

And Irene came to accept the situation. 'We were too young; we didn't stand a chance.'

Peter Head ran a very loose-knit collective called The Mount Lofty Rangers, named for the mountains that encircled Adelaide, and Bon chose to get involved. (It wasn't just a musical group; they also dabbled in art and the written word.) It was never more than a pit stop between bigger and ideally paying gigs, but it did give Bon the chance to try out some of his own songs. Bon's old Valentines buddy Vince Lovegrove, now a promoter, sat in occasionally, as did many others—over time, some 200 people were involved with the Rangers, including a post-Twilights/pre–Little River Band Glenn Shorrock.

Peter Head explained to Bon that there were two key principles to The Mount Lofty Rangers: the line-up was very fluid and they only played original music. It was just the outlet Bon needed, a huge relief from the restraints of Fraternity. Among their plans was a notion to write the great Australian musical; during Bon's tenure the Rangers did perform a week-long run of a show named *Lofty*. Head had Bon in mind for a future production of the show; he wanted

Bon to star as the lead character, named Lofty, although it never came to pass.

Among the Rangers' songs was one of Bon's most auto-biographical efforts to date, a funny, bluegrass-style ramble called 'Been Up in the Hills Too Long', which Bon and Head co-wrote. It was a less-than-subtle pot shot at life at Hemming's Farm, which ultimately didn't live up to its potential. Bon mixed downbeat observations—'I feel like a shirt that ain't been worn'—with early signs of his uncanny knack with words ('I feel like a rip that ain't been torn'). Okay, it wasn't quite 'Highway to Hell', but it was a step in the right direction.

Another song Bon sang during his brief tenure as a Ranger was a good-times, Stones-y rocker named 'Round and Round', written by Peter Head, which Bon recorded during an afternoon session at Slater Studios in North Adelaide. (Studio fee: $40.) They cut a second song, 'Carey Gully', Bon knocking over both vocals in a heartbeat.

'Perfect, first take,' Head recalled.

When 'Round and Round' did finally surface some 23 years later, it was teamed with black-and-white footage of Bon during his Fraternity days, gleefully ripping around the Adelaide Hills on his trail bike, a leather band across his forehead, and a wide grin on his face even when he took a tumble. And it was that trail bike that would have a huge impact on the next stage of Bon's life.

9

'When we met Bon for the first time, it was like we'd known him forever . . . He almost became a brother.'

—Malcolm Young

On the night of 2 May 1974, Bon was riding his bike, a Suzuki 550, in the backyard of the place he shared with the Howes when he came off, yet again. Bruce Howe pulled him aside.

'Mate,' he said, 'you're not going to last much longer if you keep doing this.'

Howe had no idea how prescient his comment would be.

The next night, after a rehearsal with the Rangers, Bon turned up at the Old Lion hotel. He was drunk and in an aggressive mood. According to Vince Lovegrove, who was at the Old Lion, an argument ensued and Bon stormed out, smashing a bottle of Jack Daniel's in the carpark before jumping on his Suzuki and roaring off into the night.

Somewhere past midnight, two grim-faced cops turned up on Irene's doorstep with the news that Bon, who was still her husband (although she hadn't seen him for almost two months), had been seriously hurt in a bike crash. He was in Emergency at The Queen Elizabeth Hospital, in very bad shape. Irene rushed to the hospital and when she caught a glimpse of Bon, she was stunned by the sight.

'He was barely recognisable,' she wrote, 'a bloodied pool of smashed jelly.'

After emergency surgery, Bon was moved to intensive care and placed in an induced coma. His injuries were horrible and numerous: he had a broken arm, broken ribs and a busted collarbone; his jaw, too, had been smashed and he'd lost a lot of teeth. There were also myriad superficial injuries—grazes, scrapes and abrasions. He was a terrible mess. As Irene recalled, his face, purple with bruises, was unrecognisable; it was 'covered in metal scaffolding'. At one point, a nurse handed Irene his broken and bloodstained helmet, thinking that Bon was dead.

'It was a very close call,' said Bruce Howe.

Within a few days Bon was conscious but in a massive amount of pain. He remained in the hospital for three weeks—when he was eventually released, his jaw was still wired shut. As a reminder of his very close call, he hung on to his bloodied motorcycle jacket. Another memento was a recurring shoulder injury that he was never able to shake. And to rub salt into his many wounds, he'd bought his now-wrecked bike on hire purchase and was forced to keep up the payments.

Mind you, he didn't lose his sense of humour; Bon took a photo of himself, sans chompers, and sent it to some friends with the caption: 'I left my teeth out on the road.'

Irene took him in, while Bon's mother, Isa, flew in from Perth to help out. She slept in a spare bedroom at Irene's house. Even though Isa knew they were separated, she realised that Bon's recovery was the most important thing, so she didn't mention their split. Bon's brother Graeme also checked in on his brother, and in an interesting twist, he took up with Fay, Irene's sister.

Bon turned 28 on 9 July, but this was hardly the type of celebration he'd hoped for, as he was still very much on the mend, and still without a band. He'd taken to smoking more pot than normal during his recovery and marked his birthday with a mixed grill of hash cookies and mushrooms. Even though he was slowly recovering and had taken a job with Lovegrove, who ran an agency called Jovan, Bon was at a low point, with no idea what to do next. He was Lovegrove's odd-jobs guy, putting up posters for upcoming gigs and playing chauffeur to visiting bands, driving them around the city in an FJ Holden that had seen better days. One of those bands he looked after was named AC/DC.

'Who are they?' Bon asked Lovegrove.

'Just some young, dinky little glam band from Sydney,' he replied, and they both got back to work.

★

The lives of Malcolm and Angus Young had taken some interesting twists since the day that Ted Albert turned up in the family lounge room and enquired about their future. Both had come to the realisation that their bands—Velvet Underground in Malcolm's case, Kantuckee in Angus's— weren't fulfilling their ambitions, so they'd joined forces in late 1973, much to the dismay of their parents. 'You'll kill each other,' they warned the brothers, who, like most siblings, often clashed. Big brother George, back from a four-year stint in the UK, took on the role of band mentor and shortly after co-producer, alongside Harry Vanda, when they signed a record deal with Ted Albert, who proved true to his word.

After a few suburban dates, AC/DC—a name suggested by their big sister, Margaret—made a big splash at Chequers, an inner-city venue that in its halcyon days had been the cabaret of choice for international acts and the watering hole for Sydney's A-list, as well as its more colourful local identities. But now it was a dingy dive for up-and-coming rock acts, operating six nights a week. AC/DC's run of shows began on New Year's Eve in 1973; they played four 60-minute-long sets each night, mixing a few originals with covers of rock-and-roll classics from The Rolling Stones ('Honky Tonk Women', 'Jumpin' Jack Flash'), Little Richard ('Lucille', 'Tutti Frutti') and Chuck Berry's 'School Days' and 'No Particular Place to Go'. When they ran out of songs, they simply played their set list over again.

'It went great,' said Angus. 'Everyone thought we were a bunch of loonies.' Angus had begun playing in his old school uniform—he'd come to get more use out of it in the band than he ever did at Ashfield Boys' High. He was not what you'd call a model student, and had left school at fifteen, avoiding likely expulsion.

The line-up was rubbery, to say the least. At their first photo shoot, with *Go-Set*'s Philip Morris, the band comprised Malcolm on rhythm guitar and Angus on lead; Dave Evans was the vocalist, while Rob Bailey played bass and Peter Clack drummed. They were an odd-looking bunch—Evans, dark haired and lanky, dressed in candy stripes and stacked heels, towered over the pint-sized Youngs, while Bailey matched an Indian shirt with satin flares and Clack sported a towering man-fro. This was not the denim-and-T-shirt look that would become as much an AC/DC trademark as their titanium-strength riffs.

With brother George at the helm, they recorded their debut single, 'Can I Sit Next to You, Girl', in January 1974. Angus was hugely impressed by George's studio acumen, as he'd relate in the documentary *Blood and Thunder*: 'He seemed to be creating things in his head.' And George's reputation—he was Oz music royalty, after all—helped AC/DC secure plenty of live work in their early months. Who wasn't going to book a band featuring two of George Young's siblings?

The single was finally released in July, reaching a modest chart peak of number 50, just before the group set out on a national tour with New York shock rocker Lou Reed. They'd already received their first notice in the music press, Malcolm telling a *Go-Set* reporter that, unlike a lot of bands doing the rounds, AC/DC understood their audience. 'Most of the groups in Australia are getting on, rather than getting it on,' he proclaimed. '[They're] out of touch with the kids who go to suburban dances.'

AC/DC were a band of the people, working class all the way down to their bootstraps. Or, in Malcolm's case, his platform heels—he was in the midst of a dalliance with glam.

★

The Lou Reed tour took AC/DC across the country and they reached Adelaide on 17 August. Bon was in the audience when AC/DC took the stage, fronting 2000 punters at Festival Hall. It didn't take long for someone to heckle

Angus: a guitarist dressed as a schoolboy, no matter how shit-hot a player he was, was fair game, especially in Adelaide.

'Hey,' someone yelled at Angus from the mosh pit, 'come on down here, mate.'

Bon, who was looking on, prepared for the inevitable flare-up. He'd been to enough gigs in Adelaide to know where this kind of heckling usually led. But not that night.

According to Bon, 'There were a dozen guys in front of the stage shouting, "Hey, hey, come on down here ya . . ."' and Angus, he walks up to the edge of the stage and screams at them, "Go and get fucked." So me, I'm looking for a microphone stand ready for the onslaught.'

Bon was impressed, both by Angus's playing—he'd been around long enough to recognise that the kid could really play—and by his gutsiness. The hecklers in the crowd went silent and the band played their set, ending with a revved-up take on the old Delta blues number 'Baby Please Don't Go', which gave Angus ample opportunity to cut loose on his Gibson. This wasn't some 'dinky little glam band'—not at all.

Bon made a mental note that the band would be back in Adelaide on 20 September. He wanted to check them out again, although he didn't think much of their singer.

It was during that Lou Reed tour that the Youngs won over another convert. While in Melbourne they played a show at the Hard Rock Café, a triple-levelled rock-and-roll hotspot operated by Michael Browning. He'd just ended his managerial relationship with Billy Thorpe, which had taken them to the UK without success, and was on the lookout for new talent. Browning's big ambition was to propel an Australian act to international stardom. He'd been tipped off to AC/DC by Sydney promoter Michael Chugg, who mentioned the Young bloodline. Browning was sold and booked them for a show on 16 August.

At first, when the band entered the venue, Browning didn't know what to make of them.

'To my surprise,' Browning wrote in his memoir *Dog Eat Dog*, 'I saw this scrawny little schoolkid walking around the [band]room . . . He looked like he'd walked off the pages of *Mad* magazine.'

His attitude quickly changed when they plugged in and let rip. Browning was blown away. 'The little fucker,' he wrote, 'was going off.' Afterwards, Browning paid the band $200 and invited them back to play the Hard Rock next time they were in Melbourne. They were a great outfit in the making, he could see that, but there was something not quite right about the singer they were working with. George Young had sensed that, too; he'd put in a call to Vince Lovegrove and asked if he knew of any rock-and-roll frontmen looking for a new gig.

'Bon Scott would be perfect,' Lovegrove replied.

★

When AC/DC returned to Adelaide, they played the Pooraka Hotel, a beer barn about fifteen kilometres north of the city. Afterwards, they were invited back to Bruce Howe's house, where a jam quickly ensued, and Bon stumbled up to the mic, slugging from a bottle of bourbon, and shouted his lungs raw. Teetotaller Angus looked on, shaking his head in disbelief; he was shocked that Bon could sing at all. 'I'd be surprised if the guy can walk, let alone sing,' he murmured to Malcolm.

But Bon impressed them on stage and off. He may have been seven years older than Malcolm, and nearly a decade Angus's senior, but a fraternal bond of sorts was formed.

'When we met Bon for the first time,' Malcolm said in 2000 on *Behind the Music*, 'it was like we'd known him forever . . . He almost became a brother.' (Over time, Bon would characterise himself as more like a 'mad uncle' to the Youngs.)

It didn't take long for Angus, too, to sense that Bon was right for AC/DC. '[He] moulded the character of AC/DC. Everything became more down-to-earth and straight ahead. That's when we became a band.'

Bon and the Youngs connected over their Scottish roots and a shared love of rock and roll—and it no doubt helped their fledgling relationship when Bon pulled Malcolm and Angus aside for a quiet word. 'I can sing better than the drongo you have at the moment,' he slurred, nodding towards Dave Evans, their current singer.

A slightly different version of events—understandable, given that this was almost 50 years ago—had Bon being encouraged by Lovegrove to stand in at the Pooraka for Dave Evans, who'd already been sacked. However it played out, it gelled. Bon was in, Evans out, although there was one other deciding factor, according to Mary Renshaw.

'Bon said he was about to start work in a factory. He walked into the premises and thought: fuck this. Then he contacted the band and left Adelaide.'

AC/DC were the best possible fit for rocker Bon Scott. Over a period that had now spanned almost a decade, he had tried his hand at bubblegum pop as a Valentine and earnest country-rock with Fraternity, and neither had been a natural fit. Now he could focus on what he knew he could do capably, if given the chance—sing rock and roll and command a stage and let his oversized personality shine brightly. As his future AC/DC bandmate Mark Evans put it, 'Bon was far better suited to wailing and causing mayhem in a gritty, bluesy rock-and-roll outfit than he would have been with the brown rice brigade. It had to be a whole lot more fun than living up in the Adelaide Hills wearing caftans, for fuck's sake.'

They had a more immediate problem to deal with, however. The Youngs needed to work out a way to leave Adelaide, because the band was flat broke.

★

Michael Browning, who was starting to see himself as something more than merely a supporter of the band, was happy to float the band enough cash to get to Melbourne, where it was agreed that they should now base themselves. Not a lot had changed since the 1960s, because Melbourne remained the epicentre of live music and Browning's Hard Rock Café was its heart and soul. And AC/DC needed a manager.

Bon's AC/DC debut, however, was in Sydney, on 5 October at the Masonic Hall in the southern suburb of Brighton-Le-Sands. Before heading off on this new journey, Bon asked Irene to come with him. While they hadn't reconciled, they'd slept together once during his recovery and were still on good terms. But, as she'd write, 'my heart wasn't in it'. It's highly likely that Bon was stung by her rejection.

Any ill feeling that Bon had was put on hold when he made his AC/DC debut, because it didn't take him long to find his rightful place. As the Youngs laid down the high-voltage framework, Bon's job was to sing hard, look good and get the punters involved (even if he hadn't quite nailed all the lyrics—he ad-libbed a lot on opening night, dropping the odd F-bomb to fill in the blanks). Bon wore his favourite red bib-and-brace overalls with not much underneath; his inkwork, earrings and snaggle-toothed smile completed a very rock-and-roll picture.

'The crowd was going berserk,' reported Fifa Riccobono, an Alberts staffer and AC/DC insider, who'd been asked by Vanda and Young to check out AC/DC's new recruit. 'Bon was screaming and shouting at the top of his lungs; he was really crass and really loud and quite vulgar. But everything about him said, "I am in this band, I belong to this band", which was true. He fitted in perfectly.'

Bon finally had the chance to interact with the audience more than he had with either The Valentines or Fraternity. 'It's a bit of rock and roll,' he said, as he introduced the song 'Show Business', 'so shake everything you got hanging and have a good time.' Things were shook, a good time was had, and AC/DC were in business. The next stage of Bon's life was officially in motion.

Riccobono was about to leave after the gig when she was asked if she wanted to go backstage and 'meet the boys'. It was then she learned there was much more to Bon than the wild man she'd just seen on stage. When she was introduced to Bon, he took her hand and gently kissed it. 'I thought, "That can't be the same guy". He was so charming, polite, he was so attentive, so wonderful.'

The following day, Vanda and Young asked Riccobono for her opinion of Bon. 'He fits like a glove,' she said, 'but god, he swears a lot.'

10

'I've got these young dudes behind me, kicking me in the arse. And I feel great.'
—Bon Scott

While the band was in Melbourne playing the Hard Rock Café, Michael Browning had floated the idea of managing them. A meeting was swiftly arranged in Sydney with Ted Albert and George Young, the band's two key mentors and advocates, whose okay was needed before Browning could take over. But even when they gave their approval, Browning quickly learned that this was nothing like managing Billy Thorpe, a man fond of the high life. This was all about business. And the Youngs were very insular, wary of 'outsiders'.

'I hadn't signed a band,' he said, 'I'd signed a clan.'

Browning was a big fan of Bon Scott; with him out front, he felt that AC/DC had the potential to be world-beaters. 'The band had acquired a new sense of purpose as well as a sense of humour and uniqueness,' he said. Years later, Harry Vanda, George Young's partner in The Easybeats, went one step further. He'd tell *Australian Musician* magazine that the biggest moment in Oz music history was 'the day Malcolm and Angus asked Bon to be their singer'.

Browning put each band member on $60 per week for the next six months, enough to cover food, booze and ciggies—the essentials. Alberts agreed to cover such necessities as a PA and new gear, and the band settled into new digs at 6 Lansdowne Road in St Kilda East, smack dab in the X-rated underbelly of Melbourne (one of their near neighbours was a brothel, and the sex workers quickly became buddies of the band). The band's fee for gigs ranged from $200 to $500, depending on the venue. Browning's Hard Rock Café became their second home; they played there every few weeks and regularly filled the joint. Finally, there was some order in the AC/DC house. It was something Bon hadn't experienced before in his career—a real manager, a serious record label and two talented producers, all dedicated to one band.

Bon suggested they buy a tour bus, and Browning helped them procure a 1950s-era Greyhound bus for $8000, which would be driven by Ralph the Roadie, an old mate of Bon's from Fraternity days. The front section was modified to accommodate the band; the rear half was cordoned off for their gear. But the bus was a lemon. Malcolm Young soon admitted, 'I think we've fucking pushed it further than we've ridden in the thing.' Or, as Mark Evans soon came to learn, 'You could really freeze your arse off in that blue fucker.' Neither air-con nor heating was especially reliable.

On stage, the rapport between Bon and Angus quickly developed. Early on, Bon offered the schoolboy guitarist some simple advice, which he embraced: 'Go out there and be a big kid.' After all, he was dressed for the part. He also provided Angus with this warning: 'Whatever I do, don't!' (Bon didn't make it clear if he was referring to his activities on stage or off it.) They may have been physical opposites—Bon was brawny and tattooed, Angus pencil-thin and pale, his teeth an odd shade of green—but punters couldn't take their eyes off the odd couple.

A few gigs down the line, Bon caught up with John D'Arcy, the former Valentines roadie and a mate. Bon was over the moon. 'I've got these young dudes behind me, kicking me in the arse,' he said. 'And I feel great.'

It was after another Hard Rock Café gig that Bon reconnected with Mary Renshaw and began a brief relationship. Watching Bon on stage with his new band, Mary understood instantly why people gravitated to him; he absolutely oozed charisma. 'Women loved him,' she wrote. And while Bon may not have been movie-star handsome, unlike, say, Zoot's Rick Springfield, he looked pretty good without a shirt, which is how he ended most gigs. AC/DC might have been a down-and-dirty rock-and-roll band, but they started to attract a strong female following.

Mary called him Bonny—which he wasn't crazy about, but let slide. In a candid moment Bon told her what he felt had gone awry with Irene. 'She got tired of the rock-and-roll life,' he said, with genuine regret. His bandmates cheekily referred to Bon and Mary as 'Mr and Mrs Scott', even though he had no plans to divorce Irene. Curiously, Bon gave Mary his wedding ring (which she still wears today).

Bon and Irene did meet again, during October, when he and the band had a run of dates at the Largs Pier in Adelaide. These were very sweet shows for Bon, a heroic homecoming of sorts, given the amount of time he'd spent there with Fraternity. Finally, Bon was doing what he was born to do—lead an arse-kicking rock-and-roll band. But there was a downside: before the gig, he'd dropped by Irene's place while she was at work and helped himself to whatever cash he could find in the house (which was actually her rent money). That night, at the Largs Pier, Irene confronted him. A very contrite Bon repaid her the next day.

*

Bon and the band were back in Sydney the next month to record their debut album, with George Young and Harry Vanda co-producing (George would also play bass, as the search for a full-timer continued). They locked themselves away in Alberts studio—soon to become known, justifiably, as The House of Hits—for a couple of weeks. While the instrumental tracks were being laid down, Bon would be in the kitchen, fine-tuning his 'toilet poetry'.

George Young had never met Bon before, and was a little taken aback when he laid eyes on him. 'He's been around the block more than a few times,' George said quietly, taking in Bon's chipped teeth and slightly shopworn appearance. But he also knew that Bon was a perfect fit for his brothers' band, both as a frontman and lyricist. 'He's your man, no doubt about it,' George told Angus and Malcolm. 'You're a rock-and-roll band now.' The respect was mutual; Bon said that George was 'like a brother—no, a father—to the group'.

This album, which they'd title *High Voltage*, finally gave Bon the chance to unearth some of the bawdy, funny lyrics that he'd been stockpiling for years. Harry Vanda was impressed; he grasped exactly what Bon was doing. 'The whole [lyrical] things were so tongue in cheek and naughty— but not nasty naughty.'

The standout was 'She's Got Balls', which, admittedly, was about as subtle as a Marshall stack set to maximum volume. It was Bon's tribute to Irene, written after she'd challenged him, asking: 'Why don't you write a song about me?' Irene knew Bon as well as anyone, but even she would have been surprised when he responded with an ode to a woman whose key traits, as he related, were spunk, funk, and, most crucially, balls.

With the album in the can, and slated for an early 1975 release, the band got back to work. Bon spoke with Irene, who'd started dating a barefoot guitarist from the Top End named Ian Moss, from fledgling outfit Cold Chisel. Irene was house-sharing with Mary Renshaw, who, like Irene, was now Bon's friend rather than his lover. Less than six months before, Bon had been depressed, his body and his marriage (and his beloved trail bike) in bad shape, unsure if he was ever going to make it as a rock and roller. But a lot had changed in the short time since he linked up with AC/DC. Bon said he now felt ten years younger.

And the album?

''Rene,' Bon told her over the phone, 'it's a fucking ripper.'

★

AC/DC were a perfect storm of sorts for Bon. The Young brothers shared Bon's love of high-energy rock and roll and his dream of world domination; they were great players and *they were Scots*. And the band had the perfect mentors in George and Harry, who, as producers and songwriters, were about to hit a purple patch—not just with AC/DC but with John Paul Young, Stevie Wright and various other homegrown acts. They also had the ideal advocate in Ted Albert. And Michael Browning was proving to be the savvy, driven manager they needed.

But another factor was about to come into play that had eluded Bon to this point: a TV show that had the ability to break the band nationwide. For all the exposure they offered, earlier shows such as *Uptight* and *Kommotion* were mainly state-based affairs, but *Countdown*, as this new ABC program came to be known, would have much larger reach. And it aired at the golden hour of 6 p.m. on a Sunday, when most Aussie teenagers were sitting down to dinner or recovering from a heavy Saturday night. AC/DC would prove to be the perfect act for *Countdown*; Bon and Angus became the show's favourite rock-and-roll court jesters. The band would appear on the show about 40 times between November 1974 and December 1976, while the program would help produce standout videos for the singles 'It's a Long Way to the Top (If You Wanna Rock 'n' Roll)' and 'Jailbreak'.

AC/DC were booked to make their *Countdown* debut on the fourth episode of the show, playing their latest single, 'Baby Please Don't Go'. Also on the program were Sherbet's Daryl Braithwaite, briefly flying solo, as well as Debbie Byrne, a graduate of Johnny Young's Young Talent Team. Music videos, a very new vehicle for promoting songs, were also aired; among them David Bowie's 'Space Oddity' and Suzi Quatro's 'Too Big'.

But it was Angus, not Bon, who was the star of the show. Decked out in a flowing white scarf, goggles and a leather jacket, a smouldering ciggie wedged between his fingers, Angus was perched in the cockpit of a homemade plane. It was as though Biggles had morphed with Albert Steptoe.

(Unfortunately, this was one of the many early *Countdown* episodes that were erased due to in-house cost-cutting at the government-run ABC. Staff had been instructed to recycle the tapes.)

Clearly it connected, because the band was invited back for a repeat performance on 20 December, and the single—which had actually been the B-side of the oddly schmaltzy 'Love Song', a track that AC/DC swiftly banished from their shows and memories—began to gain some radio airplay.

This time around, Angus was dressed as Zorro, while Bon was a vision in his snug red overalls, the shark's tooth earring he'd bought from Portobello Markets on full and proud display. As was a good chunk of Bon's anatomy; much of the female-heavy crowd packed inside the *Countdown* studio at suburban Ripponlea didn't know where to look.

Also on the 20 December bill were Melbourne shock rockers Skyhooks. Angus had taken to giving nicknames to local acts; glam rockers Hush were known as 'the Blue Suede Thongs', AC/DC's Alberts labelmate William Shakespeare was 'Willie Shake It', but Skyhooks, as far as Angus was concerned, didn't deserve a nickname. They were rivals. (Bon, however, did give them a nickname. He called them 'Sky(fish)hooks', which was not his best work. Neither was his other tag for the band, 'Cunthooks'. His name for Cold Chisel—'Warm Hammer'—was a bit more Bon Scott–worthy.)

Living at Lansdowne Road must have reminded Bon of his fast times with The Valentines, when their Melbourne HQ became the drop-in centre for the band's more eager female fans. The Lansdowne Road house was a sprawling if somewhat rundown place, with a sunroom at the front, several small bedrooms, and a family room at the rear of the house, which Bon quickly claimed as his domain. Also living there were Ralph the Roadie, another roadie named Tana Douglas, and Bon's mate Pat Pickett—the band's lighting director (in theory). The house was so big, in fact, that the group could set up in the hallway and jam when the mood took them.

This was a house that never rested: there was a steady procession of hookers, dealers, pimps, runaways and the rest of Melbourne's demimonde through its doors, day in, day out. A local newspaper sent a reporter to stake out Lansdowne Road and monitor activities. He came back with not so much a report but a scorecard; he estimated that at least 100 women came and went over a single week. Angus felt he needed to set the record straight when asked about this.

'It was 110,' he said, with a chuckle.

Sometimes things got heated, such as the day that a father tracked down his errant daughter. She just so happened to be in bed with Bon when he stormed into the house, yelling out her name. As Bon recalled, 'This guy comes banging on my bedroom door, loud as hell itself, and I say to him, "Fuck off, I'm having a fuck." Suddenly the door is crashed in and it turns out to be this girl's father, and he finds me on top of his daughter, who I find out is only sixteen years old. Needless to say, he beat me to a pulp.'

Bon's beating took place on the front lawn, after he'd been dragged through a bed of rosebushes. In the melee, he lost a couple of teeth and the dental plate he'd had installed after his bike crash in Adelaide. The fracas made the paper, inspiring a headline that read: 'Popstar, Brunette and a Bed: Then Her Dad Turned Up!'

The girl's name was Judy King, and she was actually seventeen at the time. They'd met at a New Year's party, when Mary Renshaw failed to show. King was a former star athlete. As Mark Evans recalled, Bon fell 'like a ton of bricks' for her. Irene Thornton wrote to Bon, suggesting he stop pursuing young women like King.

'I don't chase them,' Bon insisted. 'They chase me!'

The band saw out a very lively year with a run of dates in far-flung South Australia, as well as a show in rural New South Wales, where they were billed, in a poster in dire need of both a proofreader and fact-checker, as 'Sydney's No 1 nu-and-coming AC/DC, includes the two young brothers of Steve Wright, ex Easybeats [*sic*]'. This was followed by another gig at the Largs Pier and a New Year's Eve show at Melbourne's Festival Hall. The Festival Hall show, which also featured Hush, Kush and former Masters Apprentice Jim Keays—an old acquaintance of Bon's from the wild days of 1969's Operation Starlift—was broadcast live on radio. Clearly, the band's exposure on *Countdown* had done the trick, because they drew a crowd of 5000 people chanting, 'We want Angus! We want Angus!' before the band took the stage.

Bon's development as a frontman extended into his rapport with audiences. When he introduced 'Can I Sit Next to You, Girl' at Festival Hall he made a less-than-subtle reference to its performance in the charts. (It had hit a modest peak of number 50.)

'[This record] made it to number 100 in Sydney, number 200 in Perth—and number 1000 in Melbourne,' he joked.

Bon needn't have worried. He and the band had some songs ready to roll that would become AC/DC classics—and within a year they'd be the biggest band in the land.

11

'[Angus] taught me how to say, "please, fuck". And thank
you afterward.'

—Bon discusses manners

Given the band's very working-class background, AC/DC
weren't the kind of band to shy away from the hard slog.
They had to keep playing, keep moving—and try to keep
earning. But they still needed a permanent rhythm section.
One part of that problem was solved in early 1975, when
Phil Rudd, a lively character with a German and Irish background, came on board. He'd most recently been playing
in Buster Brown, whose singer was a small man with a large
voice called Gary (soon to be Angry) Anderson, and was
a big fan of rock's classic tub-thumpers—Cream's Ginger
Baker, Beatle Ringo Starr, and Simon Kirke of Free and
Bad Company.

A solidly built, good-looking 21-year-old, with grey-blue
eyes and a shock of fair hair, Rudd was described by *Go-Set*
as 'quite the swank young jackeroo'. He also kept some
interesting company. One of his mates rarely left the house
without slipping a pistol into the waistband of his jeans.

The search for the ideal bassist continued.

Around the time of Rudd's recruitment, the band shifted

base to the Freeway Gardens Motel, on the Tullamarine Freeway in North Melbourne, which was a little further out of town. Browning's plan was to get them away from the sin and sleaze of St Kilda, but the party simply moved with them. (In Sydney, a similar thing was happening with Kiwi expats Dragon; their manager, desperate for some stability, moved them from the dangerous inner city to the tranquil Northern Beaches. 'All that happened,' he said, 'was that the dealers went with them.')

Herm Kovac, the drummer with the Ted Mulry Gang, was at Freeway Gardens one night when Bon did a swan dive off the building's roof into the swimming pool, an act that was re-created in the 2000 rock-and-roll movie *Almost Famous* (but, according to witnesses, Bon didn't announce, 'I am a golden god!' as he leaped into the pool). Kovac couldn't watch; he genuinely feared for Bon's safety. One juicy slice of AC/DC folklore had Bon bedding three women a day for four days straight at Freeway Gardens; clearly, the man's libido had no limits. Not surprisingly, a regular visitor was one Dr Goldberg, aka the Rock Doctor, who did a lively trade in penicillin, which led to a new insider's nickname for AC/DC: they were now called 'The Seedies'.

One night, Sydney retro rockers Ol' 55, who'd only just begun touring, were invited by AC/DC's roadies to a party at Freeway Gardens. The group was thrilled, according to singer Jim Manzie. 'We were dying to meet the best rock-and-roll band in the land,' he said. When they arrived at about 1 a.m., they noticed a red Mini Minor parked near the AC/DC bus. The Mini was rocking ever so gently. As Manzie recalled, 'Closer inspection revealed the great man himself getting busy in the tiny back seat with a willing partner.

Since we had all been drinking, we thought it appropriate to help rock the car ourselves.'

Bon let fly with a flurry of curses and then emerged from the car, dressed only in his undies.

'You bunch of dickheads!' he roared.

'Where's the party?' asked Ol' 55 drummer Geoff Plummer.

'Fuck off!' roared Bon, who climbed back into the Mini and resumed his X-rated business.

The Freeway Gardens would also go down in Bon Scott legend as the site of his close encounter with a full-bodied woman named Rosie.

As was often the case with Bon's offstage encounters, there were a couple of different versions of the story. One, as Angus Young related to *Vox* magazine in 1998, related to a challenge that Bon simply couldn't resist. Bon was setting out on a post-gig tear, hitting a few clubs, when he heard someone call his name. 'From what he said [to me],' Angus revealed, 'there was this Rosie woman and a friend of hers. They [began] plying him with drinks and Rosie said to him: "This month I've slept with 28 famous people," and Bon went: "Oh yeah?!" Anyway, in the morning he said he woke up pinned against the wall, he opened one eye and saw her lean over to her friend in the other bed and whisper: "29!"'

Malcolm Young had a slightly different take. He recalled Bon pulling him aside while they were living at Freeway Gardens and speaking to him about some potential female company, who were offering to make them dinner.

'At the end of the night,' said Malcolm, 'after dinner and some drinks, big Rosie grabs Bon and says, "Right, you're mine for the night," and I ran away from the other one.

I went home. Bon woke up in the morning squashed against the wall, and he tried to get away, so she grabbed him again and got more payment for the meal.'

The encounter provided Bon with loads of great source material for a song about a large woman with a sexual appetite to match, and the track, entitled 'Whole Lotta Rosie', was knocked together in record time. It was a raw few minutes of classic AC/DC boogie, the perfect backing for Bon's funny, juicy lyric. And while that lyric could have been, in modern parlance, a textbook case of fat shaming, it was anything but. It was more a celebration of a woman who, while she 'ain't exactly pretty' and 'ain't exactly small', truly rocked Bon's world, if just for one night. When Bon howled, 'She's a whole lotta woman', he meant it in the best possible way.

★

Given that they were virtually living in each other's pockets, the personal quirks of Bon and the rest of the band were starting to emerge. Bon was a lover of creature comforts, who was just as happy curling up in the back room of Freeway Gardens with a *B.C.* comic or penning one of his 'despatches from my front' as he was bedding down with a woman.

Bon and Angus were developing a great rapport, both on stage and off. When asked by a reporter about their influence on each other, Angus confessed that he'd tidied up Bon's vocabulary. 'When I first met him,' Angus said, 'it was all "fuck, cunt, piss, shit". I introduced him to a new side of life. Sent 'im home with a dictionary.'

'He taught me how to say, "please, fuck",' Bon chuckled. 'And thank you afterward.'

Every band needs its schemer, and in AC/DC it was Malcolm, whose grand plan was to have them based in London within a year. If Bon was the balls of the band, Malcolm was the brains. Angus, meanwhile, was known as 'The Banker'; he was the only member of the group who could hang on to his $60 pay packet for more than a few hours. Being a teetotaller clearly helped; Angus's only indulgences were ciggies, chocolate milk and spaghetti bolognese. It was rare that a week went by without at least one bandmate hitting Angus up for a loan. Manager Michael Browning christened him AC/DC's 'very own Milburn Drysdale', a nod to the tight-fisted bank president in TV sitcom *The Beverly Hillbillies*.

Bon was displaying his domestic skills when Mark Evans, the final member of the classic AC/DC line-up, joined up. It was 19 March 1975, and the band was booked for a gig at the Station Hotel, one of the many rowdy Melbourne pubs that hosted live music. The Station was Evans' local, and he'd been asked to jam with them during their second set; it was a live audition, essentially. When he walked into the pub, he spied Bon ironing his bib-and-brace outfit, using the bar as his ironing board. Evans, who was a huge fan of Bon's, having seen him 'come to life before my very eyes' when he played with The Valentines, eagerly approached the singer.

'What are you like at ironing, mate?' Bon asked him. Evans was more than happy to take over, as Bon ordered a couple of drinks.

'Now you're talking,' Evans thought, as he related in his book *Dirty Deeds*. 'I'm drinking with Bon Scott.'

Well, not quite. Bon collected his drinks, walked straight

past Evans and sat down with a gorgeous female fan, leaving the bassist to finish the ironing.

After that night's jam, Evans was asked to join, but only after one final assessment. Malcolm introduced him to manager Browning, who, as Evans recalled, had two issues to address: 'Did I suit the band's image? *And how tall was I?*' Bon made reference to this, too, when he was asked just what was needed to join AC/DC. 'It's a rare type of bloke who'll fit into our band,' he told a reporter from *RAM*. 'He has to be under five foot six. And he has to be able to play.'

Nineteen-year-old Evans clearly did, because he got the job and made his formal debut with the band the next night, at the Waltzing Matilda Hotel in suburban Springvale, one of the many sizeable beer barns springing up across the country. Bon played motivator, giving Evans a pep talk as the set progressed. 'Going all right, Mike,' he shouted over the din of the rest of the band. (Years later, when Evans was given some gold records, they were wrongly inscribed with 'Mike Evans'.)

Evans' spirits lifted considerably after the gig, back at Freeway Gardens, where he was the very agreeable filling in what he called a 'rock-and-roll sandwich'.

★

High Voltage, the band's debut album, had been released on 17 February. It reached number 14 and charted for 39 weeks. These weren't quite Skyhooks stats—their debut LP clung to the number 1 spot and charted for more than a year—but it was a solid start. And, historically speaking, the album proved to have far more staying power than *Living in the 70's*.

Bon was incredibly proud of the finished album, so much so that he personally presented copies to his friends.

Bon's skills as a lyricist hit an all-time high with a new song, 'It's a Long Way to the Top (If You Wanna Rock 'n' Roll)', when they returned to Alberts studio with George and Harry in the autumn and winter of 1975 to record the *T.N.T.* album. (It says a lot about the band's work ethic that they were recording a new album when their debut had barely hit the shelves.)

While, strictly speaking, Bon didn't fit in with the type of confessional lyricists that were currently all the rage, including such locals as Richard Clapton and Kevin Johnson, he wasn't immune to a little autobiographical musing. George Young overheard Bon recite some of the lyrics in the studio, and he said that 'it's a long way to the top if you wanna rock and roll' was one of the best lines he'd ever heard in a rock-and-roll song.

'You like that, do you?' Bon asked, looking relieved. 'Good, because I've got a few more pages.' He duly showed his producer the entire lyric, and a classic was born.

'Long Way to the Top' captured everything Bon had been through in his career to date: a series of near misses, abject failures, disappointments and cheap thrills. For fear of coming on too heavy, Bon leavened his catalogue of chaos with some typical humour. 'I tell you, folks,' he deadpanned, 'it's harder than it looks.' As cautionary tales of a life in music went, it was right up there with The Byrds' 'So You Wanna Be a Rock 'n' Roll Star'—and it was the band's first great song.

All signature songs need a musical twist, and in the case of 'Long Way to the Top' it came in the shape of a set of bagpipes, purchased off the shelf of a Sydney music store for a hefty $435 and (eventually) used to great effect in the song. When George came up with the idea for adding a few blasts of bagpipes, Bon offered his services, convincing George that he'd been a piper back in the days of the Coastal Scottish Pipe Band in Fremantle, although he'd only been a drummer. He'd also done hard time playing the recorder in Fraternity; surely he could handle the challenge.

'I knew how to blow and finger,' Bon would tell Molly Meldrum, almost choking on the double entendre.

Before Bon had the chance to show that he couldn't play the bagpipes, he first proved that he had no idea how to assemble them. Nor did anyone else, as Mark Evans recalled.

'If you want a good giggle,' Evans wrote, 'get a bunch of Scotsmen with no previous bagpipe experience and ask them to put some bagpipes together.'

When they played the song live, Bon wielded the pipes like a bazooka, but he was actually playing to a backing track. Still, it added a little more razzle-dazzle to their shows, which were fast becoming must-see events due to the dynamic between Bon and Angus, and the group's super-tight playing.

The combination of Bon's lyrics, Malcolm and Angus's fireworks and the odd studio flare-up resulted in not just 'Long Way to the Top' but such other greats as 'High Voltage', 'T.N.T.' (all three released as singles), 'The Jack' and 'Live Wire'. Each would become a signature song that remained in their set list for the next 40 years, and all were powered by Bon's funny, smart, occasionally dodgy word-play. Even a throwaway Bon line like 'Stick this in your fuse box', which preceded a stinging Angus solo on 'Live Wire', perfectly matched the track's raw power.

Bon and AC/DC had hit a purple patch with *T.N.T.* Brother George could clearly sense this, because when Malcolm and Angus asked if they should be a bit more experimental, he replied with a hard 'no'. Their shit was very much together; no way should they mess with what they already had.

'That's your thing,' George said, referring to their bluesy, boozy way of playing. 'Stick with it.'

George had made what he considered to be a fatal mistake while with The Easybeats—by being eclectic, dabbling in everything from psychedelia to ska and lush ballads, they left listeners a bit confused. He didn't want his brothers to make the same mistake. They were a rock band, pure and simple. It was probably the best advice George would ever give his siblings.

Sometimes, however, Bon missed the mark. 'The Jack', Bon's ode to venereal disease, didn't stand up well under scrutiny, either when it was released or in these more woke times. (But Bon knew what he was in for when he wrote the song. '[It] may get us castrated by women's lib,' he wrote in a letter to Mary Renshaw.) Yet the song went over gangbusters live, especially when Bon began winding up punters and suggesting they had the dreaded social disease, much to their horror. It also slowed their sets down a little and gave them a chance to catch their breath.

'The Jack', just like 'Whole Lotta Rosie', was a song with a colourful backstory, as Bon would later explain to a British reporter. 'We were living with this houseful of ladies [most likely at Lansdowne Road] who were all very friendly and everyone in the band had got the jack [gonorrhoea]. So, we wrote this song and the first time we did it on stage they were all in the front row with no idea what was goin' to happen. When it came to repeating, "She's got the jack", I pointed at them one after another.' (In another version of events, Malcolm said he'd received a letter from a woman insisting that he'd given her the dreaded 'jack', even though when tested, he was infection free. Stories like this tended to grow lives of their own in AC/DC folklore.)

Angus chewed over Bon's lyric with a reporter from *RAM*. 'Playing pub gigs around Melbourne, Bon could empty a whole room of women—he'd point at 'em while we were doin' "The Jack" . . . and they'd all leave or go up the back of the room where he couldn't see 'em.' This didn't, however, stop them being fans of the band, as Malcolm pointed out. 'They still used to come 'round to the dressing room after we'd played.'

In fact, the front rows of AC/DC gigs were mainly populated by young women, as were backstage areas after their shows. They didn't seem to have any problems with Bon's raunchier lyrics; they loved the band (as did their boyfriends). Tougher, more streetwise than Sherbet, funnier and less arty than Skyhooks, and not too painful on the eyes, AC/DC were the perfect suburban rock-and-roll outfit.

★

AC/DC gigs were lively, occasionally downright dangerous affairs. Sometimes, Bon and the band didn't even get to play before trouble began, such as their notorious no-show after a run-in with Deep Purple's crew at the Sunbury Festival in January 1975, which resulted in the band returning to Melbourne without playing their set. This conflict left Bon rattled; he resented that early reports of the festival stated that AC/DC had been 'cancelled' by the promoters, when in fact they'd chosen to bail. At the same time, Bon was a Deep Purple fan, and he didn't relish clashing with acts that he admired.

Later in the year, in August, chaos ensued at Myer's Miss Melbourne Shop, of all places, when the band attempted to play the first of a proposed week of lunchtime shows. Clearly, their exposure on *Countdown* had done the trick; the audience had been at fever pitch from the moment the crew attempted to set up. Earlier in the year they'd even featured on a *TV Week* 'Giant Pin-up' poster, a spot usually reserved for cuddlier types like Sherbet. (In the shot, barefoot Bon, trying hard to suppress a grin, sported an impressive mullet and his favourite red overalls.)

At a very crowded Myer store, manager Michael Browning had a pre-gig prediction for the band: 'If this lasts more than one song, it'll be a fucking miracle.' As they attempted to play 'Live Wire', their usual opener, hundreds of their teenage fans didn't just rush the stage but also began looting the store. The band dispersed, each of them darting off in a different direction; Bon was spotted dashing like an Olympic sprinter through the ladies' lingerie department, his mate Pat Pickett at his side, dozens of overeager fans following in his wake. Mark Evans described the chaos as 'like a scene straight out of *A Hard Day's Night.*' All the subsequent shows were cancelled, while Myer staff tabulated their losses.

Bon also had a habit of injuring himself. During a big show in April 1975 at Melbourne's Festival Hall, playing alongside Kiwis Split Enz, rivals Skyhooks and Bob 'Newcastle Song' Hudson, Bon was indulging his inner Tarzan by swinging across the stage on a rope installed just for that purpose—he'd changed into a loincloth mid-concert to get into character. But Bon's radar failed; he missed the stage entirely and landed in the front row of the audience (earlier in the show he'd been dragged off stage and had his overalls ripped to shreds). He was roughed up considerably by the crowd.

'It was the wildest concert we've ever played at,' Bon told the *Melbourne Herald* afterwards, which, given the usual mayhem at their shows, was really saying something.

There'd been particularly ugly scenes during a May 1975 gig at the Manhattan Hotel in the Melbourne suburb of Ringwood. This time it was Ralph the Roadie who passed along a pre-gig warning—there was an angry mob of more than 1000 drunk punters itching for a fight, hurling beer glasses and overturning tables. 'You are all out of your minds if you go out there,' he advised. By the abrupt end of the show, Angus had a badly cut hand and the police had been called in to disperse the unruly mob, while the band anxiously sat it out backstage, hostages at their own gig. It took more than an hour to clear the joint.

Things got worse, much worse, at another riotous gig, this time at the Matthew Flinders Hotel in Chadstone. Angus was kicked and punched by punters during his 'dying bug' routine, when he'd lie on the floor and solo furiously while spinning like a Catherine wheel. In the ensuing melee, Mark Evans was knocked out cold and Phil Rudd broke his thumb, which forced him to miss several shows. Bon, shrewdly, would usually head backstage once he sensed that trouble was in the air. He was happy to leave the fisticuffs to the younger blokes in the band.

As Bon once told a radio DJ, 'We tend to think of live concerts as like the lions and the Christians—we're the Christians and the crowd's the lions.' Here was the proof.

★

Just weeks prior to the dust-up at the Manhattan, Bon had performed in front of what was probably his largest audience to date. A crowd of 10,000 gathered at the Myer Music Bowl on 20 April for the Concert for Bangladesh fundraiser which, while not to be confused with the 1971 event organised by George Harrison, had the same intention—to feed the poor and raise awareness of Third World crises. Also on the bill were The La De Da's, Jim Keays, Ayers Rock and Daddy Cool, among others.

Looking on from the crowd was one of the band's most fervent fans, a teenager named Wendy Jones.

Wendy's involvement with the band stretched back many months, to the darkest day of her young life. While out in Melbourne one night she'd been assaulted; she was taken to the George Hotel in St Kilda, where the band happened to be in the foyer. As she entered, the first person she saw was Bon. Wendy had no idea who he was, but Bon could sense that she was in serious trouble. Malcolm Young was there, too, and he helped as much as he could.

'Bon took charge of the situation,' she recalled, 'made sure I was okay, and put me in a cab home, which he paid for.'

Wendy firmly believed that, without exaggeration, Bon had saved her life.

She was still suffering the consequences of her attack six months later when a girlfriend suggested they see a new band at the Hard Rock Café. She reluctantly agreed, knowing she had to get on with her life. Wendy was startled to see that Bon was the lead singer in the band and Malcolm was the rhythm guitarist.

A strong bond was truly cemented when Wendy unfurled a homemade banner at the Concert for Bangladesh, which proudly read: 'I Do It For AC/DC'. She and Malcolm became especially close; they exchanged 'kissing cousins' necklaces. 'I guess he was the first love of my life,' she said. 'But it was all pretty innocent.'

★

Sydneysider Anthony O'Grady was one of the leading young rock scribes documenting the local music scene, and he conducted the first lengthy interview with Bon and the band, which was published in *RAM* during April 1975. Exposure on *Countdown* and in the pages of *TV Week* did wonders for album and ticket sales, but column inches in the 'serious' music press gave them something every ambitious band craved: credibility.

Bon was far and away the band's most experienced spokesman, having done his share of promo work with The Valentines, if not so much with Fraternity. So he did much of the talking. During the interview, Bon couldn't resist playing a little hard and fast with the truth.

When talking with O'Grady about his recent past, Bon mentioned that he was married. 'Which was something I wasn't ready for. I joined [AC/DC] and got divorced,' he added, which wasn't the case—he and Irene hadn't ever discussed divorce. Bon said that joining meant he had to choose between AC/DC and Irene, and 'I dug the band more than I dug the chick'. The macho pose didn't suit Bon, nor did his remarks impress Irene, who was deeply hurt (she said it was part of his 'rock star pose'). And his comment simply wasn't true—when she confronted him about it, Bon apologised, and the two remained close for the rest of his life. When they caught up, Irene sometimes prepared Bon's favourite curry, which they called the 'London Special', a reminder of their strange days in the UK with Fraternity.

Talk turned to Bon's lyrics, which, according to Malcolm, who was also taking part in the interview, may as well have been lifted directly from his diary. 'They're straight Bon, just exactly like he lives,' Malcolm told O'Grady. 'We have to censor half of them . . . and they're still outrageous.' Bon shrugged and accepted that perhaps Malcolm was right. '[My lyrics] aren't poetry, that's for sure. I don't write about flowers and trees.'

Bon was asked about his earrings. O'Grady pointed out that it was a custom for junkies to have their right ear pierced: did Bon's pierced ears hint at a drug problem?

'Nah, I'm not a druggie,' Bon replied.

He went on to tell a story about his early days in Western Australia, working on the crayfishing boat, and how one of his co-workers had his ear pierced: 'So I got one of mine done then.' As for his second piercing, Bon insisted it was done on a whim after a gig. 'I got a safety pin and told the roadie, "Stick it in here." Well, it was something to do to pass the time.'

Of course, the truth was another matter. Bon had been inspired by Rolling Stone Keith Richards to get his ears pierced, and he'd picked up his earrings at London's

Portobello Markets while shopping with Irene. Bon was becoming a dab hand at creating his own mythology.

Every now and then, however, Bon let some hard facts slip out. He returned to his past, discussing his shift from being 'just an arse shaker' with The Valentines to his desire 'to become a musician' when he joined Fraternity. But the creative frustration he felt while part of Fraternity still lingered. 'There was a lot of stuff I was writing [that] I could never give to them—and I was getting old.'

Joining AC/DC was Bon's saving grace—he made that very clear. 'These guys came along and took ten years off my age.'

By the time this interview ran—under the awkward headline 'AC/DC: Australia has punk rock bands too, you know'—the *High Voltage* LP had gone gold. By year's end, it would be Alberts' highest-selling album.

Bon told his mother that he intended to give her the gold-plated record. Isa asked, in return, that her 'Ronny' write some nice, clean songs in the future; enough with the racy lyrics. But that was about as likely as Bon taking a vow of celibacy.

Bon could sense that everything was falling into place with AC/DC. 'I reckon we'd have to be the hottest band in the country at the moment,' he declared in a letter to Irene. 'Not bad for a 29-year-old 3rd-time-round has-been.'

12

'Tell that Bon Scott to stick to music and leave the medical
stuff to the doctors.'

—Hospital staff give Ol' 55's Jim Manzie some advice

While the band was a favourite on the live club and pub
circuit, they still played the occasional school gig. One
morning in July 1975 they left Freeway Gardens for a lunchtime set at Altona North Technical High School in outer
Melbourne. The day's show was an eye-opener, according to
one of Altona North's students, who wrote about the gig on
an AC/DC website. 'The teachers were mortified—and had
no idea how loud they would be.'

Along for the ride was photographer Graeme Webber,
who during the course of the day captured two of the most
iconic Bon Scott images ever taken.

The first was a masterstroke of Bon Scott improv. Hunting
for the best place to take a solo shot, Bon suggested a dunny.
Why not? After all, he was the master of toilet poetry. Webber
shot Bon while he was standing in the stall, the door open.
Bon had undone the zip of his dangerously tight jeans; his
bird tattoo was on full display, as was a whole lot more of his
pelvic region. (This was the same tattoo that he had once
flashed to Irene and asked, 'Do you want to see the branch

they're on?') Bon, whose chompers hadn't yet been repaired after the rumble in the rosebush with an angry father, wore the ultimate in snaggle-toothed grins. It was the type of suggestive pose that only Bon Scott could get away with—in anyone else's hands it would have looked downright sleazy. Bon made it seem more playful than anything; to him it was just a giggle, nothing more.

As Webber recalled, it was all too easy. 'Bon loved the idea of working in a dunny and was keen to show off some tatts.' That shot of Bon was soon used for AC/DC's first *Juke* cover.

Bon was clearly enjoying working with Webber, because after the 'dunny shot' he invited him back to the tour bus for a smoke. That led to the second great shot of the day. Bon had slipped on his leather jacket and, before sparking up, smiled one of his broad smiles for Webber's camera, a spliff between his fingers. Bon's eyebrows were cocked just enough to indicate they were about to have a high old time.

A few weeks earlier in Sydney, Bon and the others had an equally wild time with Philip Morris, who'd photographed 'hippie Bon' in Centennial Park a few years back with Fraternity. Alberts needed promo shots for the band's single 'Jailbreak', and someone cooked up the idea of a 'guerrilla-style' night shoot. The group, along with Alberts' Fifa Riccobono, roadie Pat Pickett and manager Browning—the latter pair dressed as coppers—rolled up to Morris's studio in McMahons Point. After a few drinks, they went on a 'reccy', settling on a back street in nearby Lavender Bay for the shoot. As Morris clicked away, the entourage took turns 'tagging' the wall with spray paint, then posed in a line-up, the image inspired by the cover of Wings' recent album

Band on the Run. Bon slugged from a bottle of Stone's Green Ginger Wine concealed inside a paper bag, with which he pretended to clobber Angus in one especially lively shot as they staged a mock fight. Bon got a little too deeply into character, because he accidentally smashed the bottle, glass showering everyone.

'No one was hurt,' Morris clarified, 'but we were all in stitches. Most of the AC/DC shoots were fun but "Jailbreak" was the best.'

Those police uniforms proved handy when the band played a show later in the year at Sydney's Hordern Pavilion. Michael Browning had a plan to upstage their rivals Skyhooks, who were also on the bill. During AC/DC's set, it was agreed, they'd stage a mock fight, which would be broken up by Browning and Pickett in uniform. The idea of being arrested on stage was bound to get them some column inches—and humble their bigger-selling Melbourne peers.

But all didn't go quite to plan. Bassist Evans gave Bon what he thought was a gentle tap on the backside with his foot, but Bon tumbled off the stage and into the crowd, who just about swallowed him whole. Meanwhile, on stage, Evans and Angus staged a grapple, the others joined in and they were all dragged off stage—Bon, by this point, was barely conscious. (The audience wasn't in on the gag.) Bon was guided to a seat backstage where he sat in a daze, trying to regain his senses, his head inside a brown paper bag, sucking in deep breaths. Just then a roadie burst in, screaming blue murder about some gear that had been damaged on stage during the melee; he grabbed the tape containing the bagpipe recording that Bon depended on for his 'solo' during 'Long Way to the Top' and destroyed it.

'That fat fucker killed our pipes,' Bon gasped, before drifting back into unconsciousness.

As for Skyhooks, Bon was no great fan. 'They're a pain in the arse,' he admitted in a typically funny and frank letter to Mary Renshaw. 'We'd like to use them for support but they're not good enough. Maybe we could beat 'em up on stage and with a bit of luck get an encore. (Down boy.)'

Philip Morris also captured the band at their fast and furious best at a big outdoor show in Sydney's Victoria Park on 9 September 1975. The free gig was hosted by high-rating radio network 2SM, and performing with AC/DC were folkie Ross Ryan and former Easybeat Stevie Wright, who both had songs ('I Am Pegasus' and 'Black Eyed Bruiser', respectively) in the charts. A current 2SM promo—'AC/DC is not a nice band'—was a classic study in cutting through the crap, just like the band's music. It was also a very handy lead-in to the concert.

During an on-air interview at 2SM, Bon had been asked whether Angus's antics got in the way of his own performance. Absolutely not, he stressed. 'It's not like, "Look pal, it's my act, I'm the singer, give us a bit of floorspace," you know. If you want to make floorspace you've got to get it for yourself.'

'They were hell bent on leaving a serious impression,' Morris neatly understated when asked about AC/DC's eleven-song set, which kicked off, as always, with 'Live Wire'. As they played, Bon, decked out in a striped top, leather vest and leather pants, might have flashed back to his experience in the UK watching Brian Johnson and Geordie's guitarist, because he hoisted Angus onto his shoulders, wading into the big afternoon crowd, 'not missing a note' as Morris recalled.

'The punters'—including George Young, Harry Vanda and their families—'looked on with amazement as they moved around, the road crew trailing in their wake, making sure the leads didn't get tangled. It was fun and chaotic.'

At one point, Angus scaled the PA via a ladder, pulling off another blazing solo while standing atop the speakers, Morris documenting his every move. Bon also scaled the stack and dazzled the crowd from his perch high above the stage; it was as though he was conducting the sizeable gathering.

Morris had seen AC/DC perform in action before Bon joined—he'd photographed some of their first shows, at Chequers in the city—and was convinced that now, with Bon firmly established in the band, they were the real deal. 'Nobody beat AC/DC. It was all about the energy.'

Sydney band Ol' 55, who'd first encountered Bon *in flagrante* at the Freeway Gardens, were also on the bill. Their singer, Jim Manzie, tried to move a bass amp during their set and was electrocuted. He was zapped with 240 volts and thrown five metres through the air, ending up unconscious on the ground. He came to on the concrete floor of the dressing room, with Bon leaning over him. He had a bottle of Johnnie Walker Red—it was always red for Bon, never black—and administered a few therapeutic sips to Manzie.

'Briefly I thought I was dead,' laughed Manzie, 'and had woken up in heaven with my favourite singer taking good care of me. He had some kind words for me and told me he too had been electrocuted before. I was very groggy, literally, and was taken to hospital and held for observation.'

When Manzie mentioned to the hospital staff that Bon had given him booze after his zapping, they were aghast. It could have killed him. They had a clear message for Bon:

'You go tell that Bon Scott to stick to music and leave the medical stuff to the doctors.'

★

The local media wised up quickly to the fact that Bon provided great copy; he had colourful, usually sordid rock-and-roll stories seemingly on tap and was all too willing to share them, sometimes even embellish them (heaven forbid). Bon knew it was just part of the game. He was a good storyteller, too; in another life he could have cut it as a talk-show host.

Admittedly, the next slice of backroom debauchery was revealed by Malcolm, in a *RAM* article titled, 'The lusts of AC/DC', but Bon played a prominent role in the story. Apparently, after a particular gig, Bon and Malcolm had been invited by two women to 'come back to Granny's place', which, while it sounded a bit odd, was an offer they simply couldn't refuse. Once they'd jumped the back fence and let themselves into the house, the two couples got down to business on the lounge room floor. Bon, as Malcolm revealed, began racing around the house naked, 'turning somersaults'. It was then that Bon and Malcolm learned that 'Granny's place' meant just that, because the girls' grandmother unexpectedly returned.

Malcolm's clothes were thrown out the window, closely followed by their owner. Bon landed alongside him and the pair disappeared into the night.

In a subsequent one-on-one with Ed Nimmervoll, a writer for *Juke* magazine, Bon revealed his first reaction to AC/DC's debut single, 'Can I Sit Next to You, Girl', at a time when the group seemed to be just another bunch of glam rockers. Appearances had proved to be very deceptive.

'I thought, bunch of pooftahs! Now I'm in the band and singing the song.'

When not regaling journos with their lurid stories, Bon and the band kept on playing; their High Voltage tour kept them on the road through to September 1975, while the last three months of the year were consumed by a 'new' tour for their *T.N.T.* album, even though they didn't actually stop for a breather in between. A poster for the roadshow summed it up neatly: 'The AC/DC High Voltage tour is underway and ready to explode in your area'—which it duly did, in such unlikely spots as the Daceyville Police Boys Club, the Green Valley Marching Girls Field and Campbelltown's Catholic Youth Club, all in suburban Sydney, the Iceland ice rink in Melbourne's Ringwood, and the Sandgroper Hotel in far-flung Leederville, Western Australia. During 1975, AC/DC played more than 200 shows, travelled hundreds of thousands of kilometres—and in their downtime released two albums.

T.N.T. hit the stores on 1 December 1975. Harry Vanda, who co-produced the album with George Young, believed that this was the record that revealed the true identity of the band. 'Like, this is AC/DC, there's no doubt about it.'

The album sold 11,000 copies in its first week, eventually hitting a peak of number 2 and charting for 30 weeks, no doubt aided and abetted by yet another appearance on *Countdown* on 7 December. It was the 50th episode of the show, co-hosted by Skyhooks' Shirley Strachan and Daryl Braithwaite from Sherbet, and they rocked 'T.N.T.' It was the eleventh time during 1975 that Bon and the band had featured on the show, which now had a viewing audience in the vicinity of three million.

Back on the road, Bon hosted an after-party for fans in his room at the Commodore Motor Inn at Albury, a rural centre better known for its heritage buildings than rock and roll. He scrawled his autograph on various pieces of hotel stationery and anything else that was handy, passing them out as if they were coasters (which they were, in some cases). It was a lot more enjoyable than the drama of the following day, in Wangaratta, when the band and their crew got into a post-show scrap with some locals at the Olympic Café. Angus was thrown in a jail cell overnight to cool off (although at least one onlooker swears that it was Bon who was locked up). The show itself, staged at Wangaratta's town hall, was a blast; as a punter named Michael Croucher recalled, Bon and the band were in overdrive. 'I was mesmerised by Bon's presence in particular, and by his comical lift of an eyebrow and his cheeky grin. He was a great showman. He could sing a bit, too.'

Three days later, Bon must have taken great satisfaction from their year-ending gig, a New Year's Eve show staged at Football Park in Adelaide, which they headlined over his old band Fraternity (now with John 'Swanee' Swan on vocals), plus up-and-comers Cold Chisel, fronted by John's brother Jimmy, who'd also sung with Fraternity earlier in the year. Bon had come a long way in the two years since he last played with Fraternity; the excited talk about AC/DC among Adelaide locals made that clear. As Irene Thornton admitted, she heard more people discuss Bon's new band than she'd ever heard talk about Fraternity.

The band took the stage at 11.30 p.m., and soon after,

Bon suddenly emerged in the middle of the crowd, 'playing' his bagpipes, having the time of his life. The audience responded by sparking up a bonfire in the middle of the mosh pit, with *Countdown* host Molly Meldrum nearby, taking in the mayhem.

It wasn't a bad way to round out a crazy year.

★

As the band's seemingly never-ending tour rolled on, Bon continued to jot down his feelings and thoughts in letters, many of which he sent to Irene. He admitted to now being a daily smoker of the 'hippy stuff'. Along with his brother Graeme, he'd just taken a quick trip to Canberra in rare downtime; 'stoned, of course'. Bon also confessed that while the gypsy life could be lonely, he had no plans to settle down—his career with the band was moving way too fast. He knew this was his best shot, and probably his last.

In what was now becoming an AC/DC ritual, the band tweaked their schedule to ensure they'd be in Sydney early in the new year to record a new album with George and Harry at Alberts.

Bon and the Youngs had yet another rock-solid stash of songs ready to roll. Among them was 'Dirty Deeds Done Dirt Cheap', which would become the album's title track. It featured another of Bon's swaggering, big-balled lyrics; he snarled and growled and wailed, dropping such words and phrases as 'dirty deeds', 'cyanide', 'high voltage' and 'T.N.T.' as if they were burning his tongue. The band, as usual, whipped up a furious firestorm behind him. ('Dirty Deeds' was a keeper; they'd still be playing it well into the 21st century. It also came in at number 2 on *Ultimate Classic Rock*'s list of Top 10 Bon Scott AC/DC songs.)

The album—*Dirty Deeds Done Dirt Cheap*, eventually released in September 1976—featured other soon-to-be standards, among them 'Problem Child', while 'Ride On' was a curiosity in the AC/DC songbook: a slow, sinewy blues. Bassist Mark Evans, for one, was convinced this was an autobiographical lyric. 'It's Bon through and through,' he stated. Some of Bon's lyrics for 'Ride On' had previously turned up in letters he'd written to Irene, so he clearly didn't shy away from a spot of recycling.

'It's about a guy who gets pissed around by chicks,' Bon explained, 'and can't find what he wants.'

Bon the stand-up comic took centrestage during 'Big Balls', another of his oh-so-subtle odes to life below the waist. It was no musical masterpiece—it was more vaudeville than red-hot rock-and-roll—but Bon revelled in delivering a lyric that would have made a porn star blush as he boasted about the size, durability and capacity of his, erm, balls. If it was possible to sing with a smirk, Bon did just that during what was a companion piece to his earlier 'She's Got Balls'. He now had a matching pair, as it were.

Irene Thornton, for one, was impressed. 'Trust Bon to write a whole song about testicles,' she wrote. 'Bazza McKenzie would be very proud.'

'Squealer', however, despite some ferocious string-bending from Angus, was a misstep. It was Bon's attempt—by his own admission—to have fun with the concept of 'deflowering' a virgin, which, hardly surprisingly, came off as lecherous and seedy, even in the 1970s. 'Bon is so depraved he almost turns me off sometimes,' Phil Rudd admitted to a reporter from *RAM*. 'Some of the things he comes out with!'

'Ain't No Fun (Waiting 'Round to Be a Millionaire)' was more on the money, as Bon laughed out loud at the unlikely scenario that one day he'd make some serious cash and live among the rich and famous. At the end of the song he staged an imaginary argument with, of all people, eccentric American squillionaire Howard Hughes, demanding that he get his 'fuckin' jumbo jet out of my airport'.

Bon had joked in a recent letter to Irene that he was unlikely to marry again, not 'unless she's a millionaire'. Good news was that he now owed less than $200 on the bike he'd crashed back in Adelaide, while the downside was that he was still earning just $60 a week—virtually everything AC/DC made on the road was spent on keeping them on the road. Howard Hughes could sleep peacefully; Bon wasn't likely to move into his neighbourhood any time soon.

Interestingly, despite Bon's profusion of bawdy lyrics, 'Ain't No Fun' was a very rare case of him swearing on record, and even then it only appeared during the fade-out. Perhaps it was Bon's concession to Isa's request that he write 'nice' songs.

★

In what was a textbook case of deja vu for Bon, Malcolm Young had made it clear that they needed to get to the UK to achieve his goal of world domination. Bon had heard exactly this kind of talk when he was with Fraternity, but AC/DC were a very different beast. The band was focused and united, more like a gang than a typical group, even though it was clear that Malcolm was at the helm. Whereas Fraternity expected the world to come to them, Bon and the others knew that they'd have to start again from scratch and continue to do what they'd been doing for the past eighteen months or so: tour, tour and tour some more. And again unlike Fraternity, they had a bounty of road-hardened originals ready to unleash on a new audience, having all but dropped covers from their sets, with the exception of their rip and tear through 'Baby Please Don't Go'. AC/DC, in short, had their shit together.

Manager Browning, who shared Malcolm's dream of going global, had got out ahead of the band and helped them secure a deal with Atlantic Records, the home of the world's best jazz, soul and blues artists, but more recently it had been the label of choice for such 'supergroups' as Crosby, Stills, Nash & Young. Led Zeppelin had recorded for Atlantic. The label had also released *In the Court of the Crimson King* in the US, the album Bon had overheard while staying in Sydney back in 1971, which had influenced Fraternity's cover of 'Seasons of Change'.

Browning, with a lot of help from his sister, Coral, who was based in London and also worked in the business, sold the band primarily on the strength of some very persuasive live video footage of 'High Voltage', which was shot at Melbourne's Festival Hall by filmmaker Larry Larstead. In the clip, Bon was in full leather—waistcoat and duds—and also in full cry, working the crowd into a frenzy, as hundreds of arms reached out towards the stage like he was the second coming of Jesus Christ himself (admittedly, not all the audience footage was synched to the band's performance, so there'd been a bit of improvising in the editing suite). Regardless of its veracity, it worked.

'The clip made AC/DC look like a big-time international outfit,' Browning wrote. (It's now clocked almost ten million YouTube views.)

The deal was pure boilerplate—a $25,000 advance and a royalty rate of twelve per cent—but it was enough to help them set up in London. A date was set for AC/DC's departure: 1 April 1976. Typically, they'd keep playing virtually up to the day of their flight out of Sydney.

Bon couldn't wait to try his luck again offshore. He wrote to Mary Renshaw, who was currently in London. 'Wish we could drop in and see you over there. This country's driving us sane.' As for Britain, Bon's memories from his time there with Fraternity remained strong. 'I must admit it's not, or it wasn't, too bad,' he wrote. He also had a question for Renshaw: 'Do you sound like a to & from [i.e. a Pom—English] or what?' he asked her. 'Have you lost your accent?'

There was a fair bit of domestic business to attend to before departing. First there was a three-night stand at influential Sydney watering hole the Bondi Lifesaver in early February, a venue whose nickname, The Swap—as in 'wife swap'— hinted at what went down inside its four walls (pretty much anything). The crowd AC/DC drew was a curious mix of suburban headbangers, teen girls who'd caught them on *Countdown* and even some skinheads, along with the usual hedonists. As the band blasted the roof off the place, one particularly devoted skinhead picked up Bon's mic, which had stopped working, and, in the words of reporter Anthony O'Grady, who was in the thick of things, 'holds it high and strokes it devotedly. Then he kisses it and reverently passes it back to Scott.'

During another night at the Lifesaver, Bon was emerging from the club when he bumped into Jim Manzie from Ol' 55, who he'd 'helped' recover from an electrocution at Victoria Park the year before. Manzie's car had broken down.

'Forget it for now,' Bon told Manzie, as he fiddled about under the bonnet. 'Come with me to the Squire Inn; you can stay in my room.'

Manzie was no choirboy, but his eyes were opened wide as the night stretched into a couple of days in the company of Bon Scott. 'I got to see the famous Bon lifestyle up close and personal. I do remember the motel room door was never shut, and various fans, band members and roadies roamed in and out. The room was packed with transient people with various agendas.'

Bon rose late and got to work writing replies to letters from fans. Manzie was impressed by the man's dedication to his followers, until he read some of the content. A bunch of Polaroids were spread out on the table; after taking in their graphic content, Manzie offered some advice: 'You might want to burn those, Bon.'

Soon after, as Manzie recalled, some 'pleasant young ladies' arrived wearing school sports uniforms. Soothing massages turned into 'some lazy morning low-impact sex'.

It was quite the weekend for Manzie, who was still finding his way as a rock-and-roll singer. 'At all times,' he said, 'Bon was a generous elder rock statesman who knew how to live this new and strange life I was learning. I think my rock-and-roll education was pretty much complete after my lost weekend at the Squire Inn.'

The next time Manzie saw Bon was at a record reception party. Bon had shoved a smoked oyster up his nose and left it there like some giant booger as he worked the room. The last time Manzie saw Bon was one night in Melbourne. Manzie was staying with his band at the St Kilda Car-O-Tel motel and looked over to see Bon in an old Victorian house across the street.

'A huge lady dressed in pink was gently combing his hair as smoke wafted up from his cigarette, and steam from his coffee,' he recalled. 'Bon looked contented enough.'

★

After AC/DC's Lifesaver gig they shot a soon-to-be-famous film clip, produced again with the help of *Countdown*. On the morning of 23 February 1976, the band, along with some players from The Rats of Tobruk pipe band, piled onto a flatbed truck and got to work blasting away the cobwebs in Melbourne's CBD as they motored up and down Swanston Street 'playing' 'Long Way to the Top'. It was all very impromptu, this being a time long before council permits and endless paperwork were required for such a venture. The reaction of those on the streets was a mixture of shock, pure delight ('It's AC/DC!') and utter confusion. As one onlooker later remarked, 'It just got awesomely louder as the truck approached—and the cops were scratching their heads.'

Bon, bagpipes heaved over his shoulder, was every inch the entertainer as he mugged for the camera and worked the crowd that followed the AC/DC road train (among the gathering were some well-informed fans, plus manager Browning and Rob Booth, a former roadie for Fraternity). One stealthy fan managed to slip Bon a joint and another tried to persuade him to take her phone number as the cameras, and the truck, kept rolling.

The clip, produced for the princely sum of $400, instantly became a *Countdown* staple, and has now registered more than 35 million YouTube views, while the song was inducted into the National Film and Sound Archive's Sounds of Australia in 2012 and has featured prominently in such Hollywood hits as *School of Rock* and *Only the Brave*. AC/DC lovers Metallica blast 'Long Way to the Top' on their PA just prior to taking the stage; baseball's Chicago Cubs do likewise before their games, and it's a go-to track at big AFL and NRL matches. What better song could there be to stir up an audience?

Not long after the guerrilla filming, a gathering was held at the upscale Lazars in Melbourne to present the band with some gold records for *High Voltage*. Among those in the room were the mothers of Mark Evans and Phil Rudd, who were a little taken aback by the evening's raunchier events. Even Bon, usually the life of the party, took a back seat when a scantily clad woman emerged from inside a cake, clutching one of the prized gold records. Things got even rowdier when a belly dancer began working the room—and somehow lost her bra as she gyrated. At the business end of proceedings, Bon stepped up and gave an expletive-laden speech, while Angus opted for something simpler: 'I'd just like to thank me,' he said, with a wink.

Bon handed his gold disc to his guest Irene Thornton. 'You can think of me when you look at it,' he told her, smiling broadly.

★

During the early weeks of March, the AC/DC bandwagon rolled on—in one particularly lively day, they crossed two state borders in order to play two gigs and shoot some video footage. They also played dates in such rural spots as Castlemaine, where they performed from the back of a flatbed truck, emulating the 'Long Way to the Top' video. Bon was in especially high spirits; he arrived at the gig, staged at the local showground, lugging a bottle of Stone's Green Ginger Wine, with a female fan on each arm. The locals had never seen anything like it.

During a gig in the outer-Melbourne suburb of St Albans, a local named John Conte shot 45 minutes of the show, with the band's permission. He'd eventually sell the footage to a US collector for $6000, though he'd admit, 'I could have bought a house with what it was actually worth.' (Some of that footage would turn up on the 2007 AC/DC DVD set *Plug Me In*.)

In a final pre-departure conversation with *RAM*'s Anthony O'Grady, Bon downplayed his success rate with women, despite his lively night at Castlemaine. 'Me and Angus are out front pulling our balls off to get the crowd moving,' he explained, 'and what happens is the guys [in the crowd] watch Angus and me. But the chicks all get off on the other three. They do the least moving about on stage and they still pull more chicks than Angus or me.

'Bloody unfair it is. Being a singer ain't what it used to be; not in this band, anyway.'

★

When Bon had shifted to the UK with Fraternity, he'd had Irene Thornton with him, and he clearly also wanted someone to accompany him this time around. He all but begged John D'Arcy, the former Valentines roadie and friend, to take the trip, but D'Arcy had a young family and simply wasn't in a position to be part of his mate's entourage.

As their departure date neared, the band's immediate plans started to take shape. Soon after reaching the UK they were booked to tour through April and May with Back Street Crawler, whose main man was Paul Kossoff, the hard-living former guitarist of Free, a rock band much admired by Bon and the Youngs. It seemed like a perfect match, the ideal way to begin their UK odyssey.

Back Street Crawler were also signed to Atlantic, for a hefty $150,000—and in a curious coincidence, a track on their 1975 debut, *The Band Plays On*, was named 'It's a Long Way Down to the Top'. Unfortunately, it was another track on the LP, 'Rock & Roll Junkie', that would prove to be more prescient.

On 19 March, the day after the AC/DC single 'T.N.T.' entered the Australian Top 40 at number 37, Kossoff was travelling with Back Street Crawler on the red-eye from Los Angeles to New York. When the flight reached JFK Airport, Kossoff's absence was noted; a flight attendant found his lifeless body slumped in the bathroom, wedged against the door. The band was held on the plane for an hour as authorities tried to determine whether Kossoff had died in LA or New York. He was 25 years old.

A youthful taste for Mandrax had escalated into a full-blown heroin habit for Kossoff. He'd almost died in late 1975, when his heart stopped beating for more than half an hour. Kossoff's actual cause of death was 'cerebral and pulmonary oedema', not an overdose, but clearly drugs had wreaked havoc on the guitarist's body.

Word filtered back to AC/DC about Kossoff's demise. Bon was clearly distraught, so much so that he penned a heavy-hearted note to the editorial desk at *RAM*.

'That cunt Kossoff fucked up our first tour. Wait'll Angus gets hold of him.'

His death wasn't going to delay their departure, but it did put a serious crimp in their immediate plans. Bon and the band gathered at Sydney Airport on 1 April, preparing to board a Garuda flight. But first they mugged for the ever-present *Countdown* crew, who were documenting their final hours in Oz. There was a 'serious' sit-down with Molly Meldrum, in which Bon, nursing the first of many drinks (it was a long trip), made it clear how they'd hit the top in Oz. 'Our success is due to the taste of the public,' he said with a chuckle.

Bon and the others then filmed promos that would be aired on the show in their absence.

'Hello, this is Bon from AC/DC here,' Bon said, trying to keep a straight face, 'and although we're overseas at the moment, dining with the Queen, we haven't forgotten about you *Countdown* fans. And here to prove it is our brand-new single, "Jailbreak".'

At this point, band buddy and Alberts' labelmate Ted Mulry crashed the set, and Bon hoisted him onto his shoulders as they burst into an impromptu 'Long Way to the Top'. Then they were gone.

13

'What do you do around here, mate?'

—Bon, to former Beatles publicist Derek Taylor

Atlantic splashed out on two Daimler limos for the band, which they rode from Heathrow to their new London HQ at 49 Inverness Terrace, Bayswater, feeling very much like kings. According to Mark Evans, 'We were very impressed— if you can be impressed after 36 hours on a plane.'

Upon arrival at Bayswater, Bon, typically, snagged himself a private room, as did Malcolm and Angus, while the others divvied up whatever space remained. The buzzing centre of London was a quick ten-minute Tube ride away.

The Daimlers, however, turned out to be Atlantic's last offer of largesse for some time. Browning, meanwhile, put each member of the band on £50 a week 'walking around' money, which they'd have to survive on until they booked some live work.

The first public outing of the band was not a gig, but a meet-and-greet hosted by the record company, a chance for staff at Atlantic to get to know this ten-legged rock-and-roll beast from 'Down Under'. One of the guests was Derek Taylor, a former Liverpool journo who'd been The Beatles' press agent. In his post-Beatles life he'd been working with The Rolling Stones, Alice Cooper and Neil Young.

A line-up was quickly formed to meet a man who was one step away from British musical royalty. But, as Browning recalled, Taylor 'came on like a pompous git', and Bon simply couldn't resist giving him a serve.

'What do you do around here, mate?' Bon asked, trying hard not to laugh.

'My dear fellow,' Taylor responded sniffily, 'I'm Derek Taylor. I worked for The Beatles. You've heard of them, haven't you?'

Mark Evans, who was standing next to Bon, unleashed a beery burp right in Taylor's face. As Evans noted, 'He had no idea how close he came to a smack in the mouth, poor sod.'

But Taylor was hardly the last pretentious Englishman to speak down to AC/DC.

Events took an even weirder turn a few nights later when Bon and the band rocked up to a KISS gig at the Hammersmith Odeon. KISS were riding very high on the success of their *Alive* album and their cartoonish take on shock rock, which included an assault of fake blood and pyrotechnics, and bass player Gene Simmons' reptilian act with his tongue. But as far as Bon and co were concerned, KISS were all flash (and greasepaint), no substance. 'It was one of the funniest nights of my life,' said Mark Evans. 'No wonder they wore make-up.' Bon was a touch more politic when asked about KISS by Molly Meldrum. 'They were quite'—Bon paused, searching for the right word to describe their act—'spectacular.' In time, AC/DC would get their chance to rock the Odeon, without the need for pyros or props.

Bon's first night at renowned London venue The Speakeasy Club was just as puzzling. 'The Speak', as it was known, was rich with rock-and-roll history, having hosted everyone from Pink Floyd to Jimi Hendrix and King Crimson. In 1967, The Beatles hosted visiting Americans The Monkees at The Speak, which inspired the latter's song 'Randy Scouse Git'. AC/DC's first night there were as guests of Atlantic's London staff, and they happily imbibed the French champagne that flowed freely at their table. But they didn't know what to make of the headlining band (so much so that no one could remember their name), who, with their big hair and glitter, came on like the death rattle of glam rock. This was the opposition?

Even without playing a note, the band was starting to feel more and more confident about taking on the 'best' London had to offer—especially if acts like this were the pick of the bunch. But they were also sensing that their no-bullshit take on rock was a world apart from what excited London's taste-makers. The charts might have been clogged with the pure pop of ABBA ('Fernando') and Brotherhood of Man ('Save Your Kisses for Me') and Paul McCartney's Wings ('Silly Love Songs'), but it was punk, in the shape of the snarling, spitting Sex Pistols and the more politically charged The Clash, that was getting all the media attention. And AC/DC were definitely not a punk band.

*

With time to kill, Bon decided to revisit his past and dropped by the pub in Finchley where he had once pulled beers. Almost as soon as he walked through the doors, Bon was spotted by a local, who approached him. But rather than shake his hand and welcome him back, he whacked Bon with a beer mug. Bon went down in a screaming heap, his jaw broken, his already wayward teeth smashed to bits.

Bon never made it clear exactly what had incited such a violent response, but insisted it was none of his doing. 'It wasn't even my fight,' he said, when he was able to speak again.

Bon was admitted to hospital, where he underwent a particularly gruesome procedure: the surgeon made an incision at his hairline and used a probe with a hook attached to reconstruct his cheekbone. A few days later he returned to Bayswater, where he convalesced for a couple of weeks, nursed back to health by Coral Browning, who lived nearby. She lifted Bon's spirits with bowls of soup and a steady supply of his preferred comic books—*B.C.* remained a staple, along with *Conan the Barbarian*. Bon also wrote a lot, be they postcards home or ideas for new lyrics.

The next stage of Bon's facial reconstruction was a new set of chompers, fitted by a Harley Street specialist, at considerable cost—around $2000. (His bandmates cheekily referred to his 'Donny Osmond smile', or, when he wasn't within earshot, they called Bon 'Mr Ed', a nod to TV's talking horse.) But there was a flipside to his accident: Bon finally had the type of million-dollar smile that did justice to his ever-present grin.

During a photo shoot undertaken while he was still on the mend, Bon sported a pair of dark glasses to hide his bruised and swollen face.

The band's work situation changed, finally, when they secured a gig at a pub called the Red Cow, in West London, not far from their HQ, on 23 April 1976. The gig had been set in place by their UK booking agent, Richard Griffiths, from Headline Artists.

It was a gig that would go down in AC/DC folklore. When they first plugged in and tucked into 'Live Wire', their usual opener, there were more people on stage (what little stage there was) than in the room, but come their second set, the pub was packed to capacity with some 250 people, probably more. During their break between sets, those present had hit the phones, insisting their mates 'come down to the pub and check out this band!'

It was after AC/DC's rapturously received London debut that Bon reconnected with Margaret Smith, a lover from his days in Adelaide, the woman who he'd introduced Irene Thornton to soon after they wed. She'd undergone a make-over: she was now known as Silver Smith and was keeping company with London's rock-and-roll A-listers, The Rolling Stones among them. She'd set out on a world trip in 1974 and, while in London, had been introduced to Stones guitarist Ronnie Wood, who was her entree to the best gigs, and the biggest stars, in the city. She adapted quickly and was well established by the time she met Bon again. Smith was tiny but couldn't be missed; as she'd admit in a 2010 interview with ABC Radio in Adelaide, she 'was six and a half stone and wore four-inch heels'.

One Red Cow punter noted that in the break between sets, Bon was chatting with the locals at the bar, cadging drinks, then 'disappeared with two girls'. It's likely that one of them was Smith, because they quickly resumed the relationship that had spluttered out back in Oz all those years before.

★

The English tabloid press, especially the fickle music media, loved to imagine all Antipodean 'invaders' as a cross between Rolf Harris, Ned Kelly and Bon's beloved Bazza McKenzie. The temptation to throw the terms 'convict', 'wallaby' and 'tie me kangaroo down, sport' into every sentence proved to be simply irresistible for these budding Oscar Wildes. The treatment dished out to AC/DC, at least early on in their UK jaunt, was parochial English journalism at its most biased. (A decade later, on-the-cusp New Zealand bands such as The Chills copped similar treatment; no article was complete without at least one mention of sheep.)

On 26 April, when AC/DC played a show at the Nashville Rooms, a London venue that was fast becoming ground zero for punk, they managed to score a few column inches in *Melody Maker*, perhaps the worst culprit when it came to Aussie bashing. Littered through the review—which, admittedly, did heap praise on 'virtuoso' guitarist Angus Young—were such literary gems as 'outback rednecks' and 'macho chunder bar-proppers'. The same rag dismissed *High Voltage* just as casually, when it was released on 30 April, stating: '[It's] the same old boogie.' (The album combined tracks from their first two Oz LPs.)

'Is Britain ready for the human kangaroo?' ran a groan-worthy headline in the *New Musical Express*, alongside a snap of Angus in action.

It was a slippery slope for a band trying to build a following, because the music press could be kingmakers or career-wreckers, depending on which way the winds of zeitgeist blew, or who provided the best copy. Writers such as Caroline Coon and Nick Kent and Charles Shaar Murray wielded considerable influence; they could make or break a band in the space of a few hundred words. In the northern summer of 1976, cover stars for the *New Musical Express* were New York punk poet Patti Smith, reggae star Bob Marley, and Americans Blue Öyster Cult and Ted Nugent, while *Melody Maker* championed punk acts The Stranglers, the Sex Pistols and The Damned. A raw, rocking outfit like AC/DC was an outlier among this lot.

But the self-belief of Bon and the band wasn't simply bluster; they knew that if they kept playing hard and fast, regardless of whether there were ten people in the house or 10,000, they'd win new converts—and to hell with the critics. It was punters who bought tickets and albums, not journos.

Bon had a gauge for how well the band was faring: he put it all down to the wear and tear on Angus's knees. They were AC/DC's very own litmus test, not the words of reviewers. 'The more he shows them, bruises and all,' he told a writer from *Sounds* (who did get on the AC/DC bandwagon), 'the better we go over. We haven't been booed, or anything like that.'

A *Sounds* article entitled, 'The Fastest Knees in the West', featuring a shot of a sweat-drenched Angus in full-blooded, knee-bruising action, proved Bon's point.

'The music press is totally out of touch with what the kids actually want to listen to,' Bon told a writer from the *New Musical Express*. 'These kids might be working in a shitty factory, or they might be on the dole . . . they just want to go out and have a good time, get drunk and go wild. We give them the opportunity to do that.'

Bon understood his audience: AC/DC were working-class heroes, a band of the people. And, as it turned out, the more they played, the better the response—and they were unearthing a whole new audience in the UK, gig by gig. (They played fifteen London gigs during May 1976 alone.) Theirs wasn't the chains-and-safety-pins crowd, or the female-heavy following they'd had in Australia (whom Bon tactlessly described as '15 to 17—fuckable age'), but restless, up-for-anything suburban kids in denims and T-shirts. Speaking of which, the T-shirt that Malcolm favoured on stage summed up the band's mindset. It read: 'No Wuckin' Furries'.

★

When not revving up the local headbangers, Bon found plenty of outlets in London—he was very impressed by the availability, if not the quality, of the local product. In a letter home he noted that there was enough hash in London to keep Melbourne 'stoned for ten years'. Angus was the sole teetotaller, and he was less than impressed by his bandmates' indulgences. 'You know why they call it dope, don't you?' he'd grumble, as yet another session broke out in the lounge room at their new digs on Lonsdale Road in Barnes.

Bon, as some sections of the local media quickly learned—especially the writers from *Sounds*, which was far and away the most AC/DC-friendly weekly—could provide some very juicy and highly quotable copy, often in cahoots with Angus. On 2 June, a writer named Geoff Barton travelled with the band to a gig at the Retford Porterhouse, a three-hour trip up the A1 from London. On the long drive home, somewhere around 4 a.m., the conversation turned to the ideal end-of-night scenario. What would be perfect?

Bon pondered the question for a time, then responded rather dreamily: 'What'd be great right now would be a huge, comfortable, squashy waterbed . . . a woman lying right beside you.' To which Angus added, 'And a big pair of tits in your face.'

When asked whether he was 'AC or DC', Bon grinned and replied: 'Neither. I'm the lightning flash in the middle.'

Perhaps the gypsy life, which Bon had been living for a decade, was catching up with him. Phil Sutcliffe, a reporter from *Sounds*, asked Bon about life with no fixed address—he was rarely at the band's HQ, because they were constantly on the road, playing virtually every night in June (and continuing in that vein for much of the rest of 1976).

'None of us has had our own places to live for the past two years,' Bon admitted. 'All we've got is our parents' homes in Australia.'

It was no great shock, then, that when Bon did find some downtime, he set up house with Silver Smith. His bandmates dubbed their humble abode the Hippie Haven, while Bon and Silver were referred to, quietly, as 'Rod and Britt', a nod to jet-set couple Rod Stewart and Britt Ekland.

On stage, Bon had taken to trying out some banter on local audiences, with varying levels of success. 'This one you should know by now,' he told a crowd in Birmingham on 27 June, at a venue called the Mayfair Suite, as they tore into 'She's Got Balls'. 'It's all about your mother.' Bon then tweaked his lyrics, howling: 'She makes my heart race/Every time she sits on my face.' During 'The Jack', he asked for all those who'd suffered from a venereal disease to help him out. 'Sing the chorus with me,' Bon urged. Clearly, he'd hoped for a better response, because he then asked: 'Okay, how about all the guys who *haven't* had the jack before, you sing. There's more of you.'

Bon had tried something similar a couple of weeks earlier with an audience at the Leith Theatre in Edinburgh, stately digs that had also hosted such bands as Mott the Hoople and Thin Lizzy. First, he introduced one of their older songs as 'Can I Shit Next to You, Girl?' and he then asked for a quick show of hands to determine who had contracted what social disease, as he rattled off their names. ('Gonorrhoea, anyone? Syphilis?') 'You dirty bastards!' he chuckled, looking out over a surprisingly large number of raised hands. During 'The Jack', Bon delivered the line 'She curdled my cream' with an eye roll and a hearty snicker, more stand-up comic than denim-clad rocker. This night, like most gigs now, ended with Bon hoisting Angus onto his burly shoulders and undertaking a victory lap of the venue. Audiences loved it: not a lot of bands in the era of punk were willing to deliver this much show.

Bon's mention of John Lydon (aka Sex Pistol Johnny Rotten) hinted at a passing knowledge of punk. And if any member of AC/DC could relate to the anti-establishment ethos of punk, it was Bon, who'd been kicking against the pricks since the time he got locked up as a kid back in Freo. But Bon was no nihilist; he was a hedonist, through and through. He'd rather sing 'She's Got Balls' than 'Pretty Vacant'. And Bon rarely, if ever, talked about politics, something the punk bands railed against.

'We've got nothing to do with [punk],' Bon insisted, when asked by a writer from *Sounds*. 'We play quality rock'n'roll.'

★

Before relocating to the UK, Bon had lamented the diminished status of the lead singer, insisting that the rest of the band had more success than him with women, unlike 'the old days'. There was further proof of his theory when the group wound down their first full-scale jaunt, the Lock Up Your Daughters UK tour, with a rapturously received show at the Lyceum in London on 7 July.

This was more than just another rock-and-roll show, it was an event, hosted by influential British DJ—and AC/DC advocate—John Peel, who, as Bon noted in a letter home, 'reckons we're the band England needs now—and we agree'. The high point of the evening's entertainment, apart from the band's roaring set, was a competition—'The Schoolgirl We'd Most Like To'—that encouraged female fans of the band to dress provocatively. Proving that they were not gender biased, they'd hosted a similar event earlier in the tour, 'Best Dressed Schoolboy', that drew a big and sometimes very hairy response, as seemingly every wannabe Angus Young squeezed into ill-fitting school uniforms.

Selecting a winner at the Lyceum from the enthusiastic array of young women in fishnet stockings and short skirts, proved a challenge, but eventually one Jayne Haynes from Harrow was awarded the proverbial sash and crown. Bon couldn't take his eyes off her, but it was Mark Evans who escorted Ms Haynes home at the end of the night.

Bon was disappointed but understood that sometimes even he could be outcharmed. 'She was beautiful, really sexy. Garters. Suspenders. I was really lusting for her myself, we all were,' he confessed backstage afterwards. 'But Mark won out. He's just too handsome for me to compete with.'

14

'We're gonna be like Stormtroopers to the audience and like
the Gestapo to the groupies.'

—Bon, on the eve of AC/DC's first European tour

Bon turned 30 on 9 July 1976. It had been a long, strange
trip for the man known to his mother as 'my Ronny', from
his rough times as a kid in Freo, through his satin-and-
bubblegum days with The Valentines, getting back to the
country with Fraternity, and now, finally, scaling the ladder
with a band to which he was truly connected. He'd fallen
in love often, had his heart broken more than once and
generated plenty of heartache for others. And while he'd
maintained a public image as a macho, swaggering rocker,
that wasn't the complete picture: sure, Bon was a rough
diamond, but the man also had a lot of soul. He didn't have
a lot of close friends—his no-fixed-address lifestyle didn't
help—but those he did have were friends for life. And he
was fast becoming the best lyricist in rock and roll, a street
poet of the highest order, who had no end of personal
experiences to draw on for inspiration—some hard-won,
others plain hilarious.

Bon's bandmates decided to host a party to mark his 30th,
but as the night (and the next day) wore on, it became clear

that the guest of honour was a no-show. Bon later revealed to a journo just what had kept him away from the bash. 'I fucked my birthday in,' he chuckled, admitting that he'd been on the job from just before midnight to well after. 'It's the first birthday I've done that.'

When not busy between the sheets, Bon updated people back home with his, and the band's, latest achievements. When they travelled to Sweden in mid-July for their first dates on the Continent, a week-long stretch, he dropped a note to the Melbourne *Herald*, as noted in *My Bon*, stating that AC/DC were 'busy blowing polkas and oompah music out of the water'.

Bon also stated, for the record, that he was in total agreement with the Swedish practice of topless sunbathing, even if it caused him and the others a little discomfort. He told a prying journo how he had 'barred up' upon the sight of one especially comely sun-worshipper. 'It was 10 minutes before we could get up without offending public decency,' he chuckled, when he got into the same subject with Phil Sutcliffe from *Sounds*.

The Swedish press dubbed the band 'Australia's answer to Status Quo', which, given Bon's disastrous one-nighter opening for Status Quo back in 1972, must have tasted a little bittersweet. Crowds for their European shows were sparse, and they were living hand to mouth, feeding spare change into vending machines for croquettes and cigarettes, and sleeping on the tour bus. But back in the UK, Bon and the band's star was truly starting to rise.

★

The Marquee in London was a gathering place for taste-makers, musos and, most crucially, diehard music fans, and it had been hosting the pick of the musical crop since it opened in 1958 as a jazz venue. Not only was it the site of the first-ever live performance of The Rolling Stones, in 1962, but the Marquee had also hosted The Who, The Jimi Hendrix Experience and Led Zeppelin, just as each exploded onto the international stage. In 1964, in a makeshift studio at the rear of the venue, The Moody Blues recorded their breakthrough number 1 hit 'Go Now'.

To rock the bejesus out of the Marquee was one of the best possible ways to launch an act in the UK and beyond. It may have been a small room by Oz beer barn comparisons, capable of hosting 700 at a stretch, but the Marquee's reach was huge. It was known as the room favoured by serious punters as much as people from 'the biz'.

Fortunately for Bon and AC/DC, the Marquee's manager, Jack Barrie, was a big fan. He also admired the way that the band drew huge numbers of paying punters through the venue's doors. Barrie had been a big player in the London music scene since opening a venue named La Chasse in 1967, for a time known as the most popular watering hole in the music biz.

Barrie was such a fan of AC/DC, in fact, that he wrote to the band's label Atlantic and stated that AC/DC were 'the best band to appear at the Marquee since Led Zeppelin'. He also invited the band to stage an eight-week/eight-gig residency at the venue, beginning on 26 July. It didn't take long for word to spread that this was the must-see gig in town because a few weeks in, punters were being shoehorned into the room, all mad keen to take in this rock-and-roll phenomenon from Down Under. In his former life as a venue owner, Michael Browning had witnessed some extreme situations, but nothing quite like this: London might have been in the midst of a heatwave, but the heat and humidity inside the Marquee were even worse; it felt more like a large sauna than a music venue. 'The walls were like waterfalls of sweat,' he reported.

Of course, this only encouraged Bon and Angus—neither of whom tended to wear a lot on stage—to strip down to the bare essentials. On one memorable night, Angus skipped his usual late-gig striptease and began the night in jocks and sneakers; Bon rarely bothered with a shirt. 'This one's just to warm you up,' Bon told the gathering one night as they launched into 'Live Wire', but they hardly needed warming up: the room was hotter than hell. In a photo taken on the night, Angus solos wildly from the middle of the crowd, while Bon, standing alongside him, almost bleeds sweat—it pours off him in sheets.

Bon spoke with a reporter from Melbourne's *Herald*, trying his best to describe the scene inside the Marquee: 'The place looked like a nudist colony by the time we finished.' Photographer Michael Putland caught Bon taking a breather in the tiny space that passed for backstage at the club. Leaning against the wall, drink in hand, he is completely drained but has a satisfied look in his eyes—because the band had absolutely brained the crowd. So much for 'macho chunder bar-proppers' and bad Rolf Harris puns. London was theirs.

Countdown host Molly Meldrum flew out to shoot a segment for the show; during a vox pop with one exhausted punter, he was told that Angus was 'the best thing I've seen since [The Who's] Pete Townshend'. The band's barn-storming residency even rated a mention in the *Australian Women's Weekly*, not the type of mag inclined to cover hairy-chested rock and roll. 'We came to Britain to plunder and pillage,' Angus said, clearly relishing the moment. 'Perhaps we'll take the Tower of London. We don't want Big Ben, it keeps stopping.'

Press coverage of their concerts typically zeroed in on the 'Bon and Angus show', acknowledging that this was a band that did everything they could to entertain a crowd, but the usual condescension sometimes bubbled to the surface. 'Scott *could* be a first-class front man,' sniffed a writer from *Melody Maker*, 'instead of, as he strikes me, a poor cross between Alex Harvey and Steve Marriott. His enthusiasm did seem a trifle contrived at times.' Proving how clueless he was when it came to the fast-rising AC/DC, the same reporter dismissed Angus Young as 'not a great guitarist', instead likening him to rock-and-roll's answer to rubber-faced British comic Norman Wisdom, 'only more retarded'.

Rarely has the disconnect between critics and punters been more evident than in the case of AC/DC, because audiences flocked to the Marquee in such numbers that the band broke the venue's attendance record. Some 1000 fans managed to squeeze into the room midway through their residency.

'The heat is beyond belief,' gasped *Sounds* writer Phil Sutcliffe.

The only downside to this hot streak was a poorly received set at the Reading Festival at the end of August, which Jack Barrie helped to arrange in the wake of their Marquee success. It proved beyond doubt that AC/DC were not a band suited to playing in daylight, to a crowd that, by Marquee standards, was miles away from the stage. The audience response was tepid, despite Bon's attempts to get them motivated.

Between songs, taking on the dual role of MC and weatherman, Bon spoke with the crowd. 'Hello there. With all this rain we're having, the best thing to do about it is to cause some heat amongst ya to make it evaporate before it fuckin' hits ya, alright?'

His words achieved little because the audience barely moved a muscle; they seemed far more enthused by later sets from Manfred Mann's Earth Band and guitar-slingers Rory Gallagher and Ted Nugent. Afterwards, back at the band's Barnes HQ, a post-mortem devolved into a punch-up between the Young brothers (including big brother George, who'd flown in for the important show).

Bon had wisely opted not to get involved; as the punches flew and harsh words were exchanged, he was back at 'Hippie Haven' with Silver Smith, putting as much distance between himself and the others as possible. The phrase 'work-life balance' may not have existed at the time, but it was a concept of which Bon was fully aware.

'Unlike the rest of us,' noted Mark Evans, 'Bon had a life away from the band, something he very much needed.'

★

When not trading blows with his brothers, George Young found the time on his UK visit to cut some new tracks with the band, along with his partner in sound, Harry Vanda. On 1 September, they ducked into London's Vineyard Studios to record four songs, the pick being 'Dirty Eyes', a work-in-progress that would eventually become 'Whole Lotta Rosie'. Another track, 'Cold Hearted Man', featured one of Bon's best vocals, tough and raw. That song was included on the UK and various European editions of their 1978 *Powerage* album. Of the remaining cuts, 'Carry Me Home' would turn up on the B-side of their Australian single 'Dog Eat Dog'. It could never be said that AC/DC were the kind of band to waste a track.

On the strength of the band's record-setting residency at the Marquee, they signed up to the Cowbell Agency, which repped such stars as Rod Stewart and Roxy Music and whose co-owner, Richard Cowley, was briefly involved with the Sex Pistols. Their first booking was a nineteen-date European jaunt with Ritchie Blackmore's Rainbow—the former Deep Purple guitarist had been among the many A-listers who'd squeezed into the Marquee to witness the Bon and Angus show.

In mid-September, just before they left London for the opening night in Hamburg, Bon spoke with Anthony O'Grady back in Oz. When asked what they hoped to achieve during the Rainbow tour, Bon made his intentions very clear: 'We're gonna be like Stormtroopers to the audience and like the Gestapo to the groupies.'

Elsewhere in Australia, Irene Thornton hadn't heard from Bon in some time; she knew that he had reconnected with Silver Smith but wasn't aware that they were living together. She'd started to tire—understandably—of being referred to by mutual friends as 'Bon Scott's wife', especially given that their intimate relationship had been dead for some time, and she had her own life to get on with. 'It was slowly driving me mad,' Irene admitted. 'I really cared about him a lot, but

I wanted to be Irene again . . . not "Bon Scott's wife".' She decided to file for divorce.

Soon after, Bon reached out to Irene. It was the first time she'd heard from him in months.

'I'm sending you a waterbed,' Bon said down the line. 'They're great. You'll love it.'

Irene replied with a firm 'thanks but no thanks', yet a few weeks later his gift arrived, which she offloaded to a friend. Bon's act of generosity didn't change her mind; her application for a divorce remained. It was time for Irene to move on.

★

On tour with Rainbow, it didn't take long for Bon and the others to gravitate to the red-light heart of Germany—after all, this was a band that traded in boobs and balls and raunchiness, with a lead singer who, in the words of a writer from *Sounds*, 'has an extraordinary attraction for getting in the scandal sheets'. After a showcase gig in Hamburg, with Malcolm and Angus's older brother Alex along for the ride (he lived in Germany), they gravitated to the Reeperbahn, the city's notorious centre of sleaze. Their tour took in such hotspots as the Eros Centre, a multistorey HQ for the local working girls—a sort of sexual supermarket. During another lively night out, this time bankrolled by Earl McGrath from Atlantic Records, they looked on, between shots of schnapps, as a buxom woman and a well-hung stud got down to business on a table in the centre of a club.

'I'm glad we were out of range,' reported Mark Evans.

The band's onstage antics hit the mark, too, because the international edition of their *High Voltage* LP—which combined tracks from their first two Oz albums—sold 16,000 copies in its first week in Germany.

Back in Blighty, the AC/DC juggernaut kept on rolling. On 27 October, a live set at the Golders Green Hippodrome was filmed for BBC's *In Concert* series (though it wouldn't be screened until more than a year later, in February 1978). Bon's jeans were tight enough to squeeze the very life out of his much-discussed balls, which might have explained the slightly pained look in his eyes as he prowled the stage. A reporter from the *New Musical Express* had recently (and short-sightedly) dismissed Bon as nothing but 'muscle, mouth and bulging trousers'; the Hippodrome gig proved that he was, at least, correct on one front.

Bon was in a typically garrulous mood during the gig, introducing 'Problem Child' as 'a song inspired by none other than the Young boy here, Angus'. ('Yeah, Bon summed me up in two words,' Angus told a writer from *Total Guitar*.) By the end of the set, both Bon and Angus were drenched in sweat, and another crowd had been converted. Angus had been in particularly dazzling form—he played as if his guitar was shooting off sparks.

Interestingly, there was at least one Angus lookalike in the mosh pit, who was captured by the TV camera headbanging furiously. Little did the schoolboy guitarist on stage know that in years to come Angus-dressing would become a sport among AC/DC devotees—almost a religion, truth be told.

The biggest show of their UK odyssey to date was set to happen on 10 November at the 2500-capacity Hammersmith Odeon, the same venue where Bon and his brother Graeme had once seen Little Richard prance and pout. Tickets sold out quickly. It had barely been six months since their

London debut at the Red Cow and a lot had happened in a short time, most of it positive—and so what if their reviews were still dotted with references to kangaroos, dingoes and assorted Aussie wildlife?

Yet the Hammersmith show almost didn't go ahead. Bon, very much a man of the people, decided against a limo or a taxi and opted to catch the Tube from his place on Gloucester Road, which he shared with Silver Smith, but he got lost en route to the theatre. He'd only missed one gig before with the band, a midday set at Melbourne's Hard Rock Café, which he'd slept through. Now his bandmates were genuinely concerned he was going to miss another show—and this was far more crucial than a lunchtime set at the Hard Rock. The room was packed with eager punters, media and members of such acts of the moment as The Damned and Eddie and the Hot Rods. Anticipation was huge. And their singer was nowhere to be seen.

Much to his anxious bandmates' relief, Bon finally reached the venue with minutes to spare, shrugging off their jibes. What was the problem? He was here, wasn't he? Bon admitted he'd travelled some fifteen kilometres in the wrong direction before realising his mistake. This wasn't Bon's first travel mishap by any measure. During a drunken journey to a gig with reporter Harry Doherty, supposedly on their way to Cardiff, Bon steered the writer onto the wrong train from Paddington and they had to sit tight for 45 minutes until they reached a station where they could alight and start the trip all over again. 'We had a wee bit of a problem on the way,' he told the others when they finally reached the gig, 'and almost ended up in Glasgow.' Geography wasn't Bon's strongest suit.

The Odeon show itself was another milestone: the first of ten full houses AC/DC would play at the venue during Bon's life. Even the impossible-to-please *New Musical Express* had to admit that 'AC/DC conquered London' that night. A fan who travelled to the concert from the Netherlands summed it up precisely: 'This gig changed my life!'

Bon and the band continued touring the UK until mid-November, after which they returned to Oz for a run of dates to help top up their bank balance, and for more sessions with Vanda and Young. When they arrived at Sydney Airport in early December, the band was met by a small but enthusiastic group of female fans, wearing T-shirts that read, variously, 'AC/DC', 'Malcolm' or 'Bon Scott'. Bon happily posed for a photo flanked by two of his supporters, each with a blissful look on her face. Their hero was home.

After a rapid-fire press conference, where Bon said little beyond 'There is a shortage of good bands in England at the present', most members dispersed to reacquaint themselves with family. But not Bon, who settled into a suite at the Hyatt Kingsgate Hotel in Kings Cross, toasting his success with a duty-free bottle of 25-year-old Chivas Regal, a step up from his usual Johnny Walker Red. Life was good.

15

'I've never said "fuck" on stage yet.'

—Bon greets the press, January 1977

A few days after his return to Oz, Bon was hosting an after-party at the Southern Cross Hotel in Melbourne. The band had just played what was intended to be a secret gig at a venue called the Tiger Room at the Royal Oak pub in Richmond—until word leaked and the space swiftly filled to way beyond capacity. The venue's hugely popular operator, Laurie 'Loz' Richards, stood in the middle of the churning crowd, a satisfied man, as the band rocked some old Chuck Berry and Elvis favourites and the bar became gridlocked with thirsty punters.

Bon had seen little of his second (or was it his third?) hometown since he'd squeezed onto the back of a flatbed truck and blasted 'Long Way to the Top' to unsuspecting CBD workers almost a year before, wielding his bagpipes like a weapon. He was glad to be back and was positively revelling in his role as mine host at the Southern Cross.

Bon had rented a suite for the occasion and, as invitee Irene Thornton recalled, 'it seemed as though half the Tiger Room had gone there after the show'. Thornton and Mary

Renshaw looked on as Bon worked the room, loudly and proudly talking up everything the band had achieved in their absence. 'Bon was having a great time,' recalled Mary, who'd just moved to Melbourne and was staying with Irene. (Her Christmas card from Bon read: 'Xmas & future happiness Mary . . . Jingle Balls.')

Tired of the usual hangers-on and keen to reconnect with his real friends in the room, Bon turned on a few unlucky guests and bluntly insisted that they 'fuck off'. Irene confronted Bon about this, giving him a hefty serve. He told her that if she didn't like it, she could also leave.

'Yep, I think I will,' Irene snapped back, and with that she was gone.

A few days later, after a wild show at the Myer Music Bowl—where Bon demanded entry for a large number of ticketless fans, who were looking on from the other side of a cyclone fence—he materialised in the backyard of Irene's house, asleep in a hammock. But Irene had returned to Adelaide for a break. Instead, he sent her a birthday card from the road, which ended with a very Bon-like tag: 'If you ain't getting enough/It ain't my fault.'

The 'Giant Dose of Rock and Roll' tour itself—which the band had hoped to call 'The Little Cunts Have Done It', to the horror of the promoter—was a strange mix of wild audiences and over-the-top controversy, sparked by Angus's propensity for dropping his pants and baring his backside. Stodgy newspaper editorials, angry townspeople and radio bans turned the band's return to Oz into a grind. They rechristened the tour 'A Giant Pain in the Arse'.

Another controversy erupted when some kids cheekily began calling the phone number—'36-24-36'—cited by

Bon in the song 'Dirty Deeds Done Dirt Cheap', asking the woman who answered whether she was keen on performing some 'dirty deeds'. She turned out to be a Melbourne matron, a widow, who didn't appreciate the calls, duly voicing her concerns to a reporter. 'Pop Hit Makes Widow's Phone Run Hot!' screamed the headline in the following day's edition of the Melbourne *Truth*. And still her phone kept ringing, forcing her to change the number.

Bon didn't help matters when he slyly filled in a Q&A for Mark Evans, which appeared in the official tour program, without telling his bandmate. Evans was 'quoted' as saying, 'I'd like to make enough money to be able to fuck Britt Ekland.' This only caused more outrage. When Evans confronted him about it, Bon protested his innocence, then sat the young bassist down for a lecture. 'The girl's got feelings, too, you know,' Bon said, straining to keep a straight face.

Bon was interrogated by a *RAM* journo about Angus's bum, which was fast becoming the key talking point of the tour. Bon made it clear that he'd rather see that side of Angus than his pimply face.

'It's preferable,' he insisted, 'as far as I'm concerned.'

Angus doubled down on this when asked a similar question by a reporter from *The Border Mail*. Why did he insist on baring his bum? 'Why? Because my arse is better looking than my face.' In another interview, Angus said that he chose to bare all as a response to punters who yelled, 'Angus has no balls!'

'I eventually take off my pants and show 'em [it's not true],' he laughed.

Away from the controversy, Bon was running wild. Boozing was the order of the day; he had begun referring to himself as 'a special drunkard—I drink too much. It must be the Scot in me.' After a show in Albury (where the tour program was banned from sale), he invited each and every fan who made their way backstage to his room for drinks at the nearby Commodore Hotel. Some of them, such as fourteen-year-old local Jason James, were students, who went to school the next day with serious bragging rights, showing off their Bon Scott autographs. 'We were legends,' James laughed. Another fan snuck into the band's room at the Commodore and took photos of various band members in their undies, fast asleep. Those pics were also a big hit in the school playground.

Yet another teenage fan wrote about the experience of seeing Bon in action at a gig at Ginninderra High School, in the Canberra suburb of Belconnen. 'I can still picture Bon Scott, all sweaty, with his shirt off, screaming his lungs out! If only I knew the future, I would have got his autograph or pinched his shirt off the stage!'

After that particular gig on 9 December, the band settled into their digs for the night, a private house in the suburb of Pearce, some twenty minutes away. If they were seeking serenity they'd come to the wrong place; locals found out where they were staying and mobbed their hideout.

On stage at the Amoco Hall in Orange on 14 December— the same venue where The Easybeats played their final gig some six years earlier—Bon was in a playful mood, tweaking the lyrics of one of their more familiar songs.

'Can I sit on your face, girl?' he asked, his eyes scanning the crowd for keen female fans. 'You can sit on mine!'

Bon's mood darkened, however, when the tour reached Bundaberg in Queensland a few days later. The audience at the local showgrounds couldn't have been more passive, something Bon didn't hesitate pointing out. 'Next time we play Bundaberg,' Bon snarled from the stage, 'we'll play the local cemetery. We'll get more life out of people there.'

Fortunately, this was the second-to-last show before a two-week break. Bon drank in the new year at the Bondi Lifesaver, jamming with lewd, tattooed rockers—and kindred spirits—Rose Tattoo. Bon had introduced their singer, Angry Anderson, to the music of Scotsman Alex Harvey and he became an instant convert, and a rock-and-roll ally. Bon helped 'the Tatts' get a record deal with Alberts, which was quite the coup because no other label would touch such a dangerous-looking bunch. 'They were a great rock outfit,' Alberts' Fifa Riccobono said during an episode of ABC Radio's *Conversations*, 'but they scared the living daylights out of people.'

'Bon was as full as a state school,' Anderson told *Australian Rock Show* podcaster Denis Gray, flashing back to that night at the Lifesaver. 'He jumped up and we did two or three songs . . . I think we did "Jumpin' Jack Flash".'

The Lifesaver was a happy rocking ground for Bon. During one of AC/DC's many feverish gigs at the venue, a female punter, clearly caught up in the moment, leaped on stage, grabbed Bon's microphone and shoved it down her skirt. It remains unclear if Bon tried to retrieve it.

★

Early in the new year, Bon was back in fine form in his role as AC/DC spokesman when he sat down in Hobart with some journalists from the 'straight media' on 6 January 1977, ostensibly to promote a week of shows in the Apple Isle. Looking every inch the rock star—dark shades, a smattering of bling, nursing a drink, his recently repaired teeth gleaming white—Bon treated the assembled press with a mixture of disdain and humour. When asked whether Hobart authorities were planning to follow the lead of some mainland councils and ban them from playing, Bon said little. Instead, he slyly raised his middle finger in the direction of the TV camera that was capturing the moment.

Talk then turned to punk rock. After denying any knowledge of the Sex Pistols ('Don't wink at me,' he chuckled at one of the more wised-up members of the press), Bon simply said this: 'I see us as music. I see punk rock as nothing.'

'Do you describe yourselves as outrageous?' asked another reporter, clearly in search of a headline.

'No,' Bon replied. 'Rock and roll . . . Nothing else.'

And their biggest following in Australia—who was that?

'The police force,' Bon deadpanned.

'Many people see your use of indecent language in your act as outrageous. Do you see it as an essential part of your act?' asked another scribe, still pushing for something quotable.

Bon couldn't hold back a laugh. 'I've never said "fuck" on stage yet.'

With that, the reporters burst into laughter and the interview was over.

While Bon was toying with the local press, Michael Browning received some distressing business news. Atlantic's parent company in the USA was reluctant to pick up what was known as the 'option' on the band, which would leave them without a US label. They simply weren't sure if they were right for America. But the band had made it very clear that America was the rock-and-roll market they next intended to conquer and that simply couldn't be done without a label's backing, both in terms of financial support and promotional muscle. Phil Carson, the head of Atlantic in the UK, who'd signed the band, managed to talk his American bosses around, but there was a caveat: they were forced to surrender the advance guaranteed in their existing contract, some US$20,000. This wouldn't be the last time their American masters strongarmed the band into making a major sacrifice.

And still the Giant Dose tour stumbled from state to state. After enduring another sedate crowd, this time in the Victorian town of Moe, on 17 January, the band's crew assembled on stage and, in lieu of an encore, dropped their pants and mooned the audience.

*

It was a relief for Bon and the band in late January when they assembled at Alberts studio to record the *Let There Be Rock* album with George Young and Harry Vanda. Alberts was a safe haven, a place where they were welcomed, something that couldn't be said for many of the towns they'd recently visited.

The recent drama and controversies actually served as a tonic for the band, who channelled all their pent-up aggression into another high-octane set of songs. So much so, in fact, that while recording the title track, Angus's amplifier began shooting out sparks and smoke; there was a serious possibility that the studio might catch fire. But George Young knew a good take when he heard one and insisted that his younger brother keep on rocking. Fortunately, the studio didn't burn down, and the take was gold.

Bon wrote one of his sharpest lyrics for that title track, where he reimagined rock and roll in biblical terms. He dated the form's evolution back to 1955, a time when 'white man had the schmaltz' and 'the black man had the blues', and how, when those two forces collided, 'rock and roll was born'. Of course, there was a downside, just as Bon had aptly documented in 'Long Way to the Top', where he listed the pitfalls of a life spent in pursuit of rock's holy grail. As he observed in 'Let There Be Rock', while the players became superstars, admired and emulated by millions, 'the businessman got rich'. Not much had changed there since the early days of Elvis and Little Richard and Buddy Holly. And Bon was still earning $60 a week.

'Let There Be Rock' also made it clear where Bon's allegiances lay: he still loved the rock-and-roll classics, the same songs he'd sung in the shower as a kid that had driven his mother mad.

'I was never interested in modern-day sorta music,' he would tell writer Harry Doherty. 'I get off on all the old stuff—Elvis, Chuck Berry, Little Richard, Jerry Lee . . . all the other stuff seems poor in comparison. You put Little Richard's "Tutti Frutti" on and put the wildest thing from today next to it and it sounds timid in comparison.'

Elsewhere on the new record, Bon's X-rated alter ego emerged during 'Crabsody in Blue', which went to show that his interest in sexually transmitted diseases was right up there with the thing he had about his testicles. The title, a pun on George Gershwin's 1924 masterpiece 'Rhapsody in Blue', was laugh-out-loud funny, though it's unlikely that the scruffy working-class kids 'going off' to AC/DC were overly aware of a Jazz Age epic that its composer had described as 'a sort of musical kaleidoscope of America'.

Bon, adopting the role of narrator, was clearly enjoying himself as he documented the perils of the dreaded pubic lice. 'You start to scratch,' he wailed, as the band played a slow-burning blues behind him, 'when they start to hatch.' A cautionary tale to rank with 'The Jack', 'Crabsody', when mentioned on the Songfacts website, was given this assessment: 'This is a humorous look at the repercussions of sex without proper protection. In this case, lead singer Bon Scott sings about getting crabs.'

Enough said.

Bon explained his key inspirations to a DJ from 2JJ. 'All the songs we do are about one of three things: booze and sex and rock and roll. Things that kids think about 24 hours a day. If you ask a fifteen-year-old kid what's the most important thing to him and he'll say, "The chick in the front row at school. Or the teacher, whatever."'

★

After a final Giant Dose/Pain in the Arse show in Perth on 15 February, Bon's last-ever gig in the west, he checked in with his parents, Chick and Isa, and introduced them to Silver Smith, who was travelling with him. 'I have no idea what [they] would have made of Silver,' wrote Mark Evans. 'I figure that if Ron was happy that suited them well enough.'

It was a brief respite, an upbeat ending to a return to Oz that, apart from getting a new album in the can, had been full of frustrations. Ted Albert helped improve Bon's mood when he slipped him, and the rest of the band, a royalty cheque for $3957.29, just before they boarded their flight back to the UK.

'On behalf of the whole company,' Albert wrote in a note, 'our thanks for your efforts overseas and our best wishes for the coming year.'

16

'This was definitely one of the stranger bouts—Leo Sayer
versus Bon Scott.'
—Molly Meldrum

Ever the nomad, Bon had barely unpacked his bags before
the band hit the road again, this time for the Dirty Deeds
UK Tour, which ran from 18 February to 20 March 1977.
Things were lively from the get-go; during opening night at
Edinburgh University, those who couldn't squeeze into the
mosh pit sat on the monitor speakers at the lip of the stage.
When security guards tried to drag them away, fisticuffs
erupted. And the band hadn't yet played a note in anger.

A review of another wild show in Glasgow proved that
Bon Scott wasn't yet the household name he'd eventually
become, as the critic referred to him as 'Bob Scott' (shades
of early gigs with bassist Mark Evans, whom Bon had called
'Mike').

As on the Giant Dose tour, Bon loved to keep the party
rolling post-gig, and while in Blackpool on 20 February,
there was a photographer among his post-gig entourage.
A member of the band's crew 'borrowed' his camera and
managed to grab a shot of Bon in the toilet. That snap,
unlike the ones taken in rural Victoria a couple of years

back, never saw the light of day—much to Bon's relief, so to speak.

When the band reached their venue in Northampton on 5 March, they were confronted with an unusual problem: a van blocked the entrance, so they couldn't 'load in' and prepare for the gig. Bon and Angus came up with a simple solution: they recruited a couple of beefy locals to help them physically shift the vehicle and repaid them with backstage passes for the gig. Bon happily shouted them drinks after yet another high-voltage show.

The tour quickly gathered momentum, reaching London on 11 March, where the band filled the 3000-capacity Finsbury Park Rainbow. This was a room with its share of rock history—it was here that Jimi Hendrix first set his guitar on fire, and where, in 1971, Frank Zappa was pushed into the pit at the front of the stage by a member of the audience, snapped his leg and spent six weeks in hospital. The response to AC/DC was feverish but, thankfully, not physically threatening (nor was there any need for the fire brigade). In the crowd looking on, at Michael Browning's invitation, was booking agent and American industry heavyweight Doug Thaler, who would come to play a big role in the band's future by securing them work stateside.

Bon again touched on his 'rocker of the people' mantra when he sat down with a writer from the *New Musical Express*. He and the band had little interest in sucking up to the media. 'We're on the crowd's side,' Bon stated for the record, 'because it's a band-audience show. We're not like performing seals; we're in it together.'

Angus backed this up. 'I don't like to play above or below people's heads. Basically, I just like to get up in front of a crowd and rip it up . . . I honestly believe we give the people what they want. If we didn't, then we'd be on our way back to Australia by now.'

Back home, unbeknown to Bon, Irene Thornton received their divorce papers in the post. She could finally shake off the 'Mrs Bon Scott' tag for good. Irene had no idea where he was, or how to reach Bon, to let him know. 'I didn't think it really mattered to him,' she wrote. Meanwhile, Bon, the rock-and-roll gypsy, kept on moving, and partying, as he and the band filled venues in Leeds, Manchester, Wolverhampton and beyond. A fan's response to their show at the Fiesta in Plymouth on 7 March neatly summed up most audiences' reaction to AC/DC. His two-word declaration? 'Fuckin awesome.'

★

Countdown's fanatical support of AC/DC hadn't faded, and when they reached the significant milestone of their hundredth episode, it was a given that AC/DC would appear. Molly Meldrum put together the birthday episode—'a very special international edition', in the words of MC Gavin Wood—which would air on 3 April, just as AC/DC set out on a month-long European tour with Black Sabbath. (For Bon this must have provided a flashback to his days with Fraternity; they'd shared the bill with Ozzy and co. at the Myponga Festival way back in 1971.)

Bubbly pop star Leo Sayer, whose current single, the treacly ballad 'When I Need You', was firmly lodged in the pop charts in Australia and the UK, was the show's London host, while Meldrum co-hosted from the couch in

Melbourne. The line-up was the proverbial musical mixed grill; international acts included Bryan Ferry, Elton John, Shaun Cassidy, David Dundas and Kiki Dee, while among the many locals performing were Angus's least favourite band Skyhooks, as well as Little River Band and Renée Geyer.

'Next on the show from London,' Sayer announced, as Bon and the band prepared to lip-sync 'Dog Eat Dog', 'is a group that knows all about the land of Oz. And believe me, England is fast learning about them. Need I say any more?' The cameras quickly cut to the band—Bon wore a fur-lined coat for the occasion, a new purchase, but it didn't last too long under the red-hot studio lights. Angus skipped his school uniform altogether, playing instead in a striped T-shirt and long shorts, his head bobbing madly.

Countdown was a program that almost prided itself on chaos, sometimes on-set, often initiated by an overzealous (sometimes overindulged) Meldrum, but things could also get lively away from the cameras. After their rip and tear through 'Dog Eat Dog', Bon got into an off-camera tangle with the perennially chirpy Sayer; somehow, the much slighter Brit managed to push Bon over. Afterwards, Meldrum admitted that 'this was definitely one of the stranger bouts [he'd witnessed]—Leo Sayer versus Bon Scott'.

★

Typically, Bon and the band would return to Australia at the end of the year, to spend Christmas with their families, to tour and cut a new album. But things changed in 1977 when Bon found himself back in Oz during June to tie up some work commitments—among them, 'breaking in' new bassist Cliff Williams, who'd replaced Mark Evans—before he and the band, finally, launched an assault on the US. They'd signed a deal with booking agent American Talent International and were in the process of arranging their first US odyssey.

The group assembled at the Congregational Church in the eastern Sydney suburb of Woollahra, to shoot a video for 'Let There Be Rock'. In keeping with the biblical theme of his lyric, Bon dressed as a priest, while Angus head-banged in the guise of an altar boy, a fake halo perched on his head. Bon was in full vaudevillian mode, mugging for the camera, doing jazz hands and then stretching his arms wide as if to summon down the very gods of rock them-selves. All was going swimmingly until the big moment when Bon planned an Olympian leap from the pulpit, in which he'd soar over the band and land on the church's floor. Forgetting that, at 31, he wasn't the youngest buck, Bon hit the floor with a sickening thud and injured his leg. A nurse was summoned to his hotel room to tend to his injury, which helped ease the pain ever so slightly—but Bon was in real pain.

'I hurt my fucking ankle,' he moaned in a letter to Irene Thornton.

During their Sydney stay, Bon limped into the Bondi Lifesaver. When he was joined on stage by the rest of AC/DC—billed as 'The Seedies', a nod to their infectious time at the Freeway Gardens—it would be a night of firsts and lasts: the first time Cliff Williams played in Oz, but the last time Bon played with the entire band in Australia.

★

In late July 1977, *Let There Be Rock* was released in North America. Charts-wise, this was still very much the era of the sensitive singer-songwriter, the movement that had been one of the motivations for Malcolm and Angus to form AC/DC in the first place. (They weren't big fans.) As *Let There Be Rock* was unleashed on the American public, it was up against new albums from James Taylor (*JT*) and Crosby, Stills & Nash (*CSN*), while KISS, whom Bon and the others had found ridiculous the year before, shipped a whopping one million copies of their new album, *Love Gun*, on the week of its release. That album was produced by Eddie Kramer, who'd soon play a brief but pivotal role in the AC/DC story. Ditto KISS.

The US singles chart was soft-rock/AM radio manna from heaven—and an AC/DC nightmare. The high lord of schmaltz, Barry Manilow, was leading the way with 'Looks Like We Made It', followed closely by Andy Gibb ('I Just Want to Be Your Everything'), teen pin-up Shaun Cassidy ('Da Doo Ron Ron'), golden-haired guitar hero Peter Frampton ('I'm in You') and Barbra Streisand ('My Heart Belongs to Me'). The disco craze was soon to explode across the States, thanks in no small part to Andy Gibb's brothers in the Bee Gees.

Star Wars mania was sweeping America, too; the sci-fi flick was on its way to becoming the highest-grossing film of all time. Jimmy Carter, a rock-and-roll-loving Democrat from the Deep South, was in residency at the White House. Meanwhile, The King, Elvis Presley, was just a few weeks away from a one-way trip to Rock-and-Roll Heaven. It was a fascinating time to take on the US.

Let There Be Rock was one of several Bon Scott–era albums that only got its due props long after its release. In fact, reviews were scarce for the record during the northern summer of 1977, apart from some coverage in *Creem* that the writer lived to regret. ('These guys suck,' declared Rick Johnson.) However, writing in 2008, *Rolling Stone*'s David Fricke said the album was 'almost all killer. Scott sings "Bad Boy Boogie" and "Problem Child" like he's the enfant terrible . . . Angus' solos are pure white heat.' In a 2014 *Rolling Stone* readers' poll conducted to rate the Top 10 AC/DC songs, 'Let There Be Rock' was ranked number 10. Unfortunately, the American music bible gave the album a cursory two-and-a-half-star review upon its 1977 release.

Let There Be Rock was intended to be the album that would save their bacon in the US, or at least maintain the band's relationship with Atlantic. It would be fair to say that the record stalled at the gates, as Bon admitted to Molly Meldrum. 'It's number 150 with an arrow,' he revealed soon after its release. 'Not quite as fast as a bullet.' Okay, it was actually number 154 on the *Billboard* Top 200 chart, but Bon had made his point. Although it did reach the Top 20 in both Australia and the UK, in the US it wasn't a hit.

★

The band's first US gig was slated for 27 July at the Armadillo World Headquarters, a cavernous former National Guard armoury in Austin, Texas, and a hangout for stoned cowboys and Lone Star hippies. It was also the venue of choice for cosmic cowboy Willie Nelson, who played there often. It was hardly an AC/DC crowd, but Bon and Angus ripped the joint up as if they were playing the Marquee, despite a pot fog so dense that Angus got a contact high when he and Bon did a lap of the venue. According to Michael Browning, it was also incredibly humid inside the venue; he reported that it felt as though the band was playing 'under the shower'.

'The Texans lapped it up,' he added.

Soon after, on 6 August, Bon found himself confronted with one of the necessary evils of the music biz—a record convention, staged in Miami. These types of events were all about industry players schmoozing, networking and pressing the flesh; the music they were selling was little more than background noise. Still, Bon tried hard to work up some heat in the room when they hit the stage. 'This one,' he said, introducing 'Baby Please Don't Go', 'will get you off your arses and on your feet.' To their credit, Bon and the band blazed away despite barely being noticed.

The smile returned to Bon's face the next day when, in a stunt dreamed up by an Atlantic staffer, he and the band were given the keys to the city of North Miami. Bon dressed in a manner appropriate for such an important civic occasion, in his dangerously tight cut-off denim shorts and an oversized sun hat. In the official photo he grinned like a loon.

American groupies were a different breed to the women of the road Bon had grown accustomed to over the past dozen years. For reasons no one in the band was quite able to explain, they drew a more upscale female fan in the US, particularly in Texas, the starting point for their 1977 tour. These were free-spirited women, trust fund types, with fast cars and even faster lifestyles. But Bon was an early adopter, even before anyone had invented the term. He adjusted so quickly, in fact, that he often left the band on the bus and travelled from gig to gig with his new companions.

'Texans seemed to love AC/DC,' noted Michael Browning, 'especially the vivacious, long-legged groupies, who'd pursue the band in their flashy Pontiac Trans Ams and Chevy Corvettes . . . Once the Texan girls got what they came for, they'd simply jump in their sports cars and head off to the next destination. Never before had Bon been more in his element.'

Bon subtly referred to his new companions when he wrote home to Mary Renshaw, who was now sharing a house with Irene Thornton. After letting her know that 'the band is playing good & going over great', and that his perm was 'almost out—I'm a regular shaggy dog', Bon admitted: 'And the chicks are outta sight.'

During their first US sortie, the band was sometimes matched with unlikely headliners: Latin rockers Santana on one occasion, as well as bluesman Johnny Winter, then Illinois natives REO Speedwagon, a band that specialised in overwrought power ballads, who they first connected with in Florida and backed for several nights. Bon and the band didn't seem too concerned about who they were billed with—their main goal was to blow the headliner away and win over their share of true believers.

'America is just as big & freewheelin' as in the movies,' Bon wrote to Mary Renshaw, scrawled on some hotel stationery. 'It took a couple of weeks to get used to the size and Americanism of the place.' Bon told her that he and bassist Cliff Williams had been stopped by two cops outside a gig and 'got the up "against the wall" treatment . . . we had a laugh with them after we'd been frisked . . . [America] is full of freaks. I sincerely recommend it to you. Tell 'em Bon sent you.'

When the roadshow reached the Palladium in New York on 24 August, the band was teamed with US punks The Dictators. But unlike a lot of the British punk acts they'd encountered, The Dictators actually bothered to check out AC/DC's set. Their leader, Andy Shernoff, a Queens native, was well aware of the band's music but got a shock when he encountered them in the flesh.

'Angus [was] a midget,' he told Salon.com, many years down the line. 'Bon Scott was small, too.' Shernoff was dumbstruck—how could these 'midgets' generate such a thunderous noise? 'It's almost technically impossible!' he said.

Later that night they put in an unscheduled set at Manhattan's CBGB, a sacred (if toilet-sized) venue located deep in the heart of the seedy Bowery. Bon hit the stage running, quite literally, tearing his shirt off and flinging it into the crowd as they exploded into 'Live Wire'. At one stage, Angus, who'd been experimenting with an extra-long guitar lead, walked through the crowd playing solo and then headed outside into the street. 'So, there was little Angus,' noted an onlooker, 'while still playing, talking to the transient gents from the Palace Hotel milling outside.'

Bon was interviewed while in New York by a writer from *Punk* fanzine. So, what's the meaning of life? he was asked.

'As good a time and as short as possible,' Bon replied in a flash.

*

In late August, the AC/DC bandwagon was pointed in the direction of the west coast, where a three-night stand at influential watering hole the Whisky a Go Go awaited them. But somewhere around Phoenix, Bon decided to go rogue. He surfaced in a rowdy roadhouse, drinking beer and shooting pool with the locals, but the mood in the room turned sour when Bon began winning. As he recalled, 'I happen to look around and the whole bar is going, "Grrr".' It was at that point that Bon decided, wisely, to throw the game, pay his tab and head in the general direction of LA.

After one of their Whisky shows, with Iggy Pop and Aerosmith's Steven Tyler in the house, Gene Simmons, the blood-drooling bassist of KISS, introduced himself and invited Bon, Browning and Angus to a diner for supper. Bon decided to suppress his opinion of Simmons' band, especially when he invited them to open for KISS during some upcoming shows. KISS was a platinum-selling stadium band that was currently filling 20,000-seaters all across America. Only a fool would have knocked back his offer.

During a tour-closing two-night stand at the Old Waldorf in San Francisco, they drew 750 punters each night. Their American following was building, gig by gig.

Bon rounded out his first US visit with a trip to Disneyland. It had been a heady five weeks, so why not end it with a day at the Magic Kingdom? But there was a twist in the tale. After a gig, Bon and drummer Phil Rudd had been given a joint by a fan, unaware that it had been spiked with angel dust. As Rudd later told Mary Renshaw, they 'freaked out' after smoking the doobie and spent the day at Disneyland holding hands, trying hard to come down.

★

Silver Smith proved to be so well connected that she managed to get Bon into the studio to see The Rolling Stones recording, when the couple got together in Paris during October 1977. Bon had always been a fan—it was Keith Richards, of course, who'd inspired his double-earring look. Of late, though, the Stones had fallen from favour, due to the recent drug bust of Richards (who was awaiting trial) and the onslaught of punk—they were dinosaurs, as far as punks were concerned. In October, Sex Pistol Sid Vicious told US *Rolling Stone*, 'I absolutely despise those turds. The Stones should have quit in 1965.'

But Bon got very lucky during his weekend at the Pathé Marconi studio in the Paris suburbs. He got to see the Stones in the process of resurrecting themselves with the raw, back-to-basics *Some Girls* LP. Hearing a track like 'Respectable', with its rare three-guitar attack of Jagger, Richards and Ronnie Wood, must have left Bon itching to get back into the studio with the Young brothers. (In a curious quirk of fate, that next AC/DC record, 1978's *Powerage*, would become a favourite of Keith Richards.)

While in Paris, Bon, via a friend of Richards, met a local Paris rock band named Trust. Their singer, Bernie Bonvoison, growled in a style not dissimilar to Bon's—the title of his band's debut single, which translated to 'Don't Take Your Gun with You', sounded very much like something Bon might have written. He and Bonvoison became drinking buddies and Bon invited Trust to open for them when they next played Paris.

The band had been touring pretty much constantly since they returned from the States, but the ever-present Molly Meldrum tracked down Bon on 1 November, during a rare free day. While Meldrum had a tendency to become tongue-tied, it was clear that Bon enjoyed his exchanges with the *Countdown* host. He loved to toy with Meldrum, a man who took his interviews very seriously, unlike Bon.

Meldrum opened with a grumble—'He was a difficult man to find'—before introducing Bon, who was again wearing his fur-lined coat. When asked about the immediate future, Bon tried to convince Meldrum that Great Yarmouth, a town of some 30,000 on the east coast of England, where they were to play in a few days, was a hotspot on the rock circuit.

'I suppose you've all heard of Great Yarmouth.'

When Molly admitted that he hadn't, Bon feigned shock.

'You haven't? Let me tell you about Great Yarmouth.'

Before Bon could delve into a detailed description of the seaside resort, Meldrum sidetracked him into a discussion of punk. Bon made a face that looked as though he'd just bitten into a lemon. He'd heard the 'p' word too many times of late; enough already.

'We've got our following here,' Bon said. 'It's not New Wave, and it's not punk, it's just people that like our band, our rock band.' Punk and New Wave, he said, were 'a big fad for a while . . . but the main thing about it is that it [did] give rock music a real kick in the guts.'

And what about Europe? Meldrum asked. The band had just toured there; were the crowds different in any way? Yes, as far as Bon was concerned.

'There's a lot of freaks over there,' he stated, joking that you sometimes found more freaks outside the venue 'in the gutter'.

'They're not punk,' he continued, 'and they're not terribly young.' And they were emotional, he agreed, 'probably more so than the rest of the world'. Bon believed that audiences on the Continent were starved of quality rock and roll, hence their over-the-top reaction. 'The only rock they get is from England and America—and now Australia.'

It was clear that Bon saw the band's future in America. 'The Americans are mad,' he said. 'Anything new, they really go crazy for . . . The novelty of it was just overwhelming; the energy that the band puts out—they just couldn't believe it.' Typically, this was becoming a tad too serious for Bon, who then feigned a dodgy American accent. 'They're pretty laid-back over there, and then this band comes along that rocks its arse off, man.'

Meldrum, to his credit, had set out to treat Bon seriously, but the man himself couldn't resist winding up his interrogator. Teasing Molly—or 'Ian', as Bon referred to him, a nod to their shared history ('They still call you Ian, do they?')—was an itch he couldn't resist scratching. When Meldrum admitted he was having a little microphone trouble, Bon rolled his eyes and replied: 'You shouldn't have the mic down there, Ian.'

As they wrapped up, Bon admitted to Meldrum that he was a tad road weary. 'We've been working non-stop since before I started with the band. You've got to have a break occasionally.' But that break was some time off yet.

Soon after, Bon told a writer from *RAM*, 'if you don't show your arse to Molly Meldrum on *Countdown*, you're fucked. You just don't get on TV and your records aren't played on radio.' This was a touch too much. Once again, in search of a quotable quote, Bon had engaged his mouth before his brain.

★

Come 16 November and the band was back in America, this time for a six-week run of dates. AC/DC were again the 'support act du jour', opening shows for KISS, the Blue Öyster Cult and Canadian prog rockers Rush. They also shared bills with UFO, a UK heavy metal outfit, whose bass player, Pete Way, had met Bon the year before—he'd even been in the audience when AC/DC broke attendance records at the Marquee. They grew closer during this tour. Way, like Bon, was working class, coming from Enfield, in the north of London. He liked Bon personally and also loved the band.

In 2016, he would tell *Classic Rock* that sharing a bill with AC/DC was a very big call. 'Every night I watched Angus and Bon I thought, wow! It was like a hurricane. It was much better than UFO, and we had to go on and follow it.' Way would stand side stage and watch the band play every night of the tour. He could tell that Bon was an original. 'You can't buy a Bon Scott,' he told *Classic Rock*.

During a run of shows that took them through Knoxville, Tennessee, and Charleston, West Virginia, Bon would often greet Way in the foyer of their hotel. Regardless of the time, Bon would clap his hands together, beam a high-voltage smile and state, 'Right. Large Jack Daniel's' and lead Way in the direction of the bar.

'You'd see him first thing in the morning,' Way told *Classic Rock*, 'and he'd been with the barmaid or something, and he'd go, "Had a good workout last night."'

Bon found that his lyrics were sometimes a little lost on American audiences. On 27 November, the band head-lined a show in Atlanta, Georgia, which was sponsored by local radio FM station 96 Rock. When Bon introduced 'The Jack', he needed to explain to the confused punters exactly what he was talking about. 'It's what you call the clap,' Bon said.

American critics remained divided on AC/DC. Covering a show where they opened for KISS at the Freedom Hall in Louisville, Kentucky, on 12 December, a writer from *The Courier-Journal* wasn't sold. 'It's hard to see where groups like KISS and AC/DC can go from here,' stated music critic John Finley. Ellen Aman, a writer for *The Lexington Leader*, laid it on a little thicker. 'One bit of advice,' she wrote. 'Unless you are addicted to this sort of music, you can skip . . . a 45-minute set by something called AC/DC.' On the flipside, Howie Klein, writing in *New York Rocker* magazine, was a true believer; he likened the experience of seeing AC/DC with the cathartic vibe of a Patti Smith show. 'There are just some bands ya gotta see live.'

After a tour-closing gig in Pittsburgh with the Blue Öyster Cult, Bon settled into his seat on the flight back to Sydney, content with the year he'd had and looking forward to a break. He was to spend Christmas in Sydney with Silver Smith, who'd joined him during the US tour. Then he and the band would set about making the best album, to date, of their careers.

17

'Are there any virgins in Glasgow?'
—Bon introduces 'The Jack'

Little did Bon know, as the band regrouped at Alberts studio in January 1978, that he was about to record his final record with dream team George Young and Harry Vanda. They'd been crucial to AC/DC, not only as producers—they'd brilliantly honed the band's raw, primal sound—but also as advisers and mentors. It was George who'd told his brother Malcolm, upon hiring Bon, that he was the right guy for the job, even though he looked as though he'd just done a bank job. 'You're a rock and roll band now,' George had told Malcolm. It was fair to say that without Vanda and Young, AC/DC wouldn't be in their current position: just a couple of steps away from being international headliners, world-beaters.

Bon had said so much himself when he'd admitted that George was like a father to the band.

Bon was in fine form during the recording of what would become the *Powerage* album, penning some of his best lyrics and delivering some powerhouse vocals. This came about, perhaps, because the band had decided against touring Oz this time around. Typically when they recorded in Australia, they'd fit in studio sessions around live dates and sometimes they were rushed. But bassist Cliff Williams had some visa hassles again, which made it impossible for him to play live, and they were still smarting from the dramas of the Giant Dose tour, so it was agreed they'd focus solely on their new record. And that focus showed in every groove of the finished album.

Bon gave the distinct impression that he was, at least for the time being, done going for cheap laughs, writing about his balls or the pleasures of groupies. Here his lyrics took a more serious turn. Perhaps it had something to do with writing for a broader audience—he now dropped such Americanisms as 'gasoline' and 'Sin City' into his lyrics—or maybe it was simply his state of mind at the time. Whatever the reason, Bon dug deep and came up with a handful of gems.

In 'Down Payment Blues', an ominous, sinewy blues in the spirit of 'Ride On', Bon didn't so much sing as act out the lyric, injecting some serious pathos into another of his street-wise tales of hard living (he drives a Cadillac but 'can't afford the gasoline'). By the song's end, he growls and wails like he's in serious pain, a guy 'with holes in my shoes', suffering a chronic case of the 'Down Payment Blues'. It was gritty, gripping stuff where, as they did throughout the album, the band kicked up a major firestorm at his back—their playing was every bit as emphatic as Bon's vocals (the furious 'Riff Raff' sounded like rolling thunder). 'Gimme a Bullet', which biographer Clinton Walker considered 'perhaps Bon's most accomplished piece of writing to date', was just as effective. Here Bon was calling for a medic, but not the ever-amenable Rock Doctor with a script for penicillin; he was experiencing some major heartache. Only a 'bullet to bite on' would help ease his pain.

Bon's savvy wordplay shone brightly during 'Sin City', his ode to Las Vegas, the home of sleaze and sin, where he borrowed the 'rich man, poor man, beggarman, thief' line from the nursery rhyme 'Tinker, Tailor'—not the first time he'd reworked a children's rhyme—only to team it with 'Ain't got a hope in hell, that's my belief'. Bon truly was on a roll.

Bon was proud of his handiwork, too. A few months later, in Edinburgh, Bon swung by the studio of Radio Forth with a new buddy, the singer from a local band called Brody, who covered 'Whole Lotta Rosie' when they played live. ('Love my friends, you know,' Bon laughed.) The DJ Bon was speaking with challenged him about the *Powerage* song 'Up to My Neck in You', which, admittedly, came on very strong.

'It isn't the most romantic song you've ever written, is it?' Bon was asked.

'That's my most ardent love song,' Bon insisted. 'It was written for a woman I loved very dearly. Still do.' Bon never revealed whether his subject was Silver Smith, or perhaps Irene Thornton—or maybe another lover. But he believed in the song.

While in Sydney, Bon spent much of his free time at the Bondi Lifesaver, which hosted gigs most nights of the week, and stayed open late. There he checked out labelmates, and friends, Rose Tattoo, who played there on 26 and 28 January. With more than a little help from their friend Bon, 'The Tatts' had just become the country's most unlikely stars, having broken through on the charts with their scorching late-1977 single 'Bad Boy for Love', which was produced by Vanda and Young.

Bon's brother Graeme joined him for a time, too; he later revealed that Bon had been trying out hypnotherapy to reduce his drinking but, given his lifestyle, Bon's boozing was inevitable. 'He'd go down to the Bondi Lifesaver,' Graeme told Clinton Walker, 'and he'd be drunk most nights, and he'd still go home on his bike.'

Sometimes Bon would ride out to the Parramatta Speedway to check out the bike races. Silver Smith, who was in Sydney too, would later recall some hairy nights tearing down the Cahill Expressway on the bike, holding on to Bon for dear life, as he weaved in and out of the traffic.

★

Come April, Bon and the band were back touring the UK, in advance of the release of *Powerage*, which was due on 5 May. *Let There Be Rock* had reached a UK peak of number 17.

'Standing to make a bit of money at long last,' Bon wrote in a letter to Irene. He and Phil Rudd were about to head to Paris 'for a root around', as Bon put it. While there, Bon reconnected with his buddies in the band Trust, who'd covered AC/DC's 'Love at First Feel' in French; it duly got banned from TV for its suggestive lyrics. Even in translation, Bon rattled the censors.

AC/DC had started performing the recently recorded 'Down Payment Blues' live. On stage in Blackburn, Lancashire, on 26 May, Bon introduced it with a pithy, 'You've probably had them—probably still got them.' It was a song that clearly connected with the band's working-class audiences in the UK, who were only just recovering from a recession that had dragged on from 1973 to 1975. The upcoming election of hardliner Margaret Thatcher, in May 1979, wasn't going to help the upward mobility of the working classes (within a few years, unemployment in the UK would rise to three million). 'Down Payment Blues' was the perfect song for its time.

Bon, meanwhile, continued polling audiences about their sex lives; he was starting to come on like rock and roll's answer to the Kinsey Report. On 30 April, while on stage at Glasgow's Apollo Theatre, Bon asked, 'Are there any virgins in Glasgow?' before he and the band tore into 'The Jack'. (No one confessed.) They returned for their encore decked out in the strip of Scotland's national football team, a gesture that the crowd lapped up.

Backstage, Bon made it known to a writer from the *Record Mirror* that headbangers and air guitarists were very welcome at AC/DC gigs. They were an egalitarian outfit. 'As long as the kids like what we're doing and keep coming to see us—that's all we care about. They can play along with us on their imaginary guitars, have a good time and really get their rocks off.'

Bon was asked about his bandmate, the schoolboy guitarist—was the uniform a keeper? Bon figured it was all part of the show. 'If you can provide something to look at,' he said, 'it makes all the difference. He'll probably be in short pants for a while yet.'

As if to prove his point, when they plugged in to play at the Locarno in Coventry on 2 May, at least a dozen Angus lookalikes—'Angis'—were in the crowd. (More than 40 years later, nothing has changed; Angus still wears the uniform, although these days it's bespoke, and the band's audience is typically jam-packed with Angis.)

★

American reporters, much like their British counterparts, were fast warming to the fact that Bon was eminently quotable, and few subjects were off limits. Most American rockers, while willing to play the media game, weren't quite as articulate, or funny, as Bon—perhaps with the exception of Van Halen's David Lee Roth, who seemed like a cross between a Californian stoner, a wisecracking stand-up and a Viking. Roth once famously stated that 'the reason the critics all like Elvis Costello better than me is because they all look like Elvis Costello'. Even Bon would struggle to top that.

When Bon got into a discussion of American groupies with a reporter, he was asked just how willing they were. Bon, as always, had the answer.

'Whether you screw 'em or not,' Bon replied, 'depends on how big their boyfriends are.'

Angus revealed perhaps a little too much when he spoke about Bon with an American mag called *Rock Gossip*. It transpired that keen letter writer Bon also got his fair share of fan correspondence, much of it X-rated. 'He gets letters from women all over the world,' said Angus, 'about how they would like to screw him and give him head . . . We used to read them and get off on them.'

Bon and the band had returned to the States in late June, this time for a 63-date slog promoting *Powerage*. All-girl group the Heathen Girls befriended Bon during this US tour; photographer Rennie Ellis caught them in a candid pose in a hotel in Atlanta. Bon was shirtless, as usual, reclining on a bed sipping something through a straw, with four smiling, big-haired Heathen Girls, including their singer, Rose Whipperr, sharing the bed with him. Bon's eyes were closed;

he was probably trying to figure out how life had worked out so well for him.

Many of the band's gigs were opening for Boston rockers Aerosmith, who were fast becoming AC/DC advocates. They helped them snag a spot on NBC's late-night music show *Midnight Special*, a program that insisted its acts perform live—a boon for AC/DC. (Years later, Aerosmith's singer Steve Tyler inducted AC/DC into the Rock and Roll Hall of Fame, wondering out loud about Angus: 'How did such big balls get in such short pants?')

On 23 July, AC/DC were poised to take part in Day on the Green, a huge summer rock festival staged at the Oakland Coliseum in California and promoted by Bill Graham. He was a Russian Jew who'd fled the Nazis and was now a legendary American music entrepreneur. Among many huge tours, Graham had promoted Bob Dylan's 1974 'comeback' and helped stage The Band's famous farewell, The Last Waltz, duly documented by acclaimed filmmaker Martin Scorsese.

Day on the Green was an extremely loud bill; Aerosmith were headlining, while Foreigner, Pat Travers and Van Halen also plugged in, playing to 50,000-plus fans. A journalist cornered Bon just before the band took the stage (at the ungodly hour of 10.40 a.m.).

'What can the audience expect?' he was asked.

'Blood,' Bon replied simply, and a song was duly born.

Their quickfire set began with 'Live Wire' and closed 40 minutes later with a fast and furious 'Rocker', and included a now obligatory lap of the stadium by Angus. During the show, Bon had 'the crowd in his hand', according to at least one punter.

Eddie Van Halen was gobsmacked when he caught Bon and co. in action at Day on the Green. The ace guitarist was in his trailer backstage when he heard what he described as a 'rubble-pounding noise' coming from the stage, as Bon and the band kicked into gear.

'I went up there and saw 60,000 people bopping up and down at the same time,' Van Halen recalled to *Guitar Player* magazine. 'I remember thinking, "We have to follow these motherfuckers?"'

Van Halen wasn't alone. Michael Browning and Foreigner's manager Bud Prager had almost come to blows that day when Prager had made it very clear that Foreigner had no intention of taking the stage after AC/DC. They were one tough act to follow. (Browning won out and Foreigner were forced to face the music.)

Bon spent much of the rest of the day reclining in one of the inflatable pools backstage, nursing a bottle of bourbon. He was also introduced to singer Sammy Hagar, a Californian native known as 'The Red Rocker' due to his ginger mane (so much for inventive nicknames). Hagar wasn't playing that day but had come out specifically to see Bon and the band do their thing. A photographer snapped them shaking hands and smiling warmly; Bon was shirtless, as usual, while Hagar wore basic black. Another of Bon's casual, on-the-road friendships had been forged.

'Bon Scott and I used to get along pretty good,' Hagar told blabbermouth.net in 2017. 'It was two singers getting together, having a couple of drinks.'

Sammy Hagar wasn't Bon's only new road buddy. Cheap Trick were a four-piece from Rockford, Illinois; their second album, *In Color*, was on its way to gold status (500,000 sales) in the US on the strength of such power-pop classics as 'I Want You to Want Me'. In early August, AC/DC shared a few bills with Cheap Trick. Their bespectacled drummer, Bun E. Carlos, and their guitarist, Rick Nielsen, a man whose fingers flew across the fretboard just as quickly as Angus's, made the effort to befriend the band. After one show, Nielsen invited Bon to dinner at a Mexican restaurant. Bon had never eaten Mexican before; after scanning the menu, he ordered a taco—and a tumbler of Scotch to wash it down.

Bon penned a lengthy letter to a woman named Valerie, the sister of his long-ago girlfriend Michelle Dali, while on the road in the States. (Bon and Valerie had had a brief fling.) In the letter he cheekily referred to himself as 'The Bon'. He apologised for not being regularly in touch, blaming the fact that he was 'always travelling or drunk or hungover'.

He also spoke about his efforts to remain sane amid the madness of non-stop touring and living large. 'Being crazy is about the only way to keep my sanity, if you know what I mean. We've worked so much since I last saw you that it's all one hell of a blur.' Bon said that he looked forward to doing as little as possible sometime soon; he hoped to spend a lazy month with his mother, Isa. The likelihood of that, however, wasn't very high: there was a lot more work to do before Bon or the band could afford to take a breather. (That letter was sold at auction in the US in 2019 for A$14,000.)

★

Vince Lovegrove, Bon's buddy from Adelaide, caught up with his former bandmate when the roadshow reached

Atlanta, Georgia, in mid-August. Lovegrove, now working as a journalist for *RAM*, was very impressed by Bon's current situation. He was staying at the Peachtree Plaza Hotel, the tallest building in America's entire south-east. Among its features were an indoor lake, half an acre in size, known to locals as 'the lagoon', and a ballroom that could seat 3500. It was a significant step up from the fleapits and chain motels the band had frequented in the recent past.

'Personal driver,' Lovegrove noted, 'ritzy hotel, the best-lookin' groupies I've ever set eyes on.' A lot had changed since their rough 'n' tumble days in The Valentines.

During their sit-down, which took place late at night after a gig with Cheap Trick at the Symphony Hall, Bon told Lovegrove that he was tired, that the grind was catching up with him. 'I've been on the road for thirteen years,' Bon reminded his friend. (They'd just played their 55th show of the US tour.)

Bon's admission might have been off the record, but Lovegrove ran his comments verbatim in his *RAM* piece, which gave the impression that he was depressed. This offended some people close to the singer. Writing in her co-authored book *Live Wire*, Mary Renshaw felt that Lovegrove had taken advantage of a clearly tired and emotional Bon in his search for a juicy quote. After all, show by show, Bon was inching ever closer to the top of the rock pile; this was hardly the time to think about chucking it in. And the Cheap Trick show had been another killer—one fan, writing years later on ac-dc.net, described it as 'incredible'. 'Bon Scott was in rare form,' wrote another. 'My mind was officially blown.'

'I believe this was possibly the only time Bon had ever

been vulnerable with Vince,' wrote Renshaw, 'and he used that against Bon.'

Yet in a conversation with Lovegrove from the same time that appeared in a TV and radio special called *Australian Music to the World*, Bon talked up the benefits of constant touring. 'The more we work, the more we tour, we get more ideas,' he said. 'It's going to get better and better. I can't see it ever coming to an end—it's like infinity rock and roll.' These were hardly the words of a rocker who'd grown tired of the grind.

And Bon wasn't in such a dark mood that hijinks were out of the question. During the course of their Atlanta catch-up, he and Lovegrove placed a prank call to Doug Lavery, the former Valentines' drummer, who was now living in the States and playing drums in Rick Nelson and The Stone Canyon Band. Lavery, who, like Bon, had come a long way since those early times, eventually twigged to the identity of his prank callers. He and Bon would reconnect soon enough.

And still the tour rolled on. A few nights later, a show at Boston's Paradise Theater was broadcast live on local station WBCN. A breathless Bon—bizarrely introduced as 'Bon Tyler'—was asked on air to say something to the listeners, just before they played 'Dog Eat Dog'. The best he could manage was, 'Hi Boston. We wish you were all here, because we're having a ball.' This gig went down in AC/DC folklore for another reason; allegedly, Angus stepped off the stage mid-solo, left the venue, jumped in a cab and a few minutes later re-emerged at the station's HQ across town, still playing. Allegedly.

Bon and Angus never missed the opportunity to get among the punters; at each and every American gig, typically towards the end of their set, Bon would grab his spindly-legged bandmate, hoist him on his shoulders and head off into the darkness of the venue. Even flying bottles and fireworks didn't stop them. During a show on 27 September with Aerosmith at the Buffalo Memorial Auditorium, things got especially lively, so much so that the headliners were forced to briefly stop their set and plead for calm. The mayhem didn't stop Bon and Angus, even if they returned to the stage with a few more bruises than usual.

★

Bon caught up with his mates from Trust when AC/DC returned to the Continent on 24 October. Trust were to open for them at a gig in Paris at the Stade de Paris, a football stadium in the northern suburbs of the city. During Trust's set, Bon wandered over to the sound desk, making sure their onstage sound was clean and loud. It was a thoroughly decent gesture on his part; typically, rock bands could be hugely competitive, sometimes to the point of sonic sabotage. Not so Bon, especially when he was mates with the other act on the bill.

Afterwards, Bon sat down and spoke with Trust's singer, Bernie Bonvoison.

'I used to be a drummer, you know,' Bon told him, before going on to point out how much better life was out front of the band. 'When you're a singer,' he explained, 'you can walk to the front of the stage and see all the chicks.'

Bon was in a slightly more serious mood a few days later when he was interviewed by a reporter from French magazine *Ecoute*. They got into a discussion of his lyrics and their relationship to the band's musical muscle. '[My lyrics] are based on the aggressiveness of the music,' he said. 'We find inspiration in the things of life, which we do not take too seriously.'

But, of course, as Bon continued, there was always the problem with the meaning of his lyrics being lost in translation. 'In Europe,' Bon said, 'words obviously don't have the same impact as in Australia . . . For example, do you see what we mean by "The Jack"? The jack is a disease that you catch by fucking . . .'

And while on the subject of interpretation, what about the band's name, Bon was asked. 'You have to solve the riddle,' pleaded Bon's interrogator.

'An AC/DC,' Bon explained, 'is a guy who alternately jumps chicks and guys. [But] we jump only chicks—and not often enough!'

During this chat, Bon admitted that his mother had written to him, asking—pleading, perhaps—that he write more love songs. Enough with the dirty ditties.

Bon was finally going to be able to discuss this in person. The band returned to Oz at Christmas, and Bon had plans to catch up properly with Isa and Chick. Just before he flew west, Bon made a confession to the Melbourne *Sun*: it had been a long time between family visits. 'I hope they recognise me.'

18

'It's a horrible place, full of old crocks who flock there
for the winter.'
—Bon, on Florida

Early in 1979, Bon and the band met with an American
producer named Eddie Kramer. The bespectacled, Cape
Town–born Kramer had worked closely with guitar
maestro Jimi Hendrix on such trailblazing albums as
Electric Ladyland and *Axis: Bold as Love*—he'd even played
the vibraphone on The Beatles' *Magical Mystery Tour*. The
35-year-old's track record was flawless.

But Kramer had just been given a tough gig—he was
to produce the next AC/DC album. On the insistence of
their American masters, the band had been forced to fire
Vanda and Young in search of a more American-radio-
friendly sound, which Atlantic felt Kramer could provide.
It was a task that no one in the band had relished, especially
Malcolm and Angus; George and Harry were family, and
family meant everything to such a tight-knit, insular outfit
as AC/DC. Bon felt the separation as strongly as anyone in
the band. But Atlantic were insistent: Vanda and Young had
to go. To their credit, Vanda and Young accepted that it was
best for the band.

Kramer arrived in Sydney to start work, and he listened to a new track called 'If You Want Blood (You've Got It)', which the band had been working on. Its lyric was inspired by the comment Bon had made just before taking the stage at Bill Graham's Day on the Green. (Bon was asked, 'What should the audience expect?' 'Blood,' he replied.) As Bon would admit during an interview with 2JJ, Kramer suggested a change to the chorus of the song, 'to a way we didn't like. In the end the only thing he did with the song we changed back.' It wasn't a good omen for Kramer, but nonetheless formal sessions were scheduled with him in Miami, Florida, over the coming months.

On 5 February, Sydney band The Ferrets, who'd had a huge hit with the Molly Meldrum–produced 'Don't Fall in Love', played a set at the Strata Motor Inn on the north side of the city. There were about 100 people in the room. Those in the know stuck around afterwards, because word had spread that a 'special guest' act would play. Among those who got the call was Philip Morris, who was as close to an official photographer as AC/DC had, having worked with them in various situations and locales, all the way back to 1974. He had, of course, also shot Bon back in his days with Fraternity, when he was more bearded hippie than lewd, tattooed rocker.

When Morris reached the venue, he spotted Alberts' Fifa Riccobono, as well as George Young and Harry Vanda. He quickly sussed exactly who was going to play. Morris headed backstage, where he introduced his girlfriend—coincidentally named Rosie—to Bon.

'Aaarrr, Rosie,' growled Bon. He'd had a few drinks and was clearly feeling good, ready to roll. And there was something about that name that brought out Bon's inner pirate.

Not everyone there knew who was to play, because, as Morris recalled, when AC/DC took the stage, 'I swear that I saw 100 jaws all drop at the same time.'

This turned out to be a unique version of AC/DC: Ray Arnott, who'd helped the band in their earliest days, played the drums; big brother George sat in on bass. Angus, meanwhile, was in street gear rather than his school uniform. The sight of three Youngs playing together was a historic moment in the band's history, but this gig would be remembered for something else.

The small venue and the casual nature of the gig didn't stop Bon and Angus from pulling all the right moves— Angus bounded from table to table while playing, spilling drinks and ashtrays in his wake, while Bon, wearing dangerously tight jeans, a dark T-shirt and a grin that never left his face, strutted across the tiny stage and mingled with the crowd, laughing out loud when Angus, as usual, dropped his pants and mooned the gathering. Even big brother George, a man known for his intense nature, burst out laughing at their antics as they powered through a six-song set.

'It was fantastic,' said Morris, 'the best surprise gig you could ever imagine attending.'

But this one-off was historic for another reason: when Bon, Malcolm and Angus took the stage, it was the last gig Bon Scott ever played in Australia.

★

Bon hated Florida. 'It's a horrible place,' he said, 'full of old crocks who flock there for the winter.' He wasn't too keen on producer Eddie Kramer, either, as it turned out. Neither was the rest of the band. The only consolation for what turned out to be a disastrous visit was that Criteria, the studio chosen for their sessions with Kramer, had plenty of great musical history.

Criteria was the studio where soul brother number one James Brown had cut his signature track 'I Got You (I Feel Good)' in 1965, while English blues guitarist Eric Clapton had recorded his best work, 'Layla' (and other assorted love songs) there, as part of Derek and the Dominos, as well as *461 Ocean Boulevard*, his stellar 1974 comeback after a lengthy, heroin-dependent exile. Florida rockers The Allman Brothers Band and Lynyrd Skynyrd—some of whom Bon had got to know while on the road—had also raised hell at Criteria. And recently the Bee Gees—Barry, Maurice and Robin Gibb—had undergone a thorough disco makeover at Criteria, crafting such body-shirted, satin-flared confections as 'Jive Talkin'' and 'Night Fever', songs that hit the charts and dance floors and airwaves like a tsunami.

But this was to be no happy rocking ground for Bon and AC/DC. Recording with Kramer promptly turned into a disaster. Kramer would later cite Bon's boozing as a big problem, saying that 'there was an obvious difficulty with the singer . . . trying to keep him in check from his drinking was a very tough call'. This may well have been true, but it appeared that the producer didn't endear himself to anyone in the band, nor did they appreciate having him foisted upon them by Atlantic. It was always going to be a challenge for Kramer.

Bon was close with Pam Swain, a DJ at 2JJ; they'd briefly been a very unlikely couple: she was a Sydney University graduate raised in the city's upscale northern suburbs, a million miles away from Bon's gypsy life and working-class roots. But she admired his sense of mirth, both in person and on record. She also knew he was the real deal, a true rocker. 'Bon's humour [is] the thing that gets you,' she said during an episode of *The J Files* dedicated to the band. 'Bon's lyrics, Bon's humour [were] the essence of [AC/DC].'

Bon spoke with her on air about what went down at Criteria, and he said there simply wasn't a connection between Kramer and the group. 'We had no relationship with him at all, no rapport.'

At first, though, Bon explained, he and the others tried to adapt. After all, Atlantic had given them an ultimatum: work with Kramer or face being dropped from the label.

As Bon told Swain, 'Atlantic Records wanted us to have two or three definite singles on the album . . . and they wanted us to go along with anything they decided and play the game . . . It was a compromise, and we didn't want to do it, but we said we would—they were paying the money, 100 grand or whatever, at the start . . . Thank you, Atlantic.'

But the problems between band and producer escalated when Kramer suggested they cover the Spencer Davis Group soul hit 'Gimme Some Lovin'—and that it also be considered as a lead single. Bon and the Youngs were great rock-and-roll songwriters; the idea of a cover, no matter how good the original song, was unthinkable.

About a month in, and after many thousands of dollars down the drain, the band agreed that they'd had enough. As Bon told Swain, 'We told Kramer we were going to have a day off and not to bother coming in . . . we snuck into the studio and put down all these ideas we had. In three weeks with Kramer we hadn't written a thing, but in this one day we cut six songs.'

Malcolm Young had already been on the phone with Michael Browning, insisting that he negotiate their way out of the mess. Browning proposed working with 30-year-old Robert 'Mutt' Lange, a Zambian-born, English-based producer on the rise, and a client of Browning's associate Clive Calder. A trained musician, Lange had just scored his first UK number 1, as producer of The Boomtown Rats' 'Rat Trap'. The 'secret' AC/DC tape from Criteria was sent to Lange, who, after some negotiation with Browning, agreed to work with the band. Kramer was duly paid off and sent packing. Sessions were booked with Lange back in the UK, at Roundhouse Studios, after a couple of weeks of fine-tuning new material in a London rehearsal studio.

Just before Bon left Miami, he had an experience that pretty much summed up what had been a disastrous trip. He had a cassette recording of a song they'd been working on, featuring some of his best lyrics yet—another story of tough living and hard rocking that was a sequel of sorts to 'Long Way to the Top', yet written from the perspective of a guy who'd clocked up some serious miles and adventures during the years in between. But the child of someone at Criteria got their hands on the tape and almost destroyed it. Fortunately, Bon was able to piece the tape together and the song was saved. It was called 'Highway to Hell'.

'Bon was good at fixing broken cassettes,' a relieved Angus told US *Rolling Stone*. 'And he pasted it back together.'

Bon's inspiration for the title of his new song came from

the Canning Highway, a sometimes perilous stretch of bitumen that linked his hometown of Fremantle with Perth, which was known to locals as the 'Highway to Hell'. It was also a perfect metaphor for life in a rock-and-roll band, as Angus explained to *Guitar World* magazine. 'All we'd done is describe what it's like to be on the road for four years, like we'd been . . . You crawl off the bus at four o'clock in the morning, and some journalist's doing a story and he says, "What would you call an AC/DC tour?" Well, it *was* a highway to hell. It really was. When you're sleeping with the singer's socks two inches from your nose, that's pretty close to hell.'

The new lyrics that Bon had been writing were, to some extent, a reaction to his work on *Powerage*, which he now considered 'too serious'. He decided it was time to return to the raunch of his earlier work with the band; this would be on ample display in such new songs as 'Girls Got Rhythm', 'Get it Hot' and 'Beating Around the Bush' (which he'd initially called 'Back Seat Confidential'). Bon had decided to lighten up on the metaphors and get down to X-rated business.

When Bon commenced working with Mutt Lange in March 1979, it was no bromance at first sight. While recording 'If You Want Blood (You've Got It)', they butted heads. Bon struggled for breath while singing the song, and Lange offered him some advice about breathing techniques. 'If you're so fucking good,' Bon told him, 'you do it.' Lange, who'd trained as a singer, took on the challenge and demonstrated to Bon exactly what he wanted him to do, without as much as leaving his chair. Bon nodded his head, decided to accept his producer's advice and got on with the recording.

In a lighter moment, he spoke with Lange. Bon had heard that Lange had described his voice as sounding like a 'weasel in heat'. 'Do you reckon you can work with that?' he asked.

But Bon wasn't the only person to clash with their new producer. Lange had a very meticulous studio technique, which didn't sit so well with the entire band, who'd grown accustomed to the Vanda/Young approach of not messing about with retakes if the first take had the right stuff. Angus in particular grew tired of his perfectionism. But it became clear, over time, that Lange's demand for seemingly endless takes was for the benefit of the song they were recording, not his ego. Lange even helped with backing vocals on tracks such as 'Touch Too Much' (a song that became a favourite of Axl Rose, who'd one day sing in the band).

Ultimately, Bon was impressed by Lange and what he achieved with *Highway to Hell*.

'He really injected new life into us and brought out things we didn't know we were capable of.' Bon also acknowledged that while Lange had achieved his main goal—to make their music more palatable for US radio—he hadn't sacrificed any of their fundamental grunt. 'We were really trying to be acceptable for American radio without sounding drippy like those stupid American bands. And it works, too.'

And Lange didn't get in Bon's way when he wanted to indulge himself a little. On what would be the final track of the album, 'Night Prowler', Bon swiped a line from the Mork character played by Robin Williams in TV's hugely popular *Mork & Mindy*. 'Shazbot,' Bon sang in the closing grooves, 'na-nu.' It seemed oddly fitting that he was having a laugh, because these were the last words of Bon's to be heard on an AC/DC album.

19

'I'm 33, [but] you're never too old to rock and roll.'
—Bon Scott

Come 8 May 1979, with the new album being mixed, Bon and the team were back facing off against 'those stupid American bands', as they set off on yet another US tour. Their latest US sortie began with its share of drama—after only a few shows, on 22 May, the band sacked manager Michael Browning in the dressing room of the Tennessee Theatre in Nashville. Writing in his memoir *Dog Eat Dog*, Browning believed there were several issues weighing against him— some of them to do with Atlantic, some involving other band business. There was also a sense within the group—not accurate, as it turned out—that Browning wasn't giving AC/DC his complete attention, as he'd been approached about possibly managing Johnny Van Zandt, the brother of the recently deceased Ronnie Van Zant, from Lynyrd Skynyrd. American Peter Mensch, who managed Aerosmith, had also been whispering quietly in the ear of Malcolm Young, who was the band's key decision-maker.

'I was on the AC/DC shitlist,' Browning shrugged. 'No doubt about it.'

Browning was out, but he'd achieved a lot. He'd saved the band when they were down and out back in 1975, he'd helped them get a foothold internationally, and he'd also connected them with producer Mutt Lange, who would soon hit paydirt with the band—but sadly without Bon.

Bon's boozing hadn't slowed down; during the show in Nashville when Browning was fired, he slugged from a bottle of whisky throughout the gig. And this wasn't an isolated occurrence on the tour. This didn't prevent him finding time for the band's fans—when he and Angus mingled with some punters in the carpark before a concert in Springfield, Illinois, Bon learned that they'd missed out on tickets, despite having driven 100 miles to get to the venue. Bon slipped them backstage passes and they took in the show from the best seats in the house.

'We're not too concerned with being very artistic or sounding pretty,' Bon told Andy Secher of *Super Rock* magazine after a gig at Bradford University in Peoria, Illinois. 'We just want to make the walls cave in and the ceilings collapse. Nice clothes and fancy guitars can carry you only so far.'

Bon had unintentionally caused some mayhem during that night's show, when he encouraged the crowd to move closer to the stage. A dangerous surge ensued, although no one was hurt. (Bon's British mates UFO had opened the night.)

Bon continued to enjoy bantering with the crowds, which were growing ever larger. When they played the Day on the Green festival on 21 July—this time billed as 'Monsters of Rock', also featuring Ted Nugent and Aerosmith—a shirtless Bon cleared up any confusion surrounding his lyric for 'The Jack'.

'It's a love song,' he told the crowd of 60,000 that had filled the Oakland Stadium.

The huge painted jungle backdrop must have had an effect on Bon, because he prowled the stage like a wild beast, shaking his mane of shaggy hair, arching his back sensuously—all the while trying his best not to collide with Angus, who was also at his unstoppable, livewire best. If he was tiring of the grind, Bon was hiding it pretty well: he was on fire. During an earlier outdoor show, this time at the Tangerine Bowl, a football stadium in Florida, Bon had piggybacked Angus into the throng and then carried him back via the 50-yard line, pulling off a sort of rock-and-roll touchdown. The festival was called, appropriately, Rock Superbowl, AC/DC sharing the bill with The Doobie Brothers and Boston.

After their first time playing Madison Square Garden on 4 August, the must-play venue for anyone hoping to make it in the Big Apple, Bon boasted to a reporter that 'in a year or two we'll sell this place out ourselves. We've got the talent and we work harder than anyone.' (Bon was almost spot-on; they would sell out the venue on 2 December 1981, some two years after this show.)

During that night's set at the Garden, Bon, with Angus on board, raced through the orchestra pit and into the audience, while chairs were being tossed around by a rowdy crowd. 'AC/DC killed it,' noted one punter. 'AC/DC owned it,' insisted another.

And once again, just as they'd done in the past with such acts as Aerosmith and KISS, AC/DC were continuing to win over their peers. After opening for AC/DC at a show in Fort Worth, Texas, Hirsh Gardner, from the band New England, stated: 'Bon and Angus are the down and dirty Lennon and McCartney.' Bon couldn't have said it any better himself.

Praise, albeit sometimes grudging, was beginning to come the band's way from players on both sides of the pond. They briefly interrupted their US tour for some UK and European dates, including a couple of huge shows with The Who, one at Wembley Stadium on 18 August, the other soon after in Nuremberg, Germany, at a sprawling outdoor field where Hitler's Nazi Party once held rallies. Afterwards, Bon cosied up to Who great Pete Townshend in a hotel bar.

'You've done it again, you fuckers,' scowled Townshend. 'You stole the show.'

Bon, clearly impressed, couldn't hide his delight. The Who had incorporated a laser show into their already substantial act; to steal a gig from them was nothing short of amazing.

'That's right, Pete,' Bon said, as cocky as ever. 'So, what are you going to do up there [on stage]—fucking sleep?'

★

Back in the US in early September, Bon put in a call to Pam Swain at 2JJ. Bon was just about to play a show in the gym of the University of Nevada; the night before, playing in San Francisco, they'd been forced to turn away 2000 fans. 'California's one of our hottest areas,' Bon told Swain. *Highway to Hell* had just been released and was doing solid business in the *Billboard* album chart. During the week Bon called Swain, it was moving up the charts. 'With a bullet,' Bon stressed. 'When it goes down, they give you an anchor.'

The critical response to the album had also been strong. Until now, *Rolling Stone* magazine had been very cool on the band, barely bothering to cover them at all, but their writer Mark Coleman accepted that *Highway to Hell* was a great leap forward. '[The] album actually sharpens the band's impact by refining some of its rougher edges,' he wrote. The British music media, meanwhile, still had trouble out-and-out praising 'colonial' acts such as AC/DC. 'The Greatest Album Ever Made', screamed the *NME* headline. Under this was printed, in much smaller type, '(In Australia).'

One of the funnier reactions to the album came from a writer for the *Papua New Guinea Post-Courier*, Tye Hartall. 'Needless to say,' he wrote, '*Highway to Hell* isn't full of soft lullabies. Have you heard these guys before? Let me tell you, if you did, you'd remember it. Let's start off by saying they're loud. If the AMA ever did a study on the effect of loud rock music on the sense of hearing they'd pick these guys for sure as experimental guinea pigs . . . One thing for sure, you'll either love these guys or hate them.'

Bon mightn't have been too keen on Florida, but he could see a future in America. He nurtured plans of recording a solo album with US musicians, perhaps some of the guys from Lynyrd Skynyrd, who he'd got to know. He was also hoping to buy a house in California, as he made clear in a letter to Irene Thornton. 'It's just a nice feeling to know you can do it at last,' Bon wrote of his plans. With the new album selling strongly, Bon figured '[I] should be able to pay the rent for a couple years.' (Irene was pregnant; when Bon learned about her pregnancy, via his mother Isa, he immediately called and asked if he could be of any help.)

In signing off, Bon wrote that he was a 'very single man and having a ball right now'. He said he intended to be home for Christmas.

Bon's good times briefly came a cropper when the band played Santa Cruz Civic Auditorium on 7 September. During his nightly communion with the audience, Bon was punched in the face by a biker, splitting his lip. When he returned to the stage, a bloodied Bon announced, 'We're never going to play Santa Cruz again.' The next day, Angus, speaking with a local radio DJ, laughed it off, without knowing how ominous his comments would prove to be.

'Don't worry about Bon,' Angus said. 'He's already got his coffin ordered.'

AC/DC would never play Santa Cruz again.

Bon reconnected with former Valentine Doug Lavery when the tour reached Los Angeles on 10 September. After AC/DC's show at the Long Beach Arena, Bon sat down the front while Lavery's band plugged in to play a bar gig. Merely looking on was never going to be enough for Bon; he jumped on stage and jammed such golden-era classics as 'Johnny B. Goode' and 'Good Golly Miss Molly' with his old buddy. A nightcap at a watering hole called Randy's Bar finished up a very rowdy reunion for the pair.

As AC/DC's American audiences grew, they also became more unruly. From the stage of Chicago's Aragon Ballroom—known locally as the Aragon Brawlroom—Bon delivered a serve to some heavy-handed bouncers who were tossing punters about like rag dolls. As they were poised to play 'Highway to Hell', Bon announced: 'We'd like the security down front here to fuck off. We're having a rock-and-roll concert—and they're not rock-and-roll.'

Bon was equally pissed off when AC/DC raised a ruckus in Towson, Maryland. He dedicated 'The Jack' to security staff, 'because they're such a bunch of arseholes'.

What proved to be Bon's final US show with the band was, thankfully, more of a celebration. On 21 October they filled the 9000-capacity St. John Arena in Columbus, Ohio, on the campus of the Ohio State University, home of the Buckeyes basketball team. This time, when Bon piggybacked Angus into the crowd, he took the chance to high-five every raised hand he could reach. Dripping sweat and grinning madly, Bon was like some kind of rock-and-roll preacher, spreading the gospel according to AC/DC.

Then Bon boarded a plane for the UK. *Highway to Hell* was in the charts, he had big plans for his future and his life, seemingly, was in overdrive. It was a high time.

★

AC/DC were not the kind of band to warmly welcome outsiders, so there were rumblings on the tour bus when Bon invited Rose Tattoo's guitarist Mick Cocks to travel with him. The band had returned to England and set out on a hit-and-run tour, some 50 dates in 58 days, plugging *Highway to Hell* in the UK and throughout Europe. Cocks, who was as heavily inked as Bon—he would actually go on to form a band called Illustrated Men—shared a taste for the wild side; he and Angry Anderson had once kissed on the set of *Countdown* and been duly banned from the show. (Cross-dressing was okay, apparently, as Bon had proved.) Sometimes, when Bon was in Sydney, he'd stay with Cocks in a hotel in Kings Cross. They were good mates. (After Bon's death, Cocks would help raise the funds needed to build the statue of Bon in Fremantle, even though he knew that Bon would have laughed at such a notion.)

'Bon was one of the last true rock and rollers,' Cocks told biographer Clinton Walker. '[He was] a real person, it wasn't a business to him, it was an addiction, something he had a gut feeling for. He lived it.'

During quiet times on the road during that UK run, Bon spoke with Cocks about Irene Thornton. There were things he'd like to sort out with her, Bon said. But that, like so many other parts of his life, would remain unfinished business. 'Unfortunately,' wrote Thornton, 'we never got the chance.'

The UK tour wound down with a series of gigs at the Hammersmith Odeon, where they reintroduced older tracks 'Long Way to the Top' and 'Baby Please Don't Go' into their sets, songs that hadn't played for some time. After the last of four Odeon shows, Bon was in high spirits. 'I'm 33,' he said, '[but] you're never too old to rock and roll.'

In Paris during early December, Bon was trailed by a film crew, who were shooting what would become the AC/DC film *Let There Be Rock*. He looked good; his hair had grown out a little, and he was sporting a sharp black leather jacket.

During an on-camera interview, Bon was asked about Angus.

'I think he's kind of crazy,' he chuckled. Bon recalled seeing the band for the first time, before he joined. 'I stood there and there's this little guy in a school uniform, bag on his back, going crazy. I laughed for about half an hour. I still laugh. I think he's great.'

Angus returned serve. 'Bon's very different . . . he's a very individual person. What can I say? He's a lunatic, but he's great.'

In an attempt to show the non-musical sides of the guys in the band, the crew—filmmakers Eric Dionysius and Eric

Mistler—shot vignettes with each of them. Malcolm, a mad football fan, kicked around a soccer ball, pretending to score the winning goal in the Cup final; car nut Phil Rudd was shot at the wheel of a Porsche; Angus sketched a devilish self-portrait; bassist Cliff Williams was filmed at the controls of a World War I–era plane. The original idea for Bon—who was dressed in black leather pants and jacket—was to shoot him riding a motorbike, which was as natural to him as breathing, but when that fell through, the crew took him to Versailles and filmed him dancing, in a manner, on a frozen lake, while a live version of 'Walk All Over You' roared on the soundtrack. The segment didn't last too long; the ice began to crack, and Bon was forced to hightail it back to terra firma, where Rudd was waiting in the blue Porsche. And away they drove, Bon reclining on the bonnet of the car, a huge smile lighting up his face.

In a segment filmed on the street, Bon spoke of how he and Williams, who was a few days short of turning 30, were 'the old men of the band'. Bon then stood among a group of fans, signing autographs like the man of the people that he clearly was.

'Bon,' he was asked on camera during a walk-and-talk, 'the other boys in the band say you're great, but a little special. Do you know what they mean by that?'

'I'm a special drunkard,' he replied. 'I drink too much.'

'Do you feel you're a star?' he was asked.

'No,' Bon said, shaking his head. 'But I see stars sometimes.'

★

Back in Oz for Christmas, Bon caught up with Mark Evans, the former AC/DC bassist. Even though Bon had had trouble, initially, remembering Evans' name, they'd later become friends. Bon had even offered Evans a room in London when Evans was sacked by AC/DC, advising him to stay on in the UK where there were more opportunities. (Evans opted to return to Oz, where he went on to play with band-on-the-rise Heaven, and, much later, Rose Tattoo.) When he was in Sydney, Bon's calling card was a bottle of Scotch, which he'd leave on Evans' back step if he wasn't home.

'I want to do a solo album,' Bon told Evans when they caught up, going on to describe his musical vision. '[It's going to be] swingin' loud and nasty. Real down-home stuff. Gotta record it in the States, though. Got some good boys in mind, too.'

Evans was intrigued but puzzled; he knew that the Young brothers weren't the most amenable people when it came to their bandmates even considering extracurricular activities—this had, in part, contributed to Michael Browning's dismissal. Evans mentioned that it could be an interesting band meeting when Bon broke the news about his solo plans.

'I'll let you know how I go,' Bon said, flashing a grin. He then tore off into the night on his motorbike, a Kawasaki 900. Evans never saw Bon again.

Bon also checked in with his old mate Peter Head, his former fellow Mount Lofty Ranger, who was now living in Sydney. Bon arrived with a bottle of Scotch in hand. 'We're going out to celebrate,' he told Head. When asked about the occasion, Bon explained that he'd just had his pay increased to $100 a week. *Highway to Hell* was tracking its way to 500,000 sales in the US alone, where it peaked at number 17 and charted for an epic 83 weeks. (At the time of writing, the album has ticked over to 7 million sales in the US, a handy return, while the video of the title track is on its way to 200 million views on YouTube.)

Head knew how tough it was to earn a decent living; Bon's admission was proof. 'The public seems to think that if you are involved in pop music, you are rich,' he noted. 'In fact, it is one of the toughest businesses in the world to succeed in.'

When Bon caught up with his mother Isa, he insisted that he was on target to become a millionaire.

There were new creative sensations in Bon's world, which he recommended whenever he had the chance. One was the recently published novel *The World According to Garp*, written by American John Irving, a tragicomic tale of feminism, wrestling and cross-dressing. Perhaps Bon was drawn to the book by a comment from Irving's mother, who told *Time* magazine that 'there are parts of *Garp* that are too explicit for me'—which sounded a lot like Isa's take on Bon's lyrics. Another was Eric Clapton's latest record, *Slowhand*, a surprisingly mellow choice for the man who wrote 'Highway to Hell'.

It was almost an annual ritual for Bon to jam with a local group when he was home for Christmas. In late December 1979 he got up with the band Swanee, who were playing at the Family Inn, a suburban Sydney venue. John Swan, the band's frontman, had been Bon's successor in Fraternity, while his younger brother Jimmy had just hit the Australian Top 20 with his band Cold Chisel, Adelaide natives, and their song 'Choir Girl'.

Swan loved a tipple as much as Bon; when they did get together, high times ensued. As Swan would explain to a reporter, '[We're] rough as guts but we're Glaswegians. What do you expect? [Bon's] a good guy.' Their jam at the Family Inn was a boozy, rowdy affair.

Bon dropped in to visit Irene Thornton, who was living with her partner Nick in the Melbourne suburb of Prahran and was due to become a mother any day. (Bon also checked in with Mary Renshaw and her partner, Peter, and stayed with them briefly.) Bon was wearing a lurid orange Hawaiian shirt (a favourite that he wore in some later-era band shoots) and a broad smile. He and Nick, a fellow muso, got into a discussion about music—when Nick told him how much he loved the AC/DC track 'Girls Got Rhythm', Bon nodded. 'It's a great song,' he admitted.

During the night, Irene drove Bon to the bottle shop to stock up on beer, which Bon liked to drink in tandem with his current tipple of choice, a Rusty Nail—a lively blend of Scotch and Drambuie. Bon enjoyed ribbing Irene about her ever-expanding stomach.

'We laughed all the way to the shops. He seemed happy,' Thornton later wrote.

Bon made subsequent plans for dinner but skipped out after getting into a tear with some old mates at the Station Hotel. Bon called Irene just before he left to return to the UK. 'Still love ya, 'Rene,' he said down the line. And then he was gone.

★

In London, Bon was now living in a flat in Ashley Court in Westminster, which he shared with his new partner, a Japanese woman named Anna Baba. Silver Smith was still part of Bon's life but they were no longer a couple; she'd spent the past year back in Australia. But Bon and the band were, as ever, on the move; he was rarely at home.

There were several UK venues that AC/DC now filled as a matter of course—and revisited many times over. One of them was the 1500-capacity Mayfair Ballroom in Newcastle. When they plugged in to play on 25 January 1980, it was their seventh gig there in a little under three years—and their eighth show in nine days since flying in from Australia.

The Mayfair had recently been damaged in a fire, something Bon mentioned during an exchange with the audience. 'We're gonna hope the place doesn't burn down until we're finished,' he joked. When he introduced 'Hell Ain't a Bad Place to Be', Bon said it was a 'song from the new album about Newcastle'. He knew how to play to the crowd. 'The Jack' elicited a football-style chant from the audience, gratefully encouraged by Bon. This was the last AC/DC show featuring Bon that was bootlegged—it would become known on the black market as Nearing the End of the Highway.

Two nights later, the band plugged in for the final show of the tour, at the Gaumont (now called the Mayflower) in Southampton. It was crowd-pleasing, blood-and-thunder business as usual; they tore into 'Live Wire' as soon as the lights went down and then worked their way through a broad set that mixed up the 'oldies'—'High Voltage', 'Whole Lotta Rosie', 'T.N.T.'—with a brace of songs from *Highway to Hell*. Bon and Angus did a lap of the venue, the crowd went berserk, and the lights went up after yet another blistering take on 'Let There Be Rock'.

Bon left the stage dripping in sweat, well pleased that he'd delivered the rock-and-roll goods yet again. No one in the room, or in the band, could have imagined it was his final show. ('Bon went out in a blaze of glory,' insisted at least one fan who was in the room that night.) The band had been as powerful as ever—and he'd owned the stage.

Bon was photographed boarding the tour bus at the rear of the venue after the gig, surrounded by cheering fans, a mile-wide smile on his face.

A few weeks earlier, Bon had spoken with a reporter from Glasgow and, judging by his comments, all was perfectly fine in his world. 'I've been on the road for 15 years,' he said, 'and I have no intent to stop. We meet a lot of people, we drink lots of stuff and have fun.' Bon also knew that the band was on the verge of exploding internationally; *Highway to Hell* had been a huge breakthrough in America, and they now needed to follow it up with a monster. Producer Mutt Lange, also poised on the verge of superstardom, was set to work with them again. Malcolm and Angus had started chipping away at some new song ideas. Everything seemed to be in place for Bon to find the stardom that he'd long dreamed about, since the days back in Fremantle when he'd ride his postie's bike to the menswear shop where Vince Lovegrove worked and talk about their rock-and-roll dreams.

After a short break, Bon and the band played *Top of the Pops* on 7 February, delivering the bone-rattler 'Touch Too Much', which had just breached the UK Top 30, with their usual hairy-chested bravado. (Bon's torso was on full and proud display, his black shirt unbuttoned, his blue jeans seemingly sprayed on.) Yet oddly, the show's producers insisted that Angus only be filmed from the waist up when he tore into his solo; apparently, his schoolboy gyrations were too hot to handle for the show's audience. Bon's brawny torso, however, caused no such problem.

Bon and the band were keeping some unlikely company: also on the *Top of the Pops* bill was the Peter Pan of pop, Cliff Richard, who sang his latest single 'Carrie'; video trail-blazers The Buggles, who played 'The Plastic Age'; and The Boomtown Rats, who performed 'Someone's Looking at You'. The Rats shared AC/DC's producer, Mutt Lange. Even an appearance by Queen, performing 'Save Me', paled in comparison to Bon and the band.

After the taping, Bon headed across town to check in with Pete Way and co. from UFO, who were in the midst of a three-night stand at the Hammersmith Odeon. Bon was photographed by lensman Ross Halfin hanging back-stage with Way, wearing his favourite black leather jacket and looking every inch the rocker—in sharp contrast to Way and his leopard-skin print jacket. Both nursed drinks. It was among the last photos ever taken of Bon Scott.

20

'We're just about ready for you, Bon, maybe next week
sometime.'

—Malcolm Young

Barcelona native Silvia Tortosa was the golden-haired host of
Spanish TV program *Aplauso*, and on 9 February she introduced Bon and the band to the studio audience.

'Today on *TV Aplauso*, we receive a new group in Spain:
AC/DC. They're Australian and are considered one of the
best rock bands of the last generation . . . Today, for the first
time in Spain, AC/DC!'

It was the band's first appearance on Spanish TV and,
tragically, Bon's final appearance with the group. And Bon
wasn't looking his sharpest: his unruly hair flopped into his
eyes as he lip-synched his way through 'Beating Around
the Bush'. However, Angus, who'd recently married his
Dutch partner Ellen, was in full flight. His schoolboy's cap
went flying during the opening riff and he then delivered a
near-perfect dying bug—the move in which he lay on his
back and played while spinning wildly—as the song reached
its explosive climax. He then broke into a duckwalk worthy
of his hero Chuck Berry during 'Girls Got Rhythm', as Bon
gave him plenty of room to roam on the set. The seated

audience, an odd assortment of young and not-so-young Spaniards, politely applauded, not entirely sure what to make of the schoolboy running amok.

Four days later, back in London, Bon placed a call to Scorpio Studios, where his French pal Bernie Bonvoisin and his band Trust were recording. Since they had first met in Paris, Bon would sometimes write letters from the road to Bonvoison, as he did with many of the key people in his life. They'd become pals, a pair of rocking reprobates.

'Bon's coming to visit us,' Bonvoison informed his bandmates.

Bon arrived at the studio soon after his call. Rather than sit around and make small talk, and fully aware that Trust had recorded a cover of *Powerage*'s 'Ride On' for their self-titled debut LP, he urged them to jam the song with him. 'It just came together,' recalled Trust bassist Yves 'Vivi' Brusco. 'It was mad.'

Midway through the jam, the engineer hit the record button, and the end result was an even rawer cut than the stellar original—it sounded like some long-lost Rolling Stones blues. 'One of these days,' Bon howled, 'I'm gonna change my evil ways.' If Bon had known he was recording his musical swansong, he would have struggled to find a more appropriate epitaph. (Though never officially released, the recording was a standout of the AC/DC bootleg *Ride on, Bon!*, which compiled live cuts, curios and TV performances, dating from 1976 to 1980.)

Bon's reunion with Trust didn't end there. He and Bonvoison agreed to work on some lyrics together, for the new record Trust were cutting—an English version of their *Repression* album. In typical Bon style, what started as a creative endeavour morphed into a party that stretched over the next couple of days. When Bon hosted the band for dinner, they came well armed.

'We bought barrels of beer at the [off-licence] downstairs,' recalled Brusco. 'We knew that Bon liked drinking, so we followed suit.'

Brusco, just like the rest of the band, was a huge fan of Bon's work, but was also impressed by the man, who he really got to know during these few days together. 'He was just a really great guy who didn't play at being a rock star. A simple man but with talent and a big heart.'

Dinner was followed by some serious nightclubbing, and the party rolled on. But it wasn't strictly partying—over dinner, Bon mentioned that he had come up with some lyrical ideas for the record. He was clearly excited by the new project, his first outside of AC/DC. But Bon's high times with Trust were put on hold when the band got a call from their label, CBS, who insisted on taking them out in style to celebrate a recent gold record: they'd hired a plane and some limos for the occasion. Bonvoison and the others made plans to reconnect with Bon in the next few days, once their hangovers had faded.

At the same time, in London's E-Zee rehearsal studio, Malcolm and Angus Young had been chipping away at the bare bones of a few new songs, including 'Have a Drink on Me' and 'Let Me Put My Love into You', preparing for the big follow-up to *Highway to Hell*. On 15 February, Bon dropped by the studio. The songs were still very much sketches, so rather than get down to serious business, Bon sat behind the drum kit and jammed with the brothers. This was oddly poignant, given that when he'd first crossed paths with AC/DC, he'd offered them his services as drummer. In parting, Malcolm told Bon that they were almost good to go.

'We're just about ready for you, Bon, maybe next week sometime,' he said, as Bon headed out the door.

★

The details of Bon's final night on earth, 18 February 1980, have undergone the sort of forensic analysis rarely seen this side of the death of Doors' frontman Jim Morrison, who died (according to most reports) in a Parisian hotel bathtub in July 1971. As for Bon, there have been all kind of whispers about a drug overdose and post-death malfeasance, but all the evidence points to the simple fact that he drank too much, fell asleep in the wrong place and, tragically, died.

That night, Bon was with his friend Alistair Kinnear, who he'd met via Silver Smith. Kinnear had been invited to the debut show of a band named Lonesome No More, whose guitarist, Billy Duffy, would go on to found hard rockers The Cult. The show was at The Music Machine in Camden Town, and Kinnear had asked Bon to join him.

Kinnear, when tracked down years later by UK magazine *Metal Hammer*, said it was hardly an unusual night out for Bon. There was a free bar backstage and Bon happily overindulged. Kinnear was no match for Bon when it came to boozing, but he downed a few drinks himself. 'It was a great party and Bon and I both drank far too much. However,' he insisted, 'I did not see him taking any drugs.' Drummer Colin Burgess, who'd played in one of the first AC/DC line-ups, was also at The Music Machine and briefly saw Bon during the night.

Kinnear was somehow able to drive the singer home, but Bon's girlfriend, Anna Baba, wasn't there and he couldn't get inside. Kinnear called Silver Smith, who advised him to just let Bon sleep it off—he'd passed out by this stage—so Kinnear drove to his own flat, which was in East Dulwich. When he couldn't manage to get Bon upstairs, he decided to leave him asleep in his car, a Renault 5, which he had parked in Overhill Road. He reclined the passenger seat so that Bon could lie down; his parents were doctors, so Kinnear knew the safest position in which to leave him. He covered Bon with a blanket and left a note with his phone number and address in the car. By now it was about 4 a.m. Kinnear staggered upstairs and fell into a deep, booze-induced sleep.

When he awoke around 11 a.m., badly hungover, he asked a friend, Leslie Loads, to check on Bon. When Loads told him that he couldn't see anyone in the car, Kinnear figured that Bon had woken up and caught a taxi home, so he went back to bed. But at around 7.30 that evening, Kinnear went outside and was shocked to learn that Bon was still in the car. In Kinnear's words, he was 'obviously in a very bad way and not breathing'. Kinnear drove Bon to King's College Hospital in Camberwell, but it was too late, and he was pronounced dead on arrival. Kinnear made a statement to the police and also briefly spoke with a reporter from the *Evening Standard*.

'I truly regret Bon's death,' Kinnear told *Metal Hammer*, especially so when he learned from Silver Smith that Bon was undergoing treatment for liver damage. 'I wish I had known this at the time . . . Hindsight being 20/20, I would have driven him to the hospital when he first passed out, but in those days of excess, unconsciousness was commonplace and seemed no cause for real alarm.'

'Bon pushed the physical bounds beyond anything most of us had ever come across when it came to alcohol,' Silver Smith said in a 2010 radio interview with ABC Adelaide. 'But because he would get up and do these amazing performances every night . . . we felt that it was never going to happen, that there was something quite magical about his physicality. So, in some ways it was a shock, but in some ways it wasn't.'

Kinnear was 'devastated', according to Smith, who he called straightaway from the hospital. 'It was devastating for everybody.'

Various other calls were made—to Bon's girlfriend Anna Baba, and to Angus Young. A deeply stunned Angus, who'd never lost anyone close to him before, contacted his brother Malcolm, who spoke with the band's tour manager, Ian Jeffery.

'Bon's dead,' said Malcolm, who spoke in a monotone.

'Are you joking?' Jeffery asked.

'Would I fucking joke about a thing like that?' demanded Malcolm.

The band's manager, Peter Mensch, had the unenviable job of ID'ing Bon's body, while Malcolm took a deep breath and called Bon's family in Fremantle with the dreadful news. He figured that it should be someone from the band to make the call. After all, AC/DC had been Bon's family for the past five-and-a-bit years—and he feared that they might learn of his death from the media. 'All we were concerned about was Bon's parents—they're really nice people, they don't need this shit.'

'Most difficult thing I've ever had to do,' Malcolm would admit on an episode of VH-1's *Behind the Music*. 'Hope I never have to do anything like that again.'

The BBC radio report of Bon's death was thankfully brief, if ill-informed. They reported that, according to Kinnear, Bon was already drunk when he collected him to take him to The Music Machine for the gig and then kept right on boozing. 'Scott's known for being a heavy drinker,' said the reporter, who then added an unconfirmed and highly unlikely story about Bon being forced to briefly stop singing in 1973 while still in Australia 'because of his drug problems'.

'The suspicions are,' the reporter said, in conclusion, 'that this is the result of some heavy drinking.'

Bon's brother Graeme, who was living in Thailand, got the terrible news by telegram. Irene Thornton, who was days away from giving birth, was told of Bon's death by Isa's daughter-in-law, Val.

'I'm sorry you weren't able to enjoy your incredible success,' Irene wrote in a final note to her former husband. 'I will always miss you.'

Irene called Mary Renshaw.

'Bon's dead,' Irene said.

Mary had been in the process of writing a thank you note to Bon, who just weeks earlier had sent her a *Highway to Hell* T-shirt and windcheater, with a promise to send more merchandise when he could. In an accompanying letter, Bon thanked Mary and her partner, Peter, for 'your hospitality and understanding during my stay in Melb. Bet you all feel like you've just been freed. How's the kidneys, Peter? I'm off to pack my bags so I'll say bye till next. Happy new year. Love you both. Bon.'

Mary couldn't believe the news. *Bon was dead?*

For Bon's French buddy, Bernie Bonvoisin, whom Bon had invited to The Music Machine on the night of his death, hearing the news was like 'a big blow from an iron bar to the head'. He found it impossible to believe—he thought that Bon was bulletproof. Deep in shock, Bonvoisin went to Scorpio Studios, and as soon as he walked inside, reality hit him like a thunderbolt. Bon really was dead. 'I saw the faces of the guys in the studio . . . I sat down and cried.'

Just days before, Bonvoison and the guys from Trust had been partying with Bon and plotting a new musical adventure, and now he was gone. They were so stunned that they downed tools, stopped recording and went home to Paris to grieve for their friend. (The lyrics Bon had written with Bonvoison have never been located.)

Back in Sydney, Mark Evans got the news from a friend. At first, he thought Bon had been in an accident—'They found him in a car?' he asked. Evans had seen Bon passed out in a car more times than he cared to remember, 'head flopping forward as we sped home from a gig with low-flyin' Phil [Rudd] at the wheel', as he wrote in *Dirty Deeds*. The terrible news affected him as it did everyone else close to Bon—Evans felt as though he'd been hit with a blunt object. 'I had no legs,' he wrote. 'I felt heavy, like I'd been knocked out and I was just coming to.' The next day he went into Alberts' Sydney office to mourn his friend with those who had known Bon so well. He was told that *Highway to Hell* had just passed 500,000 sales in America, but that news seemed insignificant.

'He looked fantastic,' said Malcolm Young, flashing back to his last time with Bon, in the rehearsal studio. 'He was looking after himself. He went out, just for a drink, maybe to clear his head, and then he was looking forward to getting into his writing. He had it all ahead of him.'

The suggestion that Bon had died from a drug overdose appalled those who knew him closely. 'Bon Scott was undeniably a hard drinker, smoker and a midnight toker,' said his friend Peter Head, 'but in the ten years that I knew him, we shared a hatred for the drug heroin. Why? Because it was the only drug that had killed dozens of our friends and workmates, and/or made them unable to perform properly as a musician. We all drew the line at heroin.'

Another of Bon's friends from Adelaide, Niel Edgley, had been with him when they encountered a clearly high Stevie Wright. 'Mate,' Bon said to the former Easybeat, 'I love you like a brother. Get off that shit, for fuck's sake, before it kills you.' These were hardly the words of a closet addict.

Bon's death certificate, issued on 22 February, stated that he had died as a result of 'acute alcoholic poisoning'. It said that his was a 'death by misadventure'. Nothing more.

According to Silver Smith, the coroner's report revealed that Bon's major organs 'were like those of a 60-year-old man'. The lifestyle had taken its toll.

★

By that time, the eulogies for Bon Scott had begun pouring in from all around the world. The Alberts empire, the business and spiritual home of AC/DC, was Bon's second family, and the people there were dumbfounded, shocked.

Alberts' Fifa Riccobono was one of the people Bon wrote to regularly; sometimes he'd call her long distance from

London. ('Don't worry,' he'd say when she reminded him how pricey the calls were, 'I'm in one of the record companies' rooms and just picked up the phone.') Whenever Bon saw her in person, he'd give her a single rose. She'd spoken with Bon the week before he died. Bon was very enthusiastic about the new music he'd heard when he'd sat in with Malcolm and Angus at the rehearsal studio. 'Fifa, it's going to be brilliant,' he told her. His excitement was palpable.

Upon hearing the news from George and Harry, Riccobono was 'gobsmacked', she said, 'because I thought, *I just spoke to him and everything was fine*. I just found it impossible to believe.'

Riccobono was another close confidante of Bon's who firmly believed there was no intrigue to Bon's demise. 'There was nothing mysterious about it. It was death by misadventure.'

Ted Albert asked Riccobono to fly to Perth to be with Bon's people, to comfort them and shield them from the inevitable media onslaught. Already the upper-case headlines had started to appear: 'DEAD Aussie Rock Star', screamed the *Daily Mirror*. 'Rock Star, Left in Car "to Sober Up", Found Dead', read another daily.

'They were devastated, absolutely devastated,' Riccobono said after meeting with Bon's family.

When he had first met Bon, Ted Albert was, understandably, taken aback. Even in the wild world of rock and roll Bon was a lot to take in: in 1975, tattoos and piercings weren't commonplace, while Bon's snaggle-toothed grin made him look wilder still. But Albert, too, grew close to Bon, and understood what a great talent he was. 'We've lost a really good friend,' Albert wrote in a letter to Chick and Isa, 'a gentleman in the truest sense.' Herm Kovac, the drummer from the Ted Mulry Gang, remembered Bon that way, too. After a show in Sydney, Kovac went backstage and Bon made a point of finding a chair for Kovac's partner, despite having just played a hectic gig. 'He was such a gentleman.'

In the pages of *RAM*, Anthony O'Grady, who'd been backstage and on the bus during the band's earliest days in Australia, paid tribute to Bon. He described him as 'one of the most genuinely gentle and considerate people I've ever met'. Like almost everyone who knew Bon, O'Grady found it hard to believe that he was gone. Bon may have frequently flown close to the sun, but he had a knack for surviving—at least until now. Surely he was bulletproof, right?

'I always believed that, somehow, he'd just float to the top, ready to do it all over again,' O'Grady wrote. 'Except this time, he just floated away.'

Angry Anderson, the chrome-domed singer with Rose Tattoo, had grown tight with Bon, and felt his loss deeply—he'd be singing Bon's songs for the next 40-odd years. 'Bon was a gypsy, a vagabond, a buccaneer, a bad boy and a rock'n'roll outlaw,' said Anderson. 'He was truly a street poet, documenting in lyric and performance all that he thought, felt and cared about life.' George Young and Harry Vanda wrote a tribute to Bon that appeared in *RAM*. 'A great singer, a great lyricist, a great friend, one of a kind,' it read. 'We'll miss you.'

Bon always enjoyed winding up *Countdown*'s Molly Meldrum, but Bon knew how crucial Meldrum had been to the band's rise—and Meldrum understood the role that the band had played in building the show's huge weekly audience. *Countdown* was the biggest pop music show in the country.

'Earlier this week, there was some very, very sad news . . . for the Australian rock scene, and that was the death of one of, in my mind, the greatest Australian rock-and-rollers we've had over the past ten years . . . Bon Scott,' a crestfallen Meldrum stated on the 24 February episode of the show. 'Not only was he a friend of mine . . . but I think it's a great blow to the Australian industry and to AC/DC.'

Meldrum went on to document how close the band had been to '[becoming] one of *the* world's top supergroups'. Searching for the right words, he added, 'I mean, what can you say? Except that we at *Countdown* owe Bon and the boys a lot.'

He then played the classic 'Jailbreak' clip in Bon's honour—it was one of Bon's hammiest performances, staging his own death, killed 'by a bullet in the back'—followed by the equally hammy 'Show Business'. Meldrum then hinted that the show might just go on for AC/DC, even though no announcement had yet been made about their future. It was just all too soon.

Meldrum also spoke about Bon on air at Sydney station 2JJ. It was clear from his voice that he was stunned by Bon's death. It cut deep. 'It's going to be very hard to replace someone like Bon Scott because he's an ageless character. He had this amazing energy. He could not only belt out a really good rock-and-roll song but had an excellent voice . . . There's not many Bon Scotts in the world, I'm afraid.'

Not long before the band recorded *Highway to Hell*, 2JJ's Pam Swain had invited Bon into the studio to be a guest programmer, an indulgence that would give him the opportunity to kick back for a few hours, play his favourite records and bang on. He agreed but then seemingly disappeared, until one day, Swain, purely by chance, spotted him in the street as she was driving. She pulled over.

'Hey, Bon, you said you were going to come into the studio. What's happening, man?'

'Yeah, yeah, I'll be there,' he replied. 'But make sure you've got a bottle of bourbon and a case of beer.'

Bon came in, did the show, and didn't drink a drop for the entire three hours—'He was pretty big on the old bullshit,' Swain laughed—and then they sat and talked for another three hours off air.

'He was incredibly charming,' said Swain. 'Terrific guy.'

★

As Bon's body was embalmed and readied for the flight home to Western Australia, Angus and Malcolm also pulled themselves together sufficiently to make the long trip back for his funeral, along with the others in the band and their managers. Considerations about the future of the group weren't their priority right now; what they wanted to do was say goodbye to their friend, their (big) brother in arms. AC/DC business could wait.

Bon's Fremantle funeral on 1 March 1980 was to be a small, low-key affair, strictly for friends and family. Public wakes for Bon would be held in the pubs and beers barns across the country, by fans of the band. This was different.

Harry Vanda and George Young flew over from Sydney for the service. Maria Van Vlijmen (now Short), Bon's first girlfriend from back in the days of The Valentines, was there, too; she now ran a boutique in Perth. Mary Renshaw also flew over from the east—Irene Thornton couldn't attend, as she'd just given birth to a baby boy, who she named Lee. The service itself was very brief; the priest said a few words and that was it. There were no eulogies, no remembrances of Bon. It didn't feel right to those who knew him. 'It wasn't really a celebration of Bon's life,' noted Mary Renshaw.

As Bon's hearse drove into the cemetery, a group of fans, who had gathered there, raised their arms in the air as a salute to the man. A message was spelled out on the back of their denim jackets, which read, simply: 'RIP Bon.'

'That,' said a saddened Fifa Riccobono, 'was when I knew he was gone.'

The gathering then drove to Chick and Isa's home for the wake.

Bon's brother Graeme took Bon's death very badly and flew in from Thailand a couple of days after the service. Bizarrely, the final letter Bon had written to Graeme, in which he talked about working on new lyrics, was lost in transit—and would remain so until 1984 when it suddenly, and quite spookily, turned up in Graeme's letterbox.

Bon's body was cremated, and his ashes sprinkled in some of his favourite sites around his hometown. His grave marker, in Fremantle Cemetery, read, in parts: 'Close to our hearts, he will always stay, loved and remembered every day.' Over time, his grave site would become one of the most visited in Australia, a rock-and-roll shrine to rival Jim Morrison's Parisian resting place.

At the wake, Bon's parents had set out five seats, one for each member of AC/DC. One seat, of course, remained empty. That was for Bon. Malcolm and Angus spoke with Bon's parents about what they should do next: would it be best to end the band, as a mark of respect for Bon?

'Keep going,' the Scotts told them. 'That's what Bon would have wanted.'

Within eighteen months of Bon's death, AC/DC would be the biggest rock-and-roll band on the planet.

Epilogue

Highway to Hell, Perth, 1 March 2020

The last time an AC/DC song was heard blaring from the back of a flatbed truck was back in 1975, when Bon and the band staged a guerrilla raid on Melbourne's CBD, blasting their soon-to-be-signature song, 'It's a Long Way to the Top (If You Wanna Rock 'n' Roll)' to an unsuspecting crowd of office workers. But this is something different altogether. It's the closing day of the 2020 Perth Festival and a crowd estimated at somewhere between 100,000 and 150,000 mad-for-it music fans have assembled along the Canning Highway for an event called Highway to Hell. They are here to mark the 40th anniversary of Bon Scott's death, and to celebrate the music of AC/DC. Bon's final resting place, the Fremantle Cemetery, is just twenty kilometres away.

A ten-kilometre stretch of the highway, all the way from the Canning Bridge in Applecross to the Rainbow in Fremantle, is closed to traffic, clearing the way for a flotilla of eight trucks that will shuttle bands along the Canning, all playing, naturally, the best of AC/DC. Stages are set up at various intervals along the route, too. Roadside there are picnic tables and rollerbladers, cyclists and belly dancers, seniors in folding chairs nursing beers—and a tsunami of pedestrians. It's a sea of black Acca-Dacca T-shirts, middle-aged spreads, mullets and broad grins, just the type of good-natured chaos that Bon Scott would have loved if he'd lived to see such an event. As local writer Bob Gordon noted, 'Canning Highway has not seen this level of street drinking since the man of the hour was a wee Bonnie.' In a move that wouldn't have impressed the in-absentia guest of honour, the police shut down several boozers along the route for fear of the event getting a little *too* festive.

Bon Scott knew this road well. He'd often tear along it on his motorbike from Fremantle to Perth, where he'd hook up with his drinking buddies at the Raffles Hotel. The Canning was dangerous, in parts, and had claimed its share of unwary travellers over the years, which is why locals called it the Highway to Hell. Clearly, Bon knew what he was writing about when he wailed, 'No stop signs/Speed limit' back in 1979.

Today's trucks, however, are moving at a more leisurely speed than they did during Bon Scott's roaring days. The theme of the day is, of course, 'Highway to Hell', the last great song that Bon recorded with AC/DC, and it receives a number of treatments during the event.

The onboard performers paying tribute to the man are many and varied—there are about 1000 musicians in all. On the lead truck are the Kimberley's favourite sons, the Pigram Brothers, playing 'Highway to Hell'. Then follows six-year-old Miles Russo, decked out in tartan, making his public debut, singing 'T.N.T.' And then there's DivaLicious, sopranos Penny Shaw and Fiona Cooper Smyth, wearing devil's outfits (with horns, of course) leading the Western Australia Police Pipe Band through 'For Those About to Rock (We Salute You)'—and so what if it wasn't a Bon Scott composition? The sentiment was right. Carla Geneve & the Floors deliver a stellar 'Ride On', while Melbourne neo-punks Amyl & the Sniffers bash out 'Dirty Deeds'. Abbe May and the Southern River Band, meanwhile, rock the bejesus out of 'Jailbreak'. Soul singer Odette Mercy cranks up 'Let There Be Rock' and the crowd, as they say, goes off.

Then there's a public announcement—earlier in the day there'd been an air guitar competition, and it's now revealed that some 3722 wannabe Anguses took part, out-windmilling the previous mark by a hefty 1345 air guitarists.

Of course, it's a new world record. Bon Scott, the kind of guy who didn't do things in small measures, would have expected nothing less from his fans. But the one thing he would never have expected was an event like this, a huge gathering in his honour—at the esteemed Perth Festival, no less. During his short, fast life, Bon was a wild child, a rock-and-roll gypsy, a man intent on having a good time as often as humanly possible. But in death Bon Scott was much more—he was an icon.

Where are they now—and what happened next?

AC/DC—At time of writing, the band's album sales across an almost 50-year career total roughly 200 million, 75 million of those in the US. The worldwide sales of the seven studio albums and one live record featuring Bon are approximately 26 million, while his songs still feature prominently in their live sets. The Rock or Bust World Tour of 2015–16 grossed $220 million from 88 shows. AC/DC released their latest album, *PWR/UP*, in 2020, and it topped the charts in 21 countries.

Ted Albert—The head of the Alberts empire, the business and spiritual home of AC/DC, died from a heart attack in November 1990. He was 53.

Bernard 'Bernie' Bonvoisin—Bon's French pal from Trust became an actor, film director and composer after the band broke up in 1985.

Michael Browning—The man who managed AC/DC and helped them secure their first international record deal went on to work with Noiseworks. He published a memoir, *Dog Eat Dog*, in 2014, and for many years ran a successful homewares store.

Mick Cocks—The Rose Tattoo guitarist and Bon's UK road buddy died in 2009 from liver cancer, aged 54. He was the fifth member of the band to die from cancer.

Mark Evans—The man Bon initially called 'Mike' joined

Heaven after leaving AC/DC and subsequently became a vintage guitar expert. He played in a duo called Tice and Evans and is now bassist for Rose Tattoo.

Peter Head—Bon's fellow Mount Lofty Ranger lives in Sydney, where he still plays and teaches music. He is working with Hamish Henry's Grape Organisation, with plans to re-release music from his group Headband.

Hamish Henry—Fraternity's manager and advocate established a company called the Grape Organisation, which released a three-disc box set of Fraternity recordings, *Seasons of Change—The Complete Recordings 1970–1974*, in January 2021, through Cherry Red Records. The second disc of the set features Fraternity's winning performance at the Hoadley's Battle of the Sounds in 1971.

Alistair Kinnear—Bon's drinking partner on the night he died has seemingly dropped off the face of the Earth since last speaking about that fateful bender in 2005. One account, published in 2009, had him disappearing at sea after setting sail from Marseille while heading to Spain.

Robert 'Mutt' Lange—The producer of *Highway to Hell* went on to produce 1980's *Back in Black*, which, at time of writing, has sold 30 million copies (and was dedicated to Bon's memory). He worked with, and was married to, country-pop superstar Shania Twain.

Vince Lovegrove—Bon's Adelaide buddy and former Valentines bandmate died in a car accident near Byron Bay, New South Wales, in 2012, aged 65. In his later years he became an advocate for AIDS awareness; his son Troy and wife Suzi both died of complications arising from HIV.

Ian 'Molly' Meldrum—The *Countdown* host and butt of many of Bon's on-air jibes, published a memoir, *The Never, Um,*

Ever Ending Story, in 2014. He is an ARIA Hall of Fame inductee and lives in Melbourne.

Philip Morris—AC/DC's first photographer, who also shot Bon while he was in Fraternity, published a chronicle of his work, *It's a Long Way: From Acca-Dacca to Zappa, 1969–1979*, in 2015. He lives on the NSW Central Coast.

Anthony O'Grady—The founder of *RAM*, who was the first journalist to write extensively about AC/DC, died in December 2018.

Pat Pickett—AC/DC 'lighting technician' and Bon's close friend, went on to work with Midnight Oil and the Screaming Jets. He died in 2010.

Mary Renshaw—Bon's close friend and frequent correspondent co-wrote *Live Wire: A Memoir of Bon Scott by Three People Who Knew Him Best*, published in 2015. She lives in Melbourne.

Phil Rudd—After a period of home detention and exile from AC/DC, the drummer returned to the band in 2020 and played on their most recent LP, *PWR/UP*.

Graeme Scott—Bon's younger brother still lives in Thailand. His sons, who spoke on behalf of Bon when he was posthumously inducted into the Rock and Roll Hall of Fame in 2003, care for Bon's estate.

Isa Scott—Bon's mother, the woman who hoped he'd one day stop writing his 'dirty songs', died in 2011. She was 94.

Silver Smith—Bon's on-again, off-again girlfriend, who lived with him in London, died in South Australia in December 2016.

Irene Thornton—Bon's ex-wife wrote a memoir, *My Bon Scott* (published in the UK as *Have a Drink on Me*), which was published in 2017. She lives in Melbourne.

Harry Vanda—The former Easybeat guitarist and AC/DC co-producer is semi-retired and lives in Sydney's eastern suburbs.

Pete Way—The bassist from UFO, who was with Bon not long before he passed away, died in 2020, aged 69. He was the third member of UFO to die within a year.

Cliff Williams—Despite retiring from the band in 2016, the second full-time AC/DC bassist from the Bon era was enticed to return for 2020's *PWR/UP*.

Angus Young—The oldest schoolboy in the world is still rocking, with no indication that he plans to retire any time soon. At time of writing he is 66 years old.

George Young—The man who co-produced all but one of the Bon Scott–era AC/DC albums died in October 2017, aged 70.

Johnny Young—Bon's old Perth rival went on to host the hugely popular *Young Talent Time*, which aired from 1971 to 1988, and spawned such breakout stars as Tina Arena, Debra Byrne, Dannii Minogue and Jamie Redfern. He was inducted into the ARIA Hall of Fame in 2010.

Malcolm Young—Bon's AC/DC bandmate died from the effects of dementia in November 2017, aged 64. His last record with AC/DC was 2008's *Black Ice*, although some of his guitar work has appeared on their more recent albums.

Acknowledgements

First up a big thanks to all at Allen & Unwin, especially Jane Palfreyman, Samantha Kent and Jennifer Thurgate, and freelancers Emma Driver, Luke Causby and Camha Pham, for another pain-free writing experience. I sincerely hope our relationship, like the music of AC/DC, keeps on rolling. And rocking.

Also, a huge thanks goes out to Peter Gould, Herm Kovac, Niel Edgley, Glenn A. Baker, Jim Manzie, Bruce Elder, Pam Swain, David Café, Wendy Jones, Graeme Webber and, especially, Peter Head, whose thoughtful read and constructive suggestions really helped bring the book to life. Bruce Elder remains an ever-reliable sounding board and mentor. Mary Renshaw, whose book *Live Wire* is essential reading, was incredibly helpful with her thoughts, comments, observations and the very generous gesture of sharing Bon's letters with me.

A thunderstruck thank you for the guidance and insight provided by those who I've had the privilege of working with in the past, including Mark Evans (whose *Dirty Deeds* remains my favourite book about this great era in Oz music), Michael Browning (author of the terrific memoir *Dog Eat Dog*) and Philip Morris (his book *It's a Long Way: From Acca-Dacca to Zappa, 1969–1979* is a great snapshot of this golden age). Hopefully, I've also been able to bring something new to the much-discussed life and times of the peerless Bon Scott.

It would be remiss of me not to mention the fine work of all those who have travelled this road before, namely Clinton Walker (author of *Highway to Hell*), Murray Engleheart and Arnaud Durieux (*AC/DC: Maximum Rock & Roll*), Jane Albert (*House of Hits*) and Irene Thornton (*My Bon Scott*, published in the UK as *Have a Drink on Me*). Arnaud Durieux's AC/DC Tour History website (ac-dc.net) is an invaluable resource, as are Barney Hoskyns' website Rock's Backpages (rocksbackpages.com) and the National Library of Australia's seemingly bottomless archive, Trove (trove.nla.gov.au).

RIP Malcolm, Margaret and George Young.

And as always, love and sympathy for my family, Diana, Elizabeth and Christian, as well as Neela and Poe and our new addition, Rani. Ride on, folks.

Selected Discography for Bon Scott

The Valentines: Singles
Everyday I Have to Cry/I Can't Dance With You (May 1967)
She Said/To Know You Is to Love You (August 1967)
I Can Hear the Raindrops/Why Me? (February 1968)
Peculiar Hole in the Sky/Love Makes Sweet Music (July 1968)
My Old Man's a Groovy Old Man/Ebeneezer (February 1969)
Nick Nack Paddy Wack/Getting Better (September 1969)
Juliette/Hoochie Coochie Billy (March 1970)

Fraternity: Albums

LIVESTOCK (1971)
Livestock/Summerville/Raglan's Folly/Cool Spot/Grand Canyon
Suites/Jupiter's Landscape/You Have a God/It

FLAMING GALAH (1972)
Welfare Boogie/Annabelle/Seasons of Change/If You Got It/
You Have a God/Hemming's Farm/Raglan's Folly/Getting
Off/Somerville R.I.P./Canyon Suite

SEASONS OF CHANGE—THE COMPLETE RECORDINGS 1970–1974 (2021)
CD1: Livestock/Somerville/Raglan's Folly/Cool Spot/Grand
Canyon Suites/Jupiter Landscape/You Have a God/It/Why
Did It Have to Be Me?/Question/Seasons of Change (single
version)/Somerville (single version)/The Race Part 1/The
Race Part 2
CD2: Welfare Boogie/Annabelle/Seasons of Change/If You
Got It/You Have a God/Hemming's Farm/Raglan's Folly/

Getting Off/Somerville R.I.P./Canyon Suite/The Shape I'm In/If You Got It/Raglan's Folly/You Have a God/Seasons of Change (Hoadley's Battle of the Sounds 1971)/If You Got It (Hoadley's Battle of the Sounds 1971)

CD3: Second Chance/Tiger/Going Down/Requiem/Patch of Land/Cool Spot (alt. version)/Hogwash/Chest Fever/ Little Queenie/The Memory/Just Another Whistle Stop/ No Particular Place to Go/Livestock/Rented Room Blues/ Get Myself Out of This Place (A.K.A. Getting Off)/That's Alright Momma

AC/DC: Charting singles with Bon Scott

Baby Please Don't Go/Love Song

First charted: 31/3/75 (Aus). Weeks on chart: 18. Highest position: #20

High Voltage/Soul Stripper

First charted: 21/7/75 (Aus), 28/6/80 (UK). Weeks on chart: 22 (Aus), 8 (UK). Highest position: #10 (Aus), #36 (UK)

It's a Long Way to the Top (If You Wanna Rock 'n' Roll)/Can I Sit Next to You Girl

First charted: 22/12/75 (Aus), 28/6/80 (UK). Weeks on chart: 19 (Aus), 3 (UK). Highest position: #9 (Aus), #55 (UK)

T.N.T./I'm a Rocker

First charted: 8/3/76 (Aus). Weeks on chart: 18. Highest position: #19

Jailbreak/Fling Thing

First charted: 28/6/76 (Aus). Weeks on chart: 19. Highest position: #10

Dirty Deeds Done Dirt Cheap/R.I.P. (Rock in Peace)

First charted: 18/10/76 (Aus), 28/6/80 (UK). Weeks on chart: 18 (Aus), 3 (UK). Highest position: #29 (Aus), #47 (UK)

Love at First Feel/Problem Child

First charted: 14/2/77 (Aus). Weeks on chart: 9, Highest position: #63

Dog Eat Dog/Carry Me Home

First charted: 18/4/77 (Aus). Weeks on chart: 5. Highest position: #60

Let There Be Rock/Problem Child*

First charted: 6/2/78 (Aus). Weeks on chart: 6. Highest position: #82
*Aus release B-side was 'Let There Be Rock (Part 2)'

Rock 'n' Roll Damnation/Sin City*

First charted: 17/7/78 (Aus), 10/6/78 (UK). Weeks on chart: 8 (Aus), 9 (UK). Highest position: #83 (Aus), #24 (UK)
*Aus release B-side was 'Cold Hearted Man'

Highway to Hell/If You Want Blood (You've Got It)*

First charted: 3/9/79 (Aus), 1/9/79 (UK), 8/12/79 (USA). Weeks on chart: 20 (Aus), 4 (UK), 9 (USA). Highest position: #24 (Aus), #56 (UK), #47 (USA)
*US release had 'Night Prowler' on the B-side

Touch Too Much/Live Wire (Live) and Shot Down in Flames (Live)

First charted: 2/2/80 (UK). Weeks on chart: 9. Highest position: #29

Whole Lotta Rosie (Live)/Hell Ain't a Bad Place to Be

First charted: 28/6/80 (UK). Weeks on chart: 8. Highest position: #36

AC/DC: Albums with Bon Scott

HIGH VOLTAGE (1975/1976)

AUS (1975): Baby Please Don't Go/She's Got Balls/Little Lover/Stick Around/Soul Stripper/You Ain't Got a Hold on Me/Love Song/Show Business

INT (1976): It's a Long Way to the Top (If You Wanna Rock 'n' Roll)/Rock 'n' Roll Singer/The Jack/Live Wire/T.N.T./ Can I Sit Next to You Girl/Little Lover/She's Got Balls/ High Voltage

First charted: 10/3/75 (Aus). Weeks on chart: 39. Highest position: #14 (Aus), #146 (USA)

T.N.T. (1976)

AUS: It's a Long Way to the Top (If You Wanna Rock 'n' Roll)/ Rock 'n' Roll Singer/The Jack/Live Wire/T.N.T./Rocker/ Can I Sit Next to You Girl/High Voltage/School Days

First charted: 5/1/76 (Aus). Weeks on chart: 30. Highest position: #2

DIRTY DEEDS DONE DIRT CHEAP (1976)

AUS: Dirty Deeds Done Dirt Cheap/Ain't No Fun (Waiting 'Round to Be a Millionaire)/There's Gonna Be Some Rockin'/Problem Child/Squealer/Big Balls/R.I.P. (Rock in Peace)/Ride On/Jailbreak

INT: Dirty Deeds Done Dirt Cheap/Love at First Feel/Big Balls/ Rocker/Problem Child/There's Gonna Be Some Rockin'/ Ain't No Fun (Waiting 'Round to Be a Millionaire)/Ride On/Squealer

First charted: 4/10/76 (Aus). Weeks on chart: 24. Highest position: #5

LET THERE BE ROCK (1977)

AUS: Go Down/Dog Eat Dog/Let There Be Rock/Bad Boy Boogie/Overdose/Crabsody in Blue/Hell Ain't a Bad Place to Be/Whole Lotta Rosie

INT: Go Down/Dog Eat Dog/Let There Be Rock/Bad Boy Boogie/Problem Child/Overdose/Hell Ain't a Bad Place to Be/Whole Lotta Rosie

First charted: 4/4/77 (Aus), 5/11/77 (UK). Weeks on chart: 20 (Aus), 5 (UK). Highest position: #19 (Aus), #17 (UK), #154 (USA)

POWERAGE (1978)

AUS/USA: Rock 'n' Roll Damnation/Down Payment Blues/ Gimme a Bullet/Riff Raff/Sin City/What's Next to the Moon/ Gone Shootin'/Up to My Neck in You/Kicked in the Teeth

UK/EUR: Rock 'n' Roll Damnation/Gimme a Bullet/Down Payment Blues/Gone Shootin'/Riff Raff/Sin City/Up to My Neck in You/What's Next to the Moon/Cold Hearted Man/Kicked in the Teeth

First charted: 26/6/78 (Aus), 20/5/78 (UK). Weeks on chart: 16 (Aus), 9 (UK). Highest position: #22 (Aus), #26 (UK), #133 (USA)

IF YOU WANT BLOOD YOU'VE GOT IT (LIVE) (1978)

Riff Raff/Hell Ain't a Bad Place to Be/Bad Boy Boogie/The Jack/ Problem Child/Whole Lotta Rosie/Rock 'n' Roll Damnation/ High Voltage/Let There Be Rock/Rocker

First charted: 11/12/78 (Aus), 28/10/78 (UK). Weeks on chart: 15 (Aus), 59 (UK). Highest position: #37 (Aus), #13 (UK), #113 (USA)

HIGHWAY TO HELL (1979)

Highway to Hell/Girls Got Rhythm/Walk All Over You/ Touch Too Much/Beating Around the Bush/Shot Down in Flames/Get It Hot/If You Want Blood (You've Got It)/Love Hungry Man/Night Prowler

First charted: 15/10/79 (Aus), 18/8/79 (UK). Weeks on chart: 15 (Aus), 40 (UK). Highest position: #13 (Aus), #8 (UK), #17 (USA)

BONFIRE (1997)

CD1: Live from Atlantic Studios, 1977

Live Wire/Problem Child/High Voltage/Hell Ain't a Bad Place to Be/Dog Eat Dog/The Jack/Whole Lotta Rosie/Rocker

CD2: *Let There Be Rock: The Movie*—Live in Paris (Part 1)

Live Wire/Shot Down in Flames/Hell Ain't a Bad Place to Be/ Sin City/Walk All Over You/Bad Boy Boogie

CD3: *Let There Be Rock: The Movie*—Live in Paris (Part 2)

The Jack/Highway to Hell/Girls Got Rhythm/High Voltage/

Whole Lotta Rosie/Rocker/T.N.T./Let There Be Rock
CD4: *Volts*
Dirty Eyes/Touch Too Much/If You Want Blood You Got It/
Back Seat Confidential/Get It Hot/Sin City/She's Got Balls/
School Days/It's a Long Way to the Top (If You Wanna
Rock 'n' Roll)/Ride On
CD5: *Back in Black* (remastered)
Hells Bells/Shoot to Thrill/What Do You Do for Money
Honey/Given the Dog a Bone/Let Me Put My Love into
You/Back in Black/You Shook Me All Night Long/Have
a Drink on Me/Shake a Leg/Rock and Roll Ain't Noise
Pollution

Chart information is derived from the following sources:
www.billboard.com
www.officialcharts.com
Australian Chart Book 1970–1992 (compiled by David Kent)
The Book: Top 40 Research 1956–2010 (Jim Barnes and Stephen
Scanes)

Bibliography

Adams, Cameron: '10 of the most amazing AC/DC moments', news.com.au, 15 April 2014

Adams, Cameron: 'John Swan honoured for musical contribution in Australia Day awards', news.com.au, 26 January 2017

Aman, Ellen: 'Get out the earplugs for KISS concert', *Lexington Leader*, 16 December 1977

Anon: 'At the Haydon Centre, Manuka, yesterday happiness was a "beat"', *Canberra Times*, 4 July 1966

Anon: 'AC/DC nipped', *Juke*, 25 June 1975

Anon: 'AC/DC to export an album', *TV Times*, 7 February 1976

Anon: 'AC/DC creates another rock concert riot', *TV Week*, 27 March 1976

Anon: 'AC/DC score heavy overseas workload', *RAM*, 9 April 1976

Anon: 'AC-DC', *The Australian Women's Weekly*, 6 October 1976

Anon: 'Vice squad at AC-DC concerts', *Papua New Guinea Post-Courier*, 3 December 1976

Anon: 'Sweet and sour notes', *Australian Women's Weekly*, 2 March 1977

Anon: 'Treble exposure', *Record Mirror*, 3 June 1978

Anon: 'AC/DC madness', *Juke*, 14 October 1978

Anon: *Ecoute* magazine, November 1978

Anon: Interview with Eddie Kramer, www.loudersound.com

Anon: *Best* magazine, December 1979

Anon: 'Propos de Bernie Bonvoisin, le chanteur de Trust, sur Bon Scott' (Interview with Bernie Bonvoisin, singer of Trust, on Bon Scott), Highway to AC/DC, November 1982, http://highwaytoacdc.com

Anon: 'George Young interview', *Let There Be Light*, no. 5 & 6, 4 September 1992

Anon: *Riff* magazine, May 2003

Anon: The night Bon Scott died, https://onlyrocknrollsite.wordpress.com/2016/02/21/the-night-bon-scott-died/

Anon: 'The 50 most significant moments in Australian pop/rock history', *Australian Musician*, 19 June 2007, https://australianmusician.com.au

Anon: 'Rose Tattoo frontman remembers Bon Scott', Blabbermouth.net, 1 March 2008, www.blabbermouth.net

Anon: 'Farewell to loveable larrikin', *Sunshine Coast Daily*, 17 March 2009

Anon: 'Sammy Hagar: "I wanna be the oldest living rock star on the planet one day"', Blabbermouth.net, 23 November 2017, www.blabbermouth.net

Anon: 'Phil Rudd interview: "KISS were like a cartoon band"', Skiddle, 7 September 2017, www.skiddle.com

Anon: 'Bon Scott "Highway to Hell" tribute draws 150,000 fans', The Music Network, 3 March 2020, www.themusic-network.com

Apter, Jeff: *High Voltage: The Life of Angus Young*, Melbourne: Nero Books, 2017

Apter, Jeff: *Malcolm Young: The Man Who Made AC/DC*, Sydney: Allen & Unwin, 2019

Apter, Jeff: *Friday on My Mind: The Life of George Young*,

Sydney: Allen & Unwin, 2020

Apter, Jeff: *Chasing the Dragon: The Life and Death of Marc Hunter*, Sydney: Hardie Grant, 2012

Armitage, Laura: 'Forty years since AC/DC played Year 12 formal at Ivanhoe Grammar for $240', *Herald Sun*, 7 May 2015

Barnes, Jim & Stephen Scanes: *The Book: Top 40 Research 1956–2010*, Gorokan, NSW: Scanes Music Research, 2011

Barton, Geoff: 'AC/DC high on orange Smarties', *Sounds*, 22 May 1976

Barton, Geoff: 'AC/DC: The fastest knees in the west', *Sounds*, 12 June 1976

Barton, Geoff: 'Same old song and dance (but so what?)', *Sounds*, 20 November 1976

Barton, Geoff: 'A long way to the top: How AC/DC conquered the world from the back of a van', *Classic Rock*, no. 68, July 2004

Barton, Geoff: 'What really happened on the night Bon Scott died?', *Classic Rock*, no. 76, 9 July 2016

Beaujour, Tom: 'AC/DC's Angus Young discusses Bon Scott and the "Bonfire" Box Set', *Guitar World*, January 1998

Bennett, Lachlan: 'Memories of AC/DC concerts in Queenstown, Devonport', *The Advocate*, 20 November 2017

Bisset, John: 'John Bisset interview', AC/DC Collector, 2003, www.acdccollector.com/interviews.htm#JOHN

Bisset, John: 'Interview for AC/DC Back in Black website', John Bisset's Website, 2006, www.johnbisset.nz/Interview ACDCbackinblack.htm

Blake, Mark: 'The short life and tragic death of Paul Kossoff', *Classic Rock*, 26 July 2018, www.loudersound.com

Bonomo, Joe: 'The night AC/DC stormed CBGB', Salon,

5 November 2017, www.salon.com

Brinton, Robert: 'Spanish Fly', *Disc*, 21 April 1973

Brown, David: 'The dirtiest group in town', *Record Mirror*, 13 November 1976

Browne, Geoff: 'Scott, Ronald Belford (Bon) (1946–1980)', *Australian Dictionary of Biography*, 2018, http://adb.anu.edu.au/biography/scott-ronald-belford-bon-27533

Browning, Michael: *Dog Eat Dog*, Sydney: Allen & Unwin, 2014

Byrne, Bob: 'Adelaide's own Woodstock, the Myponga Pop Festival', Adelaide Remember When, 22 September 2014, www.adelaiderememberwhen.com.au

Capone, Alesha: 'High Voltage for AC/DC anniversary at St Albans Secondary College', *Herald Sun*, 4 March 2016

Carr, Roy: 'Is Britain ready for the human kangaroo?', *New Musical Express*, 16 October 1976

Cashmere, Paul: 'AC/DC's first setlist from 40 years ago', Noise11, 31 December 2013, www.noise11.com

Catterall, Tony: 'Magnificent assault on eardrums', *Canberra Times*, 13 December 1976

Coleman, Mark: *Highway to Hell* review, *The Rolling Stone Album Guide*, Virgin Books, 1992

Conroy, John: 'Vintage voltage: When AC/DC rocked Albury', *The Border Mail*, 11 February 2010

Coon, Caroline: 'Live review', *Melody Maker*, 8 May 1976

Creswell, Toby, Craig Mathieson & John O'Donnell: *The 100 Best Australian Albums*, Melbourne: Hardie Grant, 2010

Cross, Ian: 'Tiny Angus is cult figure', *Canberra Times*, 14 December 1978

Deane, Roy. 'Sex Pistols diary: 1976', Rockmine, 2019, www.rockmine.com/Pistols/SexDates.html

di Perna, Alan: 'AC/DC: Hard as a rock', *Guitar World*, 6 February 2008

Dimery, Robert (ed.): *1001 Albums You Must Hear Before You Die*, London: Quintet Publishing, 2005

Dodomo, Giovanni: 'Destroy your brain with AC/DC', *Sounds*, 15 May 1976

Doherty, Harry: 'AC/DC Marquee London live review', *Melody Maker*, 21 August 1976

Doherty, Harry: 'Current affairs: Harry Doherty travels to Cardiff to see how AC/DC are steadily working their way to the top', *Melody Maker*, 5 March 1977

Doherty, Harry: 'The Who/The Stranglers/AC/DC/Nils Lofgren, Wembley Stadium—Close encounters of the Wembley kind', *Melody Maker*, 25 August 1979

Dome, Malcolm: 'AC/DC's first British gig', *Classic Rock*, 23 April 2019, www.loudersound.com

Donovan, Patrick: 'For a piper, it's a long way to the top from the back of a flatbed truck', *The Age*, 13 February 2010

Elder, Bruce: 'AC/DC by name and nature', *The Age*, 29 January 2010

Eliezer, Christie: 'AC/DC spray their piece', *RAM*, 11 December 1976

Elliott, Paul: 'AC/DC: Cash for questions', *Q*, September 2003

Elliott, Paul: 'Angus Young on life in one of the world's biggest rock bands', *Total Guitar*, 19 August 2020

Engleheart, Murray & Arnaud Durieux: *AC/DC: Maximum Rock & Roll*, Sydney: HarperCollins, 2006

Evans, Mark: *Dirty Deeds: My Life Inside and Outside AC/DC*, Sydney: Allen & Unwin, 2011

Feliu, Luis: 'More than a little sunburn', *Canberra Times*, 1 December 1978

Finley, John: 'Kiss, Kiss, bang, bang, at Fairgrounds Concert', *Courier-Journal*, 11 December 1977

Flavin, Ian: 'AC/DC hiding from a gunman', *Rock Star*, 5 March 1977

Foss, John: 'Bon Scott and the day he was busted by the cops in Jan Juc', *Forte*, 26 July 2016

Francos, Robert Barry: 'AC/DC at CBGBs', *Ffanzeen*, 8 November 2008, https://ffanzeen.blogspot.com

Fricke, David: 'AC/DC shrug off a death and rock on', *Rolling Stone*, 30 October 1980

Frost, Amber: 'Sharpies: The mulleted rocker kids of 70s Australia', Dangerous Minds, 24 June 2013, www.dangerous minds.net

Gordon, Bob: 'Highway to Hell review: Perth pulls off joyous AC/DC covers concert for the ages', *Guardian*, 2 March 2020

Granger, Bob: 'The lusts of AC/DC—Band bids for supreme punkdom', *RAM*, 20 September 1975

Greene, Andy: 'Readers' poll: The 10 best AC/DC songs', *Rolling Stone*, 15 October 2014

Greene, Andy: '10 classic albums *Rolling Stone* originally panned', *Rolling Stone*, 25 July 2016

Grow, Kory: 'Metallica's Lars Ulrich: My 15 favourite metal and hard rock albums', *Rolling Stone*, 22 June 2017

Grow, Kory: 'Hipgnosis' life in 15 album covers', *Rolling Stone*, 2 May 2017

Hartall, Tye: 'AC/DC Highway to Hell: "My ears rang for a year"', *Papua New Guinea Post-Courier*, 7 December 1979

Head, Peter: 'Bio', Peter Head Music, 2019, https://peter headmusic.com/bio

Head, Peter: 'Peter Head interview', AC/DC Collector, 2001,

www.acdccollector.com/interviews.htm#PETER

Hoctor, Michelle: 'It's a long way to the top . . . from AC/DC's early days in Corrimal', *Illawarra Mercury*, 5 February 2010

Kaplan, Ira: 'AC/DC's high-voltage sonic assault', *Rolling Stone*, 16 November 1978

Kent, David: *The Place of* Go-Set *in Rock and Pop Music Culture in Australia, 1966 to 1974*, Master's thesis, University of Canberra, 2002, https://researchsystem.canberra.edu.au/ws/portalfiles/portal/33678050/file

Kent, David: *Australian Chart Book 1970–1992*, Sydney: Ambassador Press, 1993

Klein, Howie: 'AC/DC hit California', *New York Rocker*, November 1977

Kusko, Julie: 'A family reunion for the Easybeats', *Australian Women's Weekly*, 15 October 1969

Lewis, Dave: 'Sex + drugs + rock & roll = AC/DC?', *Sounds*, 20 May 1978

Locker, Melissa: 'Catching up with Cheap Trick's Rick Nielsen, 35 years after *Live at Budokan*', *Time*, 3 May 2013

Lovegrove, Vince: 'Fraternity: 5+1+1=7—More than just a pop group', *Go-Set*, 18 September 1971

Mason, Darryl: 'Bon Scott on AC/DC: "The Beatles, The Rolling Stones . . . We're better. Who needs them? They're last year's model"', The Orstrahyun, 28 May 2011, http://theorstrahyun.blogspot.com

McAleer, Dave (ed.): *The Warner Guide to US & UK Hit Singles*, London: Little, Brown, 1994

McFarlane, Ian: *The Encyclopedia of Australian Rock and Pop*, Sydney: Allen & Unwin, 1999

McNeill, Phil: 'I wallaby your man', *New Musical Express*, 8 May 1976

Mustaine, Dave: 'The record that changed my life', *Guitar World*, 15 January 2014

Meldrum, Ian 'Molly' & Jeff Jenkins: 'Molly Meldrum tells of his interview with Prince Charles and how he punched on with the Sex Pistols' Johnny Rotten', *Herald Sun*, 19 October 2014

Mitchell, Georgina: 'Cheap Trick's Rick Nielsen "would be in the Angels or AC/DC right now' if plan to move to Australia had gone ahead', *Newcastle Herald*, 19 September 2014

Moore, Tony: 'Cloudland: Inside Brisbane's dead queen of the ballrooms', *Brisbane Times*, 3 May 2017

Morris, Philip: *It's a Long Way: From Acca-Dacca to Zappa, 1969–1979*, Sydney: Echo, 2015

Myponga Music Festival & The Grape Organisation: 'About', Myponga Music Festival, 2020, www.myponga71.com/about

Najem, Gemma: 'Bon Scott's letter to sister Valerie to be auctioned', *The West Australian*, 30 January 2019

Nimmervoll, Ed: 'AC/DC', *Juke*, 4 June 1975

O'Grady, Anthony: 'Australia has punk rock bands too, y'know', *RAM*, 19 April 1975

O'Grady, Anthony: 'Gonna be a rock'n'roll singer, gonna be a rock'n'roll band', *RAM*, 23 April 1976

O'Grady, Anthony: 'AC/DC would really like to be as successful here as they are in England, but . . .', *RAM*, 14 July 1978

O'Grady, Anthony: 'Zoot singer an enduring mainstay of rock scene: Darryl Cotton, 1949–2012', *Sydney Morning Herald*, 30 July 2012

O'Hanlon, Seamus & Shane Homan: 'Music city: Charting the history of Melbourne pop and rock', *Lens*, 17 April 2018, https://lens.monash.edu

Renshaw, Mary, D'Arcy, John & D'Arcy, Gabby: *Live Wire*, Sydney: Allen & Unwin, 2015

Rogers, Bob & Denis O'Brien: *Rock 'n' Roll Australia: The Australian Pop Scene, 1954–1964*, Sydney: Burbank Production Services, 2008

'Rot AC/DC': Letter, *Australian Women's Weekly*, 2 March 1977

Sealey, Irving: 'AC/DC: The lusty boys from Down Under', *Rock Gossip*, no. 1, 1979

Secher, Andy: 'Plug into AC/DC', *Super Rock*, vol. 3, no. 1, 1979

Shaw, Oliver: 'That time the Rolling Stones and the Sex Pistols had a row', *Interview*, 29 August 2019

Simmons, Sylvie: 'AC/DC celebrate their quarter century', *Mojo*, December 2000

Sinclair, David: 'AC/DC: Phew! Got away with it, readers!', *Q*, December 1990

Soave, Daniela: 'Kerrang! Whang! Crunch! It's AC/DC!', *Sounds*, 18 August 1979

Stewart, Tony: 'AC/DC: Hammersmith Odeon, London', *New Musical Express*, 20 November 1976

Strangleman, Tim. 'Thatcher and the working class: Why history matters', Working-Class Perspectives, 23 April 2013, https://workingclassstudies.wordpress.com

Super Seventies Rocksite: 'CREEM magazine 1975 & 1979 reader's polls', Super Seventies Rocksite, https://super seventies.com/creem.html

Sutcliffe, Phil: 'More songs about humping and booze', *Sounds*, 24 July 1976

Sutcliffe, Phil: 'The dirtiest story ever told', *Sounds*, 28 August 1976

Sutcliffe, Phil: 'AC/DC: *Let There Be Rock* review', *Sounds*, 22 October 1977

Sutcliffe, Phil: 'AC/DC: Sex, snot, sweat and school kids—The Mayfair, Newcastle', *Sounds*, 29 October 1977

Sutcliffe, Phil: 'No cord wonder', *Sounds*, 12 November 1977

Tait, John: *Vanda and Young: Inside Australia's Hit Factory*, Sydney: NewSouth, 2010

Telford, Ray: 'Don't be fooled by the name', *Sounds*, 13 October 1973

Thornton, Irene: *My Bon Scott*, Sydney: Pan Macmillan, 2014 (published in the UK as *Have a Drink on Me*, Falmouth: Red Planet Books, 2019)

Walker, Clinton: *Highway to Hell: The Life and Death of AC/DC Legend Bon Scott*, Sydney: Pan Macmillan, 1994

Wall, Mick: 'AC/DC: The making of *Highway to Hell*', Louder, 6 November 2013, www.loudersound.com

Wardlaw, Matt: 'AC/DC's Cheap Trick Connection: Malcolm Young was the "main man"', Ultimate Classic Rock, 18 November 2017, https://ultimateclassicrock.com/

Wendleton, Jason: 'Classic albums revisited: *Dirty Deeds Done Dirt Cheap*', Defending Axl Rose: An Abnormal Music Blog, 30 July 2012, https://defendingaxlrose.com/

Wheatley, Glenn: *Paper Paradise: Confessions of a Rock 'n' Roll Survivor*, Sydney/New York: Bantam, 1999

Wilkening, Matthew: 'How AC/DC brought their live show to the studio with "Let There Be Rock"', Ultimate Classic Rock, 23 June 2015, https://ultimateclassicrock.com

Wilkening, Matthew: '10 surprising things we learned during AC/DC's "Ask us anything" session', Ultimate Classic Rock, 17 November 2014, http://ultimateclassicrock.com

Wilkening, Matthew: 'Top 10 Bon Scott AC/DC songs', Ultimate Classic Rock, 9 July 2015, https://ultimateclassicrock.com

Young, Emma: 'Lost Perth's AC/DC memories: "3 hours straight and Angus was cranking"', *Sydney Morning Herald*, 30 November 2015

Zuel, Bernard: 'Albert Productions, the label behind AC/DC, rocks up 50 years', *Sydney Morning Herald*, 10 August 2014

Audio/Video

'AC/DC', *Behind the Music* [TV program], Gay Rosenthal Productions/Santo Domingo Film & Music Video, 2000, www.youtube.com/watch?v=lhl4-SSiD68

'AC/DC—Angus Young [and Stevie Wright] talks about the passing of Bon Scott', YouTube, www.youtube.com/watch?v=nJWjtdMGtIk

'AC/DC—Bon Scott interview—Hobart—6 January 1977', YouTube, www.youtube.com/watch?v=r7DZa-wJYQM

'AC/DC—Bon Scott interview—London—1 November 1977', YouTube, www.youtube.com/watch?v=rxJuhlryBb4

'AC/DC—Bon Scott: The Pirate of Rock 'n' Roll' [*Let There Be Rock* DVD bonus feature], YouTube, www.youtube.com/watch?v=buVvK4nUOOU

'AC/DC—Interview Sydney Airport (Countdown ABC—1 April 1976)', YouTube, www.youtube.com/watch?v=Aah Zb0lsT2U

'AC/DC: Vince Lovegrove Part 4', YouTube, www.youtube.com/watch?v=Fbonvy6IfQk

'Angry Anderson', *Australian Rock Show* [podcast], ep. 123, 13 February 2020, www.australianrockshow.com/show-archives22.html

'Angus and Malcolm Young on how they founded AC/DC', YouTube, www.youtube.com/watch?v=Gwb-SNVb4Vo

'Angus talks about playing in AC/DC', YouTube, www.youtube.com/watch?v=2jOY4RPAPE0

'Angus Young [talks] about AC/DC's first singer', YouTube, www.youtube.com/watch?v=GFSUySHjjzY

'Aplauso—Actuación de AC/DC' [AC/DC on Spanish TV show *Aplauso*], 1980, www.rtve.es/alacarta/videos/aplauso/chicos-ac-dc-tocan-plato-aplauso-1980/317139/

Blood and Thunder: The Sound of Alberts [TV program], Beyond International/Bombora Film & Music, 2015

'Bon Scott—The classic 1978 interview', YouTube, www.youtube.com/watch?v=-7Yuo-QoQi0

'Bon Scott and Angus Young 11/8/1978—"it's like infinity rock and roll"' (excerpt from Vince Lovegrove's *Australian Music to the World*), YouTube, www.youtube.com/watch?v=g3LKdpOeXwQ

'Fifa Riccobono—Godmother of Australian music', *Conversations*, ABC Radio National, 14 September 2020, www.abc.net.au/radio/programs/conversations/fifa-riccobono-australian-music-alberts-acdc-vanda-and-young/12640482

'Silver Smith interview', ABC Radio Adelaide, February 2010, www.youtube.com/watch?v=r5nr1HSwip8

'Tribute to Bon Scott by Trust former bassist Yves "Vivi" Brusco', YouTube, www.youtube.com/watch?v=x9ALnaihMD4

Websites

AC/DC Collector: www.acdccollector.com
AC/DC Tour History: www.ac-dc.net
AllMusic: www.allmusic.com
Discogs: www.discogs.com
Go-Set charts: www.poparchives.com.au/gosetcharts
Highway to AC/DC: www.highwaytoacdc.com

History of Rock'n'Roll in Western Australia: http://members. optusnet.com.au/perthrocks/

MILESAGO: milesago.com

Songfacts: songfacts.com